HIKE
SOUTHERN CALIFORNIA

Hike SOUTHERN CALIFORNIA

A DAY HIKER'S GUIDE

BY
JOHN McKINNEY

TheTrailmaster.com

HIKE Southern California, A Day Hiker's Guide

Portions of this book appeared in the author's hiking column in the *Los Angeles Times*, plus *Westways*, *Los Angeles* and *Sunset* magazines.

Design, Layout and e-book by Lisa DeSpain
Cartography by Tom Harrison, Mark Chumley, Helene Webb
Cover illustration: *Santa Ynez Mountains* by Nadya Penoff
HIKE Series Editor: Cheri Rae

Published by Olympus Press and The Trailmaster, Inc.
www. TheTrailmaster.com (Visit our site for a complete listing of all Trailmaster publications, products, and services.)

ACKNOWLEDGEMENTS: For their cooperation, field- and fact-checking, the author wishes to thank the rangers and administrators of the Cleveland, San Bernardino, Angeles and Los Padres national forests, Los Angeles County Department of Parks and Recreation, Orange County Harbors, Beaches and Parks, California Department of Parks & Recreation and the National Park Service. Re-hiking many of the hikes in this book was a particular pleasure with friends, family members (particularly my son, Daniel). Many thanks to Dan Simpson for generously sharing his knowledge of the San Gabriel Mountains. And thank you, fellow hikers, for the feedback! My decision about hikes to add (and subtract) to the new edition of this guide was definitely influenced by your trail reports and passions for a particular pathway. You've made the hiking experience better for everyone. Please continue to stay in touch via TheTrailmaster.com.

PHOTO CREDITS: Courtesy California State Parks, pp. 247, 295; Jon Foster, p. 257; Chuck Graham, p. 83; Tom Kenney, p. 111; Lynne Malone, p. 37; Mission Inn, p. 189; Cara Moore, p. 27; Cheri Rae, p. 149; Stan Shebs, p. 319; Jarek Tuszynski, p. 305; Dan Waters, p. 55.

HIKE SOUTHERN CALIFORNIA

A DAY HIKER'S GUIDE

MOUNTAINS
CHAPTER 1: SANTA BARBARA

CHAPTER 2: VENTURA COUNTY
OJAI

MOUNTAINS

CHAPTER 3: L.A. MOUNTAINS SAMPLER
HOLLYWOOD HILLS

VERDUGO MOUNTAINS

SANTA SUSANA MOUNTAINS

CHAPTER 5: SAN GABRIEL MOUNTAINS
FOOTHILLS AND FRONT COUNTRY

11

CHAPTER 10: SAN DIEGO AND BEYOND

SAN DIEGO

PALOMAR MOUNTAINS

CUYAMACA MOUNTAINS

COAST

CHAPTER 11: SOUTHERN CALIFORNIA COAST

CHAPTER 13: JOSHUA TREE NATIONAL PARK

CHAPTER 14: PALM SPRINGS

A WORD FROM
THE TRAILMASTER

➡ Hike to Bear Canyon, Deer Flat and Lizard Rock. Hike up Mt. Baldy, Mt. San Gorgonio and Mt. San Jacinto. Hike to The Arrowhead, The HOLLYWOOD Sign, and The Bridge to Nowhere. Hike to Aspen Grove, Sycamore Canyon and Oak Creek. Hike to Pine Mountain, Torrey Pines and the Champion Lodgepole Pine. Hike around Anacapa, Catalina and Santa Cruz islands. Hike to Seven Falls, Eaton Canyon Falls and San Antonio Falls.

Southern California offers the hiker a diversity of environments unmatched by any other region in the U.S. Other regions of the country have high peaks, pine forests, vast deserts and lovely shorelines, but only Southern California has all of these environments. And four-season hiking, too!

By some accounts, if Southern California were a country, its economy would be the world's 16th largest, ahead of Indonesia and behind South Korea. And if Southern California were a country, it would likely rank as one of the most ecologically diverse nations in which to take a hike.

Southern California hikers can choose trails in four national forests (Los Padres, Angeles, San Bernardino and Cleveland) three national parks (Santa Monica Mountains National Recreation Area, Channel Islands National Park, Joshua Tree National Park) and two distinctly different deserts—the Mojave and the Colorado.

Since the publication of my first guide in 1981, trails have come and gone, improved and declined. The first edition of "Day Hiker's Guide to Southern California" featured accounts of just 52 hikes; this most recent guide collects nearly 150 of my favorites, including 25 new ones.

While trails and this guide have changed greatly over the years, my mission to inspire readers to take a hike in this wonderful land we call Southern California has not.

"Southern California has more miles of trail than most states," I wrote in my first hiking guide. "There's a trail waiting to take you wherever you want to go."

➡ Hike to Lost Palms, Palm Canyon and Fortynine Palms. Hike up Mt. Hollywood, Mt. Wilson and Mt. Lowe. Hike to Devil's Slide, Devil's Backbone and the Devil's Punchbowl. Hike to Mt. Zion, Angel's Vista Point and Holy Jim Falls. Hike Ojai Valley, La Jolla Valley and Little Round Valley. Hike across Henninger Flat, Chantry Flat and Monkey Flower Flat. Hike to Fish Creek Meadow, Slushy Meadow and Tin Can Meadow.

The Trailmaster's new collection of the best day hikes in Southern California has been updated in three ways:

1) Fire Reports: Southern California—particularly the San Gabriel Mountains, Santa Monica Mountains, and Santa Barbara area—has been scorched by wildfire. Consequently, I've removed accounts of some hikes that pass through terrain too toasted to enjoy and subbed hikes out of the fire zone.

2) Trail Changes: We've made many minor updates. For example, Link Trail in the Verdugo Mountains is now called the Vital Link Trail. (Who knew it was so crucial?) And that unsigned spur trail we used to follow to the top of Sandstone Peak now has a big sign with an arrow: Sandstone Peak, Highest Peak in the Santa Monica Mountains, elevation 3111 feet.

3) Trailhead Changes: Surprisingly, I've found that trailheads change as much or more as trails! Park agencies seem to like to change where visitors are supposed to park and where hikers are supposed to start their hikes. The good news is that most trailheads have improved signage and better parking, and many have added restrooms. The bad news is that such improvements come at a cost—more places where you have to pay to take a hike.

I'm pleased to report that most of the trails included in this guide—classics, near-classics and even some of my more eclectic, even eccentric choices, are in pretty good condition. Thank you park agencies and volunteer trail-builders!

My decision about which hikes to keep and which to add in the new edition of this guide was definitely influenced by feedback from my fellow hikers. Thanks to all of you who wrote—from the Girl Scout troop leader in Orange County to the newly retired fellow who made it his goal (and achieved it!) to complete each and every hike in the last edition of this guide.

I love hearing about your experiences on the trail. While I'm the first to grouse about how we're spending too much time online and not enough time outdoors, I like it that assorted social media make it easy for us to share our hiking experiences. Please continue to stay in touch via TheTrailmaster.com.

➡ Hike the Chino Hills, Hollywood Hills and San Joaquin Hills. Hike up Sandstone Peak, Simi Peak, and Saddleback Peak. Hike to Suicide Rock, Rattlesnake Canyon and Prisoner's Bay. Hike in the San Gorgonio and San Jacinto and Cucamonga Wilderness. Hike to Inspiration Point in the Santa Ynez Mountains, Inspiration Point in the Santa Monica Mountains and Inspiration Point in the San Gabriel Mountains. Hike to Cold Spring, Icehouse Canyon and Winter Creek. Hike to Red Rock, Black Rock and the Wonderland of Rocks.

Jerry Dunphy, perhaps L.A.'s most popular TV newscaster of the 1980s and 1990s, concluded every broadcast with his signature sign-off: "From the desert to the sea, to all of Southern California, a good evening."

It was a wonderful line—suggesting the diversity, the scope, even the grandeur of the Southland. From my hiker's perspective, it made me feel how lucky we are as Southern Californians to have such a land, one that extends from the vast Mojave Desert to Malibu Beach with many mountains in the middle!

A lot of mountains in Southern California! Take a hike in more than a dozen mountain ranges: the Santa Ynez Mountains, Topatopa Mountains, Santa Susana Mountains, Santa Monica Mountains, Verdugo Mountains, San Gabriel Mountains, San Bernardino Mountains, San Jacinto Mountains, Santa Rosa Mountains, Santa Ana Mountains, Cuyamaca Mountains, Palomar Mountains…

And head for the hills. SoCal has a half-dozen or more hills to climb: the Anaheim Hills, Puente Hills, Hollywood Hills, Simi Hills, Chino Hills, San Joaquin Hills...

Hike to the top of a hill or mountain above the SoCal metropolis and I guarantee you'll get a great workout—and much more. You'll likely find the hike to the top as wonderful as the views from the summit, the journey every bit as rewarding as the destination. Whatever you see or experience along the way, you'll return home with a slightly different perspective on Southern California.

Today in our frenzied modern world, often so separated from the natural world, this "hiker's perspective" is more important than ever. Hikers get big-time mental, emotional and physical benefits from time on the trail. Hiking helps restore the sense of peace and tranquility that our souls require and our hearts desire.

Hike smart, reconnect with nature and have a wonderful time on the trail.

Hike on.

—John McKinney

CHOOSE A HIKE
YOU'RE SURE TO LIKE

First decide on the kind of hike you'd like to enjoy. A walk for the whole family? A long solo trek in the wilderness? An after-work work-out? A first-date excursion? A scout or youth group outing?

Next decide where you want to hike. About 150 hikes plus some options are described in this guide so it may be quite a challenge to select one! Want some help narrowing the field? Check out my recommended "Best Hikes."

After you pick a hike in your geographical area of interest, read the corresponding trail description.

In matching a hike to your ability, consider mileage and elevation, as well as the condition of the trail, terrain and season. Hot, exposed chaparral, or a trail that repeatedly goes steeply up and down can make a short walk seem long.

Use the following guidelines:

- **Easy** A hike most suitable for beginners, children or anyone looking for mellow day on the trail is under 5 miles long and requires an elevation gain less than 700 to 800 feet.
- **Moderate** A hike in the 5- to 8-mile range, with less than a 2,000-foot elevation gain. You should be reasonably fit for these. Pre-teens often find the going difficult.
- **Strenuous** A hike longer than 8 miles, particularly one with an elevation gain of 2,000 feet or more, is for experienced hikers in at least average condition. Those hikers in top form will enjoy these more challenging excursions.

My introductions to the hikes describe what you'll encounter in the way of plants, animals and panoramic views and outline the natural and human history in the region. I'll also point out what's best about a hike and, if there's a downside, what's best to avoid.

Season is the next item to consider. Although Southern California is one of the few regions in the country that offers four-season hiking, some climactic restrictions must be heeded. You can hike some of the trails in this guide all of the time, all of the trails some of the time, but not all of the trails all of the time. Check with the various park agencies and U.S. Forest officials for the latest trail and weather conditions before you hit the trail.

Visit TheTrailmaster.com for tips about what to pack, what to wear, and how to hike over various kinds of terrain.

BEST HIKES

FOR WATCHING WHALES
Pt. Dume above Zuma Beach, Cabrillo National Monument

FOR SUNSET-VIEWING
Crystal Cove State Park, Keys View, Joshua Tree National Park
Inspiration Point, Will Rogers SHP

TO A CLASSIC PEAK
Mt. Wilson, Mt. Baldy, Mt. San Jacinto, Mt. San Gorgonio

FOR ROMANCE
Any beach walk! Any island hike! Charmlee Wilderness Park,
Santa Barbara's Mission Canyon, Ojai Valley, Antelope Valley
California Poppy Reserve, HOLLYWOOD Sign

FEATURING WATERFALLS
Switzer Falls, Eaton Canyon Falls, Sturtevant Falls, San Antonio Falls,
Holy Jim Falls, Tenaja Falls, Tahquitz Canyon Falls

FOR TREE-HUGGERS
Cheeseboro Canyon (oaks), Santa Rosa Plateau Preserve
(Englemann oaks), Joshua Tree National Park (Joshuas), Palm Canyon
(palms), Henninger Flats (tree nursery), San Bernardino Mountains
(Aspen Grove), Santa Susana Mountains (big-cone Douglas fir)

ON THE BEACH
Carpinteria Beach, Point Dume, Crystal Cove,
San Clemente State Beach

FOR AUTUMN COLOR
Placerita Canyon, Palomar Mountain State Park, Sycamore Canyon in Point Mugu State Park, Aspen Grove in San Bernardino Mountains

TO FIND WILDFLOWERS
Reagan Ranch area, Malibu Creek State Park, Charmlee Wilderness Park, Nicholas Flat in Leo Carrillo State Park, Santa Rosa Plateau, Antelope Valley California Poppy Reserve

ALONG NATURE TRAILS
O'Neill Regional Park, Heaps Peak, Idyllwild County Park, Torrey Pines State Reserve, Devil's Punchbowl, The Living Desert, Santa Barbara Botanic Garden

TO TAKE GUESTS FROM OUT-OF-TOWN
Santa Barbara's East Beach, Ojai Valley, Big Santa Anita Canyon, Echo Mountain, Malibu Creek State Park, Point Dume, Laguna Coast Wilderness Park, Mt. Hollywood, the HOLLYWOOD Sign

INTO HISTORY
Mt. Lowe Railway Trail, Arroyo Seco, Will Rogers State Historic Park

WITH KIDS
Placerita Canyon, Malibu Creek State Park, Big Santa Anita Canyon, Rattlesnake Canyon, Carpinteria State Beach, Point Dume

TO PALM OASES
Palm Canyon (Palm Springs), Forty-nine Palms (Joshua Tree National Park)

WITH EXCELLENT VISITOR CENTERS (LARGE ONES)
Joshua Tree National Park, Channel Islands National Park, Griffith Park Observatory

WITH EXCELLENT VISITOR CENTERS (SMALL ONES)
Catalina Island Conservancy, Santa Rosa Plateau Ecological Reserve, Eaton Canyon Nature Center, Devil's Punchbowl County Park, Torrey Pines State Reserve, Idyllwild County Park

HIKE SMART

SIX TIPS TO STAY ON THE TRAIL— AND KEEP FROM GETTING LOST

- Watch for way-marks. Parks are marked with basic trail mileage signs and in many other ways, including blazes, disks, posts and cairns.

- Be aware of your surroundings. Note passing landmarks and natural features. Stop now and then to compare your progress on the ground to the route on the map.

- Think for yourself. Just because you're in the middle or at the end of the line of hikers doesn't mean you can switch over to autopilot and stop paying attention to where you're going.

- Eyes in the back of your head. Look behind you frequently. Knowing where you came from always gives you a better feel for where you're going and prepares you for the return trip.

- Put the trail into words. Sharing what you see and what you expect to see when with your trail companion can confirm whether you're on the "same page" in regard to the hiking route. Two heads are better than one, four eyes better than two, when it comes to staying on the trail.

- Here comes the sun. Use the east-rising, west-setting sun and its respective position to the trail to help you in your orientation.

Southern California
Geography Made Easy

The land we call Southern California is an island, ecologically isolated from the rest of the continent by a combination of geographic and climatic factors. Helen Hunt Jackson once said of Southern California: "It's an island on the land." Carey McWilliams popularized the phrase in his definitive history of the region, *Southern California: An Island on the Land.*

The land's island nature is apparent when you enter it from the north or east. When you round Point Conception and the north-south orientation of California becomes east-west, it is obvious that you have entered a unique geographical province. If you come to Southern California from the east through Cajon Pass or San Gorgonio Pass, the change is immediately evident. Light is softer, the climate more temperate.

The land includes seven counties: Santa Barbara, Ventura, Los Angeles, Orange, Riverside, San Bernardino and San Diego. Usually, only those parts of San Bernardino, Riverside and San Diego counties "west of the mountains" are in Southern California, but a case can be made for including all of them and adding Imperial County as well. Geographically and ecologically, Southern California's northern boundary is at Point Conception.

Southern California is protected from the Mojave Desert by the San Bernardino and San Gabriel Mountain Ranges on the east and walled off from the San Joaquin Valley by other Transverse Ranges.

Compass directions can be confusing to both newcomers and old-timers. "Up the coast" in other parts of the world is usually taken to mean north, but it's not north in Southern California. To travel north from L.A you head directly into the Mojave Desert, crossing east-west trending mountains in the process. If you traveled a straight line, as the crow flies, from San Bernardino to Santa Barbara, you would travel 137 miles west and only 27 miles north.

Southern California may be geographically cockeyed, but we day hikers ought to get our bearings before heading for the hills. We need to find a few landmarks and consult a map. Orienting yourself to Southern California isn't that difficult. Consult the map on the following pages, and try the accompanying geography exercise.

Use the locator map above or get yourself an Auto Club map of California or similar-sized map. Spread it on the floor. Or beam-up a map on your tablet or laptop.

Put your right thumb on Santa Barbara, your right pinkie on San Diego and spread your fingers in as wide a fan as you can manage. One of the first things you may notice is that your palm covers the L.A. Basin. (Don't sell L.A. short; you're covering up some good hiking in the Verdugo Mountains, Hollywood Hills and new and upgraded parklands.) Look at your thumb. Above it is Pt. Conception, the northernmost point of Southern California. Above Santa Barbara are the Santa Ynez Mountains and beyond are those parts of Los Padres National Forest we call the Santa Barbara Backcountry.

Along your index finger are the San Gabriel Mountains and the Angeles National Forest. Your middle finger is in the San Bernardino

SOUTHERN
CALIFORNIA

San Gabriel Mts.

San Bernardino Mts.

San Bernardino

Joshua Tree
National
Park

San Jacinto
Mts.

Santa Ana
Mts.

Santa Rosa
Mts.

Palomar
Mts.

Anza-Borrego
Desert State
Park

San
Diego

Cuyamaca
Mts.

MEXICO

Hélène Webb

Mountains; at the eastern terminus of this range is Mt. San Gorgonio, the highest peak in Southern California.

Between your middle and ring fingers, paralleling the coast in
Orange Country are the Santa Ana Mountains, protected by the
Cleveland National Forest. At the tip of your ring finger at the north
end of Anza-Borrego Desert State Park lie the Santa Rosa Mountains. Take note of the Colorado Desert and farther to the north, the
vast Mojave Desert.

Due east from your pinkie is the southern part of Cleveland National Forest, as well as the Palomar and Cuyamaca mountain ranges.

Now that you're oriented, raise that right hand of yours and
pledge to preserve, protect, and enjoy these places.

Some of the very best hiking in Southern California is along trails through the mountain canyons right behind the city of Santa Barbara. The creekside paths, the mountain tracks, and the marvelous views of the Pacific, the islands and "America's Riviera," add up to world-class walking.

Typically, Santa Barbara's front country trails start in lush canyon bottoms, zigzag up the dry canyon walls, and follow rock ledges to the crest. Soft south light illuminating the Santa Ynez Mountains makes the range all the more magical to the hiker.

CHAPTER I

SANTA BARBARA

HIKE ON.

SAN ROQUE CANYON

JESUSITA TRAIL

To Moreno Ranch is 2.6 miles round trip with 700-foot elevation gain; to Inspiration Point is 7.2 miles round trip with 1,200-foot gain

Fortunately for hikers, the Depression of the 1930s forced San Roque Country Club to cancel its plans and much of San Roque Canyon became parkland rather than a golf course.

Jesusita Trail extends 4.5 miles east-west from San Roque to Mission canyons. Between the canyons is a high ridge with viewpoints, including official Inspiration Point. Creekside flora, handsome rock formations, avocado orchards, grassy meadows, power lines and panoramic views are all part of the Jesusita experience.

The trail was a flashpoint for the 2009 Jesusita Fire, which burned more than 8,000 acres and destroyed 80 homes. San Roque Canyon's native flora has since recovered nicely and local volunteers have done wonders to re-hab Jesusita Trail.

DIRECTIONS: From Highway 101 in Santa Barbara, exit on Las Positas Road and drive north two miles. Continue on San Roque Road, 0.4 mile past its intersection with Foothill Road to the Cater Water Filtration Plant.

THE HIKE: Descend Jesusita Trail, soon pasing a left-branching path that leads to Stevens Park. About 0.5 mile out, hike past a picnic table and at 0.75 mile reach a signed junction. Arroyo Burro Trail forks left; stay right with Jesusita Trail.

The path curves and ascends to an open meadow; follow the narrower path along its left edge. About a mile out, cross San Roque Creek, then re-cross it again a few more times. Jesusita Trail parallels a private ranch road and eventually meets it.

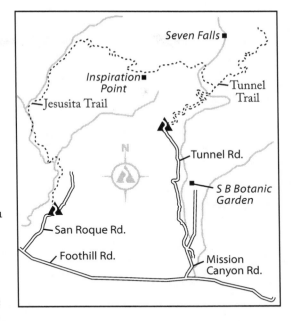

Follow trail signs and continue across Moreno Ranch to the top of a hill and a vehicle gate. Pass through a smaller pedestrian gate to a shady vista point, picnic table and a drinking fountain (the only one found along a Santa Barbara Trail!).

Inspiration Point-bound hikers will continue down the dirt road into the shady confines of the canyon. Emerge on open, chaparral-cloaked slopes and get grand views of Santa Barbara and the ocean. Passing handsome sandstone formations, travel under power lines to the ridgeline and a junction with the Edison power-line road.

Head left along the road to meet footpaths leading left (north) and south (right). The leftward path is Jesusita Trail and it leads down into Mission Canyon. Reach Inspiration Point by descending east on the power-line road a short distance.

Look sharply right for a narrow, unsigned connector trail leading 0.2 mile or so to Inspiration Point, a cluster of sandstone boulders. views from the 1,750-foot point include the city and coastlines of Santa Barbara and Ventura.

Rattlesnake Canyon

Rattlesnake Canyon Trail

From Skofield Park to Tin Can Meadow is 3.6 miles round trip with 1,000-foot elevation gain; to Gibraltar Road is 6 miles round trip with 1,500-foot gain

Rattlesnake Canyon Trail is serpentine, but otherwise far more inviting than its name.

The joys of hiking the canyon were first promoted by none other than the Santa Barbara Chamber of Commerce. In 1902 the chamber built "Chamber of Commerce Trail," an immediate success with both tourists and locals, though both trail and canyon continued to be called Rattlesnake.

In the 1960s, the city of Santa Barbara purchased the canyon as parkland. A handsome wooden sign at the foot of the canyon proudly proclaims: Rattlesnake Canyon Wilderness.

The canyon was severely burned in the Tea Fire of November 2008, but the chaparral community in particular has recovered quite well from the devastation. Red-berried toyon, manzanita with its white urn-shaped flowers, and purple hummingbird sage cloak the slopes.

DIRECTIONS: In Santa Barbara, follow State Street to Los Olivos Street. Head east and proceed a half mile, passing by the Santa Barbara Mission and joining Mission Canyon Road. Follow this road past its intersection with Foothill Road and make a right on Las Canoas Road, continuing to the trailhead, located near the handsome stone bridge that crosses Rattlesnake Creek. Park alongside Las Canoas Road.

THE HIKE: From the Rattlesnake Canyon Wilderness sign, head north and soon rock-hop across the creek. A brief ascent leads to a trail that parallels the east side of the creek.

After a half mile, an unsigned trail veers off to the right. (One of The Trailmaster's favorite byways, this narrow path leads along and above the east bank of Rattlesnake Creek and reunites with the main trail in about a mile.)

Soon after the junction, the main trail draws near the creek and crosses it. The path then ascends past remnants of a small stand of planted pines and into the open for good vistas of coast and ocean. Continue to a creek crossing and notice (you can't miss it, really) a large flat rock in the middle of the creek known by locals as "Lunch Rock."

The trail crosses the creek again, continuing along the west bank to open, grassy Tin Can Meadow, named for a homesteader's cabin constructed of chaparral framing and kerosene can shingles and sidings. For the first quarter of the 20th century, Tin Can Shack was a canyon landmark, mentioned in guidebooks of that era. A 1925 brushfire destroyed the shack.

The apex of the triangular-shaped meadow is a junction. The trail bearing left leads 0.75 mile and climbs 500 feet to an intersection with Tunnel Trail. To the right, Rattlesnake Canyon Trail climbs 0.75 mile and 500 feet to meet Gibraltar Road. The hiker's reward is an unobstructed view of the South Coast.

Mission Canyon

Tunnel Trail, Jesusita Trail

From Tunnel Road to Seven Falls is 2 miles round trip with 400-foot elevation gain; to Inspiration Point is 4 miles round trip with 800-foot gain

Seven Falls has long been a popular destination for hikers. "A pleasant party spent yesterday up Mission Canyon visiting noted Seven Falls and afterward eating a tempting picnic dinner in a romantic spot on the creek's bank," the *Santa Barbara Daily Press* reported in 1887.

This easy family hike follows Tunnel Trail, joins Jesusita Trail for an exploration of the seven little falls and numerous cascades found in the bed of Mission Creek, and ascends to Inspiration Point for sweeping coastal views.

Tunnel Trail was used by workers to gain access to a difficult city waterworks project. Upper Mission Canyon was severely scorched by the 2009 Jesusita Fire. The riparian flora on the canyon bottom looks pretty good; the open slopes along the paved road are recovering more slowly.

DIRECTIONS: From Highway 101 in Santa Barbara, exit on Mission Street. Turn east to Laguna Street, then left and drive past the historic Santa Barbara Mission. From the mission, drive up Mission Canyon Road, turning right for a block on Foothill Road, then immediately turning left back onto Mission Canyon Road. Drive 0.3 mile to a distinct V-intersection, veer left onto Tunnel Road and drive a mile to its end. Park alongside the road. This is a particularly popular trail in the late afternoons and weekends; you might have to park quite some distance down the road from the trailhead.

THE HIKE: From the end of Tunnel Road, hike past a locked gate onto a paved road. Enjoy far-reaching city and ocean views.

About 0.75 mile from the trailhead, the road makes a sharp left and crosses a bridge over the west fork of Mission Creek, where a waterfall spills over some boulders.

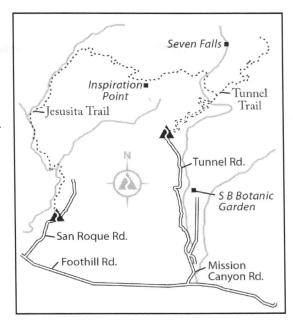

Beyond the bridge, hike a short distance under handsome oaks to a junction. (Tunnel Trail angles northeast, uphill, leading three miles to East Camino Cielo.) Join dirt Jesusita Trail, which soon descends to Mission Creek.

At the canyon bottom, you can hike up-creek into a steep gorge that was cut from solid sandstone. Rainwater rushing from the shoulder of La Cumbre Peak has cut away at the canyon's sandstone layers, forming several deep pools. Use caution; reaching the waterfalls—particularly the higher ones—requires quite a bit of boulder hopping and rock climbing. Even when there's not much water in the creek, it can be tricky going. (More cascades and pools are located down-canyon from the trail crossing.)

From the creek crossing, Jesusita Trail switchbacks steeply for one mile up the chaparral-cloaked canyon wall to a T-junction with a power line road atop a knoll. Cross the road, walk a few moments east, and join the path for the 0.2-mile hike down from the ridgeline to Inspiration Point. The view from the cluster of sandstone rocks at the 1,750-foot viewpoint includes a long length of coastline, the Channel Islands, Santa Barbara and the Goleta Valley.

Santa Barbara Botanic Garden

Canyon, Pritchett, Easton Trails

1 to 3 miles round trip

Nestled in the rugged landscape of Mission Canyon, the Santa Barbara Botanic Garden is truly a treasure, a living museum. Pathways leading through California's ecosystems allow quick getaways from city life. The garden, home to more than 1,000 species of native trees, shrubs and flowers, is a place to linger and learn.

Founded in 1926, this 65-acre enclave is devoted to the display, protection and research of native species. Ecosystems represented include meadows, desert, chaparral, woodland, arroyo, and the Channel Islands. Magnificent redwoods thrive in a grove located on the flat streambed along Mission Creek.

Among the ongoing programs offered by the garden are lectures, docent-led tours, field trips to other gardens, classes and workshops. A herbarium, library, year-round nursery and well-stocked garden bookstore are also attractions to plant lovers.

Easton Aqueduct Trail honors the late Robert Easton, a fourth-generation Californian, fine writer of California-themed books, and long-time conservationist, who worked diligently to protect the South-Central Coast and the Santa Barbara backcountry. I've linked this pathway and several other trails into a clockwise route around the garden. Begin the hike at the main entrance at 1212 Mission Canyon Road. Have fun and improvise: You can make a tight circle for a one-mile walk or take every side trail and enjoy a three-mile excursion.

DIRECTIONS: From Highway 101 in Santa Barbara, exit on Mission Street and head east to Laguna Street. Turn left and, keeping the Santa Barbara Mission on your left, you'll soon join Mission Canyon Road. When you reach a stop sign at Foothill Road, turn right, and then make an almost immediate left back onto Mission Canyon Road. Travel 0.2 mile to a distinct V-shaped intersection. To reach the main entrance: At the above-mentioned V-intersection, keep right on Mission Canyon Road and follow it a half mile

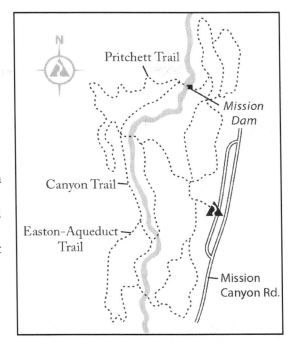

to nearly to road's end, where you'll find the Santa Barbara Botanic Garden. Park in the garden's lot. There is a fee to enter the garden.

THE HIKE: From the garden's main entrance, as you pass the entry kiosk and approach the bookstore, turn left on the brick pathway and walk past the Discovery Garden and the Home Demonstration Garden. Join the path heading down into the canyon. Carefully cross the creek then veer left on signed Easton Aqueduct Trail.

The trail zigzags through the Island Section (plants from the Channel Islands), nears Tunnel Road, then drops to a small bench. Continue on a short descent to Mission Dam and a footbridge over Mission Creek. Enjoy the lovely scene and the restful sound of cascading water.

Join the wide path along the canyon bottom to the redwoods, and then ascend a brick path to the meadow section of the garden. Walk the fringe of the meadow, passing a picnic area, a display of California native orchids, an information kiosk and even a display of desert flora, before returning to the garden shop and entry.

Find Shangri-La around Ojai Valley with engaging trails in the foothills above the avocado ranches, citrus orchards, and lovely town. Sunsets are spectacular, especially Ojai's famed "Pink Moments."

Ventura County offers the hiker a generous sampling of lonesome canyons, skyscraping peaks, oak woodlands, sparkling rock formations, waterfalls and wildflower-strewn meadows. The county also boasts an engaging selection of trails near population centers—perfect for fitness hikes and quick getaways into nature. "Overlooked and underrated," is the way The Trailmaster characterizes the trails of Ventura County.

CHAPTER 2

VENTURA COUNTY

HIKE ON.

OJAI VALLEY

PRATT, FUELBREAK ROAD, SHELF ROAD TRAILS

Loop from Stewart Canyon to Gridley Road is 6.5 miles round trip with 800-foot elevation gain

The 10-mile-long, 3-mile wide Ojai Valley, surrounded by coastal mountain ranges has always had a sequestered feeling. The native Chumash called this region Ojai, meaning "nest."

Four trails at the edge of town combine to form a loop hike and offer fine vistas of the lovely valley, which has spawned an artists colony and music festival as well as a number of health resorts, faith-based enclaves and spiritual retreats. Ojai Valley was the setting for Shangri-La in the 1937 movie "Lost Horizon."

Gridley and Pratt are Ojai's most easily accessible and popular north-south trails. East-west trending Fuelbreak Road and Shelf Road connect to Gridley and Pratt to create a memorable hike. Fuelbreak Road Trail is the wilder of the two with grander views, while Shelf Road is more multi-use with lots of dog-walkers

This loop hike offers great vistas of the town and valley: Ojai's harmonious Spanish architecture, sweet-smelling citrus groves and the sometimes misty, sometimes mystical Ojai Valley.

DIRECTIONS: From Highway 33 in the heart of downtown Ojai, turn north on North Signal and drive 0.8 mile to a water tank and a signed road on your left. Turn left and drive 0.3 mile on this road, past Ventura County flood control works and Stewart Canyon Debris Basin to a turnaround and parking.

THE HIKE: Join signed Pratt Trail and hike briefly west then north along Stewart Creek. The path dips into brushy, boulder-strewn Stewart Canyon, zigzagging beneath oaks and tangled understory of native and nonnative shrubs. Signs, lots of them,

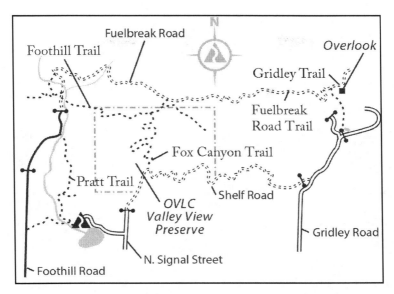

clearly define private property and public right-of-way. The path meanders behind some lovely residential gardens and meets a paved road that leads to a gate and forest boundary at the 1-mile mark. Get your bearings at the handsome map/display and hike on.

Continue on dirt road past a water tank and a signed junction with Foothill Trail, then past Foothill Connector Trail and onward to a Y-junction. Pratt Trail goes left, but you go right on the USFS Fuelbreak Road.

The dirt road alternately dips and rises and, just as you begin to wonder if the trail will ever deliver a view, climbs eastward out onto open slopes for great vistas of Ojai Valley. Shangri-La, indeed.

Continue to a gate at the end of Fuelbreak Road Trail, a vista point and a junction. Gridley Trail (dirt road) ascends left to Gridley Spring (see hike description). Descend right down a brushy draw 0.5 mile to a cul de sac at the top of Gridley Road. Walk down Gridley Road 0.3 mile to Shelf Road on your right.

Follow Shelf Road, closed to vehicle traffic, west into the hills. Skirting orange trees and avocado groves, Shelf Road serves up views that are just a little less-dramatic than those offered by higher Fuelbreak Road. After 1.7 miles of travel, reach a gate and North Signal Street, which you'll follow 0.2 mile south down to the turnoff for the trailhead. Turn right and walk 0.3 mile back to the trailhead.

VENTURA RIVER PRESERVE

RICE CANYON, WILLS CANYON TRAILS

5-mile loop with 400-foot elevation gain

Explore an intriguing section of the Ventura River and tributary creeks with a hike in Ventura River Preserve once known as Rancho El Nido. Well-signed footpaths and old ranch roads weave through the 1,591-acre preserve, a diverse environment with oak woodland, chaparral-covered hillsides and sunny meadows.

At the turn of the 21st century, Rancho El Nido appeared destined for development of an upscale residential community and golf course. The Ojai Valley Land Conservancy raised funds to purchase the spread and the preserve opened to public use in 2003.

The rancho was planted in oranges in the 1920s, and one of the highlights of this hike in the west end of the Ojai Valley is meandering through an orange grove gone wild. If the trees were tended, the scene would make a perfect postcard or lovely label for a wooden orange crate.

For a great intro to the delights of Ventura River Preserve, hike up Rice Canyon and down Wills Canyon. Both canyons boast strategically placed benches from which to contemplate the inspirational scene.

DIRECTIONS: From Highway 33, about 3 miles south of Ojai, turn west onto Highway 150 (Baldwin Road) and go 0.2 mile to Rice Road. Turn right and drive 2 miles to Meyer Road, go left 0.2 mile and, as the road bends sharply right and continues as Oso Road, head straight through an open gate (note sign with preserve hours) and follow a narrow lane with sizeable speed bumps to parking and Oso trailhead.

THE HIKE: The signed path soon leads to a crossing of the Ventura River, which flows about half the year. Usually you can

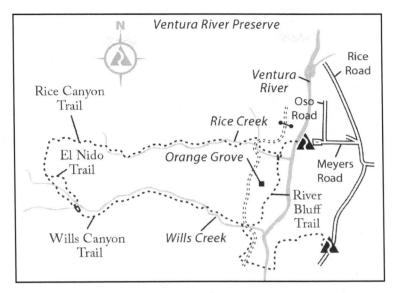

rock-hop across the river, sometimes you need to wade and once in a while, after a storm, the river is a rain-swollen torrent, crossing impassable and you need to find another place to hike.

The trail leads west through the old orange grove and bends south to a bridge and a fork with a connector trail leading 0.5 mile south to Wills Canyon Trail and signed Rice Canyon Trail. Hike west along the north side of Rice Creek, soon crossing paved Canal Road and a bridge over a canal. Restoration efforts underway will re-divert Rice Creek waters from the irrigation canal back into its original creek bed.

The path parallels the oak and sycamore-shaded creek, passes through a gate and enters Los Padres National Forest. A modest ascent leads to ridgeline views of the Ojai Valley. Bend south to meet a narrow dirt road, pass through a cattle gate and re-enter the preserve. Observe lovely El Nido Meadow and continue the descent into Wills Canyon, to a footbridge and a junction with Wills Canyon Trail.

Descend along Wills Creek, passing a junction with Fern Grotto Trail, to the mouth of the canyon and a bench offering a fine view of the Ventura River watershed. Cross Canal Road and join River Bluff Trail, which leads north past the historic orange grove. Traverse a drainage canal, re-cross the Ventura River and return to the trailhead.

GRIDLEY CANYON & NORDHOFF PEAK

GRIDLEY TRAIL

From Gridley Road to Gridley Spring is 5.6 miles round trip with 1,300-foot elevation gain; to Nordhoff Ridge is 12 miles round trip with 2,600-foot gain; to Nordhoff Peak is 14.2 miles with 3,300-foot gain

German-born Charles Nordhoff was one of the 19th century's biggest boosters of California. An editor with the New York Evening Post, Nordhoff traveled extensively around the Golden State in 1870-1871, and wrote *California: for Health, Pleasure and Residence*, an enormously popular book that prompted much visitation and settlement.

He wrote about a beautiful valley located inland and, as a result, the peaceful hamlet here quickly grew into a town. Grateful townspeople named it Nordhoff in 1874. Nordhoff it was until 1916 when the anti-German sentiment of World War I prompted a change of name to Ojai.

Nordhoff's name remains on the 4,425-foot peak that forms a dramatic backdrop for Ojai. Reward for the steep ascent to Nordhoff Peak are splendid views of the Ojai Valley, the coast and Channel Islands. The hike to Gridley Springs is a more moderate hike with great valley vistas. The Thomas Fire (December 2017) blackened the slopes of Gridley Peak; the trail is not as pretty as it was pre-fire, but it's passable.

DIRECTIONS: From the intersection of Highways 33 and 150 in Ojai, proceed on 150 (Ojai Avenue) through town. About 2 miles from the intersection, look for LPNF Ojai Ranger Station on the left, proceed another 0.5 mile, turn left on Gridley Road and drive

1.7 miles to its end at a cul-de-sac, find parking and the trailhead.

THE HIKE: Gridley Trail climbs a brushy draw, overhung with tall ceanothus on a gentle 0.5 mile ascent (over private property; courtesy, please) to a vista point near a curious citrus grove (Ojai Pixie tangerines) and a junction with signed Fuelbreak Road Trail.

Stay right and follow a crumbling dirt road above avocado groves planted on steep slopes. The route enters

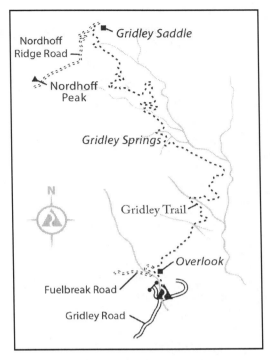

Gridley Canyon, climbing to the northwest (and thankfully cooler) side of the canyon, highlighted by ferns and maple.

You'll find a horse trough at Gridley Spring, but not much else is left of the former trail camp. Nevertheless, the spring named for an early homesteader still flows, and it remains a nice rest stop.

Continue along the dirt road (narrowing into trail) into an east fork of Gridley Canyon. The switchbacking trail makes a rigorous ascent, passing the occasional gathering of bay-trees watered by seasonal springs. Look above at the superb succession of sedimentary rocks displayed by the Topatopa Mountains.

Nearly 3 miles from Gridley Spring, reach Gridley Saddle (3,800 feet) and Nordhoff Ridge Road. Turn left (west) and ascend 1 mile to the turnoff to the fire lookout and continue another 0.2 mile to the top of Nordhoff Peak. Vistas to the west include the high peaks of the Topatopa range; to the north, the Pine Mountain range; to the south is Ojai Valley, with Lake Casitas and the Pacific beyond.

LOS ROBLES TRAIL SYSTEM

OAK CREEK CANYON, LOS ROBLES TRAILS

From Oak Creek Canyon to Angel Vista Point is 8 miles round trip with 500-foot elevation gain

Perched on an elevated plateau that extends between Westlake and the Oxnard Plain lies the lovely, oak-studded, mountain-surrounded Conejo Valley. The valley, which crowns the eastern edge of Ventura County, certainly hosts its share of suburban developments, but retains a charming, pastoral side that offers some delightful hiking.

The network of pathways exploring the Conejo Valley is often referred to as the Los Robles Trail System. Los Robles and companion trails link Conejo Valley with the extensive trail system in the Santa Monica Mountains. At the valley's west end, Los Robles Trail ties into Point Mugu State Park; an intrepid hiker could hike across the valley then over the mountains to the Pacific Ocean in the course of a day.

The trail, along with the terrain it traverses, is oriented east-west. Los Robles Trail was developed—and is maintained—as a multi-use path, meaning the hiker can expect to see an occasional horseback rider and many mountain bikers. Connector trails extend from Westlake, Thousand Oaks and several neighborhoods to Los Robles Trail.

The middle section of Los Robles Trail offers a pleasant introduction to hiking the Conejo Valley and the region's trail system. Begin in pleasant Oak Canyon at the edge of Thousand Oaks and enjoy the winding path and fine valley vistas.

DIRECTIONS: From Highway 101 (Ventura Freeway) in Thousand Oaks, exit on Moorpark Road and drive 0.5 mile south to Greenmeadow Avenue. Turn right (west) and proceed 0.4 mile to road's end at the parking lot for the Conejo Valley Arts Council Center and the signed trail.

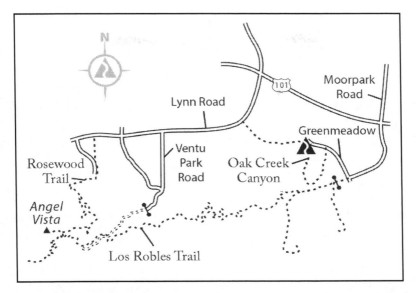

THE HIKE: Walk among the oaks on Oak Creek Canyon Whole Access Trail, a footpath designed to assist the blind learn more about the great outdoors. Interpretive stations with text written in Braille describe the lovely surroundings.

After 0.25 mile, the path bends east and junctions. An eastern leg of the canyon trail loops back to the trailhead; instead, head briefly south to connect with Los Robles Trail.

Stick with Los Robles Trail (West) at a couple of junctions. The path tunnels through the high chaparral, climbs gently on a mile-long set of switchbacks, and delivers good Conejo Valley views at about the 2-mile mark.

The trail dips into a canyon, crosses a private road, and climbs again. Los Robles Trail meets Rosewood Trail (which descends to Lynn Road) at a signed junction. Stick with Los Robles Trail, descending steeply to cross a private dirt road and then making a brief final ascent to Angel Vista Point, where a welcome picnic table offers a place to relax and enjoy Conejo Valley vistas. Near the table is a higher point offering a 360-degree panorama of the Santa Monica Mountains extending east-west, the Ventura-Oxnard Plain, the Channel Islands and Pacific Ocean.

Retrace your steps to the Oak Creek Canyon Loop trail and take its eastern leg through a chaparral section back to the trailhead.

WILDWOOD REGIONAL PARK

MESA, LIZARD ROCK, WILDWOOD CANYON TRAILS

To Lizard Rock with return via Wildwood Canyon is 5 miles round trip with 400-foot elevation gain

A tranquil retreat on the outskirts of Conejo Valley, Wildwood Regional Park preserves 1,732 acres of canyon-land and rocky cliffs. The park is bounded by Conejo Creek and its two seasonal branches—Arroyo Santa Rosa and Arroyo Conejo—and features Paradise Falls, a year-around waterfall.

From the 1930s to 1960s, Wildwood Canyon was a popular location for movies (such as "Spartacus" and "Wuthering Heights") and TV Westerns, including "Dodge City" and "The Rifleman." The park still looks like a scene from a western movie with Mount Clef Ridge rising dramatically from a mesa and resembling a kind of Monument Valley in miniature.

The park boasts an extensive trail system offering trails for hikers of all abilities. Families with small children can take a stroll along Wildwood Creek and check out Paradise Falls, a year-around waterfall. This route tours the heart of the park, and offers many options and sights-to-see.

DIRECTIONS: From the Ventura Freeway (101) in Thousand Oaks, exit on Lynn Road and drive 2.5 miles north to Avenida De Los Arboles. Turn left and proceed 1 mile to the park entrance and a parking area.

THE HIKE: Follow a dirt fire road, soon veer right onto Mesa Trail, and hike past a junction with Santa Rosa Trail (leading to Mountclef Ridge). The road splits, with the route straight ahead crossing the mesa to Lizard Rock. Bear left on a short connector path

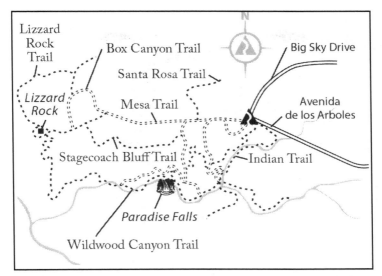

to Stagecoach Bluff Trail, which heads west along the lip of Wildwood Canyon. Many stagecoach chases and robberies were filmed along this route.

Continue on Stagecoach Bluff Trail, joined by trails coming in from the north from Mesa Trail and Box Canyon, to the summit of Lizard Rock. The rock's resemblance to a lizard is dubious, but the lizard's-eye view from atop the rock is excellent: to the north are the Los Posas Hills and far north, the Los Padres National Forest backcountry; to the south is Conejo Valley. To the northeast are the Santa Susana Mountains, and to the east are the Simi Hills. To the west are the Camarillo Hills and Oxnard Plain.

After taking in the view, hike south downhill on Lizard Rock Trail, switchbacking toward Hill Canyon Water Treatment Plant. The path bends east into the bottom of Wildwood Canyon and crisscrosses the creek on footbridges. Pass benches, picnic tables, restrooms, a drinking fountain…is this a luxe hike or what?

Contemplate Paradise Falls and look up at Teepee Overlook and a big faux teepee. Continue on the path up-creek, pass Little Falls Picnic Area, cross branch of Conejo Creek on a wooden bridge and join signed Indian Creek Trail heading northeast.

Ascend this trail through lush creekside flora, keeping an eye out for Indian Creek Falls below. At a junction, take the left fork and walk amidst old oaks back to the trailhead.

Simi Peak

China Flat Trail

To China Flat and Simi Peak is 4-mile loop with 1,000-foot elevation gain

"The map is not the territory," wise explorers counsel. That old adage seems to apply to the Simi Hills, which appear as little more than a narrow band between suburbs on the map, but on the ground present some challenging territory to hike. The Simi Hills have a distinct identity when viewed up-close. Somehow the sky-scraping sedimentary rock formations seem all the more awesome towering over flatland neighborhoods.

The reddish-orange sandstone outcroppings of the Simi Hills, dating from the Tertiary and Mesozoic periods 60 to 80 million years ago, form a dramatic backdrop and it's easy to see why these rugged hills were a popular setting for Western movies.

China Flat Trail is an excellent (but not easy) introduction to the Simi Hills. It leads to China Flat, perched on the wild west side of the National Park Service's Cheeseboro Canyon Site. The trail's return loop contours high over the shoulder of 2,403-foot Simi Peak, highest summit in the Simi Hills.

A one-block neighborhood stroll links trail's end with the trailhead.

China Flat Trail is a bit of a misnomer; the trail is anything but flat. And China Flat itself, while of more level relief than surrounding Simi peaks, will never be confused with one of those truly flat Flats found in other mountain ranges.

DIRECTIONS: From the Ventura Freeway (101) in Westlake Village, exit on Lindero Canyon Road and head north 4 miles. A few blocks from the trailhead, Lindero Canyon Road bends east.

Look for the signed trailhead on the left (north) side of the road between King James Court and Wembly Avenue. Park on Lindero Canyon Road.

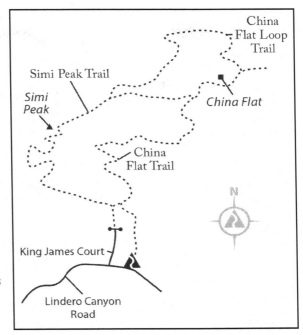

THE HIKE: Follow the trail north up a short, steep hill. Here a connector trail rising from King James Court meets the path. Continue on the main (China Flat) trail as it ascends past a sandstone formation. After climbing some more, the path gentles a bit and contours east to an unsigned junction. Keep to the left (north) and begin a stiff climb toward the ridgeline.

Finally the trail gains the ridge and you encounter another unsigned junction. Bear left and continue an ascent along the ridge to a saddle and yet another trail junction. Take the left fork (trekkers bound for Cheeseboro Canyon will take the right fork.) and begin a moderate descent.

Views from the shoulder of Simi Peak include Westlake Village, Agoura Hills and other communities clustered on the Ventura-Los Angeles County line, as well as the peaks of the Santa Monica Mountains.

The trail ends at a gate on King James Court. Follow this short street one block down to Lindero Canyon Road and your vehicle.

CHEESEBORO CANYON

CHEESEBORO CANYON TRAIL

To Sulfur Springs is 6.6 miles round trip with 100-foot elevation gain; to Sheep Corral is 9.2 miles round trip with 200-foot elevation gain

It's the old California of the ranchos: oak-studded potreros, rolling foothills that glow amber in the dry months, emerald green in springtime. It's easy to imagine vaqueros rounding up tough Mexican range cattle.

For years this last vestige of old California faced an uncertain future, but thanks to the efforts of conservationists it was saved from golf course and suburban development. Cheeseboro Canyon was placed under the stewardship of the Santa Monica Mountains National Recreation Area.

From the days of the ranchos to 1985, Cheeseboro Canyon was heavily grazed by cattle. Grazing altered canyon ecology by displacing native flora and allowing opportunistic plants such as mustard and thistle to invade. The National Park Service re-colonized native flora and eradicated non-natives.

The canyon's handsome scenery—big old oaks and dramatic sedimentary rock formations—offers stellar nesting areas for owls, hawks and other birds of prey. According to the National Park Service, Cheeseboro Canyon is believed to have the largest concentrations of birds of prey nesting areas in the U.S. outside Alaska.

DIRECTIONS: From the Ventura Freeway (101) in Agoura, exit on Chesebro Road. Loop inland very briefly on Palo Comado Canyon Road, then turn right on Chesebro Road, which leads to the National Park Service's gravel entrance road and parking lot.

THE HIKE:
Note a possible return route, Modelo Trail, snaking north up the wall of the canyon, but follow the fire road east into Cheeseboro Canyon. The fire road soon swings north and dips into the canyon amidst valley oaks. Pass a signed intersection with Canyon Overlook Trail, a side trail that leads east 0.7 mile to a knoll overlooking the Lost Hills landfill.

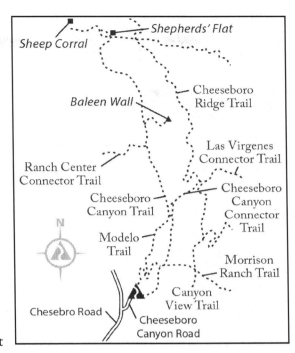

Sheep Corral
Shepherds' Flat
Cheeseboro Ridge Trail
Baleen Wall
Las Virgenes Connector Trail
Ranch Center Connector Trail
Cheeseboro Canyon Connector Trail
Cheeseboro Canyon Trail
Modelo Trail
Morrison Ranch Trail
Canyon View Trail
Chesebro Road
Cheeseboro Canyon Road
N

Stay left at a junction with a connector trail leading to Cheeseboro Ridge Trail, pass a picnic area at the 1.6-mile mark and continue through valley oak-dotted grassland and coast live oak-lined canyon. Watch for mule deer browsing in the meadows.

The old road crisscrosses an (usually) all-but-dry streambed. A bit more than 3 miles from the trailhead, observe the white cliffs of Baleen Wall to the east and soon your nose will tell you that you've arrived at Sulphur Springs. Turn around here or continue another 1.3 miles up a narrowing trail and narrowing canyon to Shepherds' Flat and an old sheep corral.

You can continue a bit farther on the trail to a junction with Palo Comado Canyon Trail and head south on this path back to the trailhead. Ranch Center Trail, a 1.1-mile long path, connects Palo Comado and Cheeseboro canyons, as does the 1.5-mile Palo Comado Connector Trail. The latter path leads to a junction 0.7 mile from the trailhead. Modelo Trail leads along the western ridge of the canyon for a good view of Cheeseboro Canyon and one of the finest remaining oak woodlands in Southern California.

UPPER LAS VIRGENES CANYON

EAST LAS VIRGENES CANYON, LASKEY MESA TRAILS

From Las Virgenes Road to Laskey Mesa is 5.5 miles round trip with 500-foot elevation gain; many shorter and longer options possible

From atop the ridge on the southeastern corner of Upper Las Virgenes Canyon Open Space Preserve, commanding vistas of two altogether different vistas and visions of Southern California are revealed to the hiker. Eastward and southward the San Fernando Valley suburbanopolis sprawls across Los Angeles County. Westward beckons a magnificent, nearly untouched landscape of rolling grassland, oak-dotted slopes and the dramatic summits of the Simi Hills, miles of wildland extending across Ventura County.

The preservationist vision prevailed here after a decade-long battle that pitted conservationists and celebrity allies such as Rob Reiner and Martin Sheen versus Washington Mutual with a $2 billion plan that called for construction of 3,000 homes, a golf course and a shopping mall on what was then known as Ahmanson Ranch. The enormous savings institution (now defunct) agreed to sell the land to the Santa Monica Mountains Conservancy in 2003.

Natural resources include the headwaters of Malibu Creek and 4,000 valley and coastal live oak trees. The preserve is a prime raptor habitat.

The rolling hills and broad mesas located on the far eastern edge of Ventura County have been a favorite location for filmmakers since the silent movie era. The Laskey Company owned the ranch, which boasted both a close proximity to studios and an almost complete lack of development. Among the movies filmed at Laskey Mesa, as

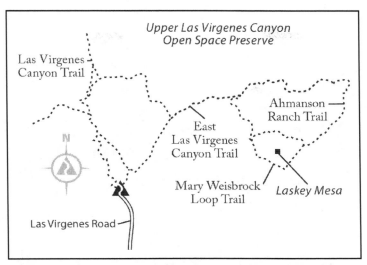

it was then known, were "The Charge of the Light Brigade," "They Died with Their Boots On," and "Gone with the Wind."

The 2,983-acre preserve offers 15 miles of trails and dirt roads, and the hiker looking for more can continue to the upper reaches of Cheeseboro Canyon. An excellent introduction to the preserve's attractions, this hike meanders across wide grasslands and amidst oak woodland to the broad plateau of Laskey Mesa.

DIRECTIONS: From Highway 101 in Calabasas, exit on Las Virgenes Canyon Road and drive north 1.5 miles to road's end, the main trail leading into Upper Las Virgenes Canyon Open Space Preserve, and curbside parking.

THE HIKE: From the trailhead gate, hike 0.3 mile along the park's main dirt road leading along the west side of Las Virgenes Creek to a junction. Branch right on East Virgenes Canyon Trail and ascend grassy rolling hills. In 0.5 mile note a left-branching trail (optional longer return loop) and continue another mile to a junction with Laskey Mesa Trail.

Join this path and descend westward. Make a big bend southward to join Mary Weisbrock Loop Trail (both trails loop around the 1,391-foot mesa), round the south side of Laskey Mesa to a trail gate, pass ranch buildings and head north on Ahmanson Ranch House Trail. Return to East Las Virgenes Trail, descend west 1.1 miles over oak-dotted slopes to the junction with Laskey Mesa Trail, and retrace your steps to the trailhead.

From Runyon Canyon to Mt. Hollywood to the HOLLYWOOD Sign, take a hike on the truly wild side of Hollywood. I love hiking through Griffith Park and the famed Hollywood Hills.

Other L.A. mountains aren't so well known. The Verdugo Mountains—a range 13 miles long and 3 miles wide—is surrounded by millions of people who live in metropolitan Los Angeles, yet relatively few know the range's natural attractions or hiking trails. Pathways in the Baldwin Hills offer great city views and an air traffic controller's view of LAX. The Puente Hills, which rise from 400 to 1,400 feet in elevation, offer San Gabriel Valley residents a natural backdrop and hikers many miles of trails to roam.

CHAPTER 3

L.A. MOUNTAINS SAMPLER

HIKE ON.

GRIFFITH OBSERVATORY

EAST AND WEST OBSERVATORY TRAILS

**From Ferndell to Griffith Observatory is 2.5 miles round trip
with 500-foot elevation gain**

Griffith Observatory opened to the public in 1935 and has been
an L.A. cultural institution, tourist attraction, and L.A. landmark in
every sense of the word ever since. The observatory has been featured
in many films including that James Dean classic, "Rebel Without a
Cause," as well as "The Terminator" and "Transformers."

The observatory, planetarium and extensive array of space and
science exhibits, combined with lectures by leading astronomers and
scientists, have interpreted the wonders of the universe for generations of schoolchildren and an enthusiastic public. Closed in 2002
for an extensive $93 million renovation, the observatory reopened
in 2006, retaining its Art Deco exterior and adding all new exhibits,
the Leonard Nimoy Event Horizon Theater and Café at the End of
the Universe. The 2007 Griffith Park Fire came dangerously close to
Griffith Observatory.

This hike crosses upper Ferndell and joins West Observatory
Trail for a climb up the south-facing slope of Mt. Hollywood to the
observatory. Hikers get vistas of the L.A. Basin from downtown to
the Pacific Ocean. Extend this hike by continuing to the top of Mt.
Hollywood (see hike description) or by beginning in lower Ferndell
(see hike description).

DIRECTIONS: From Los Feliz Boulevard, one block east of
Western Avenue, turn north on Fern Dell Drive and proceed about
0.3 mile to the Trails Café. The trail begins at an opening in the
fence opposite the café. Park along the road above or below the
trailhead.

THE HIKE:
Across from Trails
Café, walk through
the opening in the
fence and soon
cross two bridges to
the east side of the
brook to join a wide
path (the main path
coming up from
lower Ferndell).
Head right (east)
under the shade of
a mixed forest of
oak, sycamore and
redwood. The picnic
ground has plenty of
tables and is a great
place for a post-hike
lunch stop, as is the Trails Café.

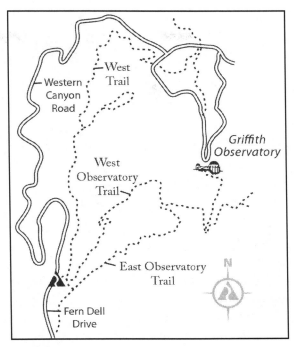

Soon you'll pass a footbridge over a stream on the left; this leads
to West Observatory Trail (which meets the eastern path near the
top) and West Trail; both are great alternate return routes. Proceed
straight, and soon glimpse the observatory. More ascent yields more
views: Mt. Hollywood and Mt. Lee with the famed Hollywood sign,
and downtown Los Angeles, about 5 miles away as the crow flies.

After bending north, East Observatory Trail meets its western leg
and the two proceed in tandem southeast to a major intersection.

Take the road on the right and ascend north 0.25 mile to the
eastern end of the observatory. Those hikers bound for Mt. Hollywood should walk to the well-signed trailhead at the north end of
the Observatory parking lot.

My favorite return route (adding a mile to this short hike) is a
descent through Western Canyon; walk a short way up the trail to
Mt. Hollywood to join West Trail at Western Canyon Road.

MT. HOLLYWOOD

MT. HOLLYWOOD TRAIL

From Griffith Observatory to Mt. Hollywood is 3 miles round trip with 500-foot elevation gain

Griffith Park's best-known hike leads to the top of 1,625-foot Mt. Hollywood, the park's premiere peak. Mt. Hollywood is not the mountain crowned by the historic Hollywood sign; however, the trail to it delivers great views of Mt. Lee and the bold HOLLY-WOOD lettering across its summit. Mt. Hollywood can be hiked by way of several different trails but the route from Griffith Observatory is by far the most popular.

On clear days the entire basin is spread out before you from the San Gabriel Mountains to the Pacific Ocean. Sometimes mounts San Gorgonio, Baldy and San Jacinto can be seen. The view at night can be spectacular, too.

Griffith Observatory opened to the public in 1935 and has been a cultural institution, tourist attraction and L.A. landmark ever since. Closed in 2002 for an extensive renovation, the observatory reopened in 2006, retaining its Art Deco exterior and adding all new exhibits and a theater.

In 2007, the great Griffith Park Fire burned more than 800 acres of parkland and came dangerously close to the complex. The observatory has long been an iconic movie location, most recently playing a starring role in the 2016 blockbuster, "La La Land."

Artist-writer Dante Orgolini, an immigrant of Italian descent, began planting a two-acre retreat of pine, palm and pepper trees high on the south-facing slope of Mt. Hollywood in 1965. British-born retired insurance agent Charlie Turner took over as caretaker in 1978 after Orgolini's death and, for the next 15 years, until he was nearly

90, hiked to the garden virtually every morning to tend the plants. The trailhead for Mt. Hollywood is named for Turner.

DIRECTIONS: From Los Feliz Boulevard, take Vermont Avenue into the park. Follow signs to the observatory and park in the north end of the lot farthest from the observatory near the signed and landscaped Charlie Turner Trailhead.

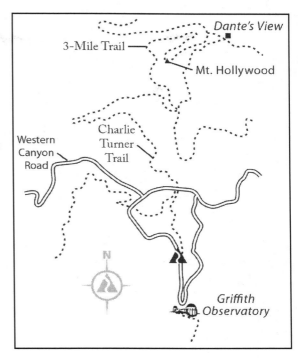

THE HIKE: A brief ascent along the narrow ridgeline dividing Vermont Canyon on the east and Western Canyon on the west leads to Berlin Forest. Among the trees planted by L.A.'s German sister city officials, is a whimsical sign pointing northeast to Berlin, 6,000 miles away.

The path traverses the top of the Vermont Canyon Road tunnel and about 0.9 mile out reaches a four-way junction on the brushy shoulder of Mt. Hollywood. The left branch loops around the west side, the right around the east side.

Ascend the right (east) branch of the Mt. Hollywood Trail to Dante's View, where a water fountain and picnic tables suggest a rest stop for hikers. Dedicated volunteers maintain the garden. Continue the short distance to the top of Mt. Hollywood and enjoy the view.

Return the way you came or descend the western loop of the Mt. Hollywood Trail past Captain's Roost, a rest stop, to a junction with Charlie Turner Trail.

Hollywood Sign from Brush Canyon

Brush Canyon, Mulholland, Mt. Lee Trails

From Canyon Drive to Bronson Caves is 0.5 mile round trip; to HOLLYWOOD Sign is 6.4 miles round trip with 1,100-foot elevation gain

Visit two Hollywood landmarks—the Bat Cave and the HOLLYWOOD Sign—on this hike that begins in Brush Canyon.

"To the Bat Cave, Robin." With that cry, Batman and Robin of TV fame hopped into the Batmobile and sped to their hideaway—not a set built on a studio back lot, but a real cave in Griffith Park. Many old TV shows including "Star Trek," countless Westerns, and low-budget horror movies were filmed in the "Bronson Caves."

Now that Canyon Drive trailhead has become a favorite trailhead for a hike to the HOLLYWOOD Sign, expect lots of company on the trail from SoCal hikers and visitors from across the US and around the world.

DIRECTIONS: From Franklin Avenue, on the southern boundary of Griffith Park, turn north on Bronson Avenue or Canyon Drive (the streets soon join and continue as Canyon). Follow Canyon Drive a winding mile through the hills into Griffith Park. Park alongside the road near a picnic area or in a small parking lot by the trailhead at road's end.

THE HIKE: Those heading directly for the Bronson Caves will locate the trailhead on the right (east) side of Canyon Drive. Join a fire road and hike south a short distance to the caves.

Walk past an info board with a large park map and join the fire road (Brush Canyon Trail). The trail passes handsome sycamores that line the canyon bottom but once the trail begins climbing northeast it leaves the trees behind and Brush Canyon lives up to its name. Chaparral flora frame views of the HOLLYWOOD Sign and Mt. Hollywood.

After 1.25 miles and a stiff 600-foot gain,

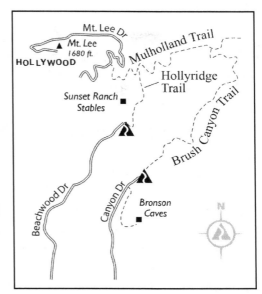

reach an overlook (great views of metro LA) and soon thereafter a signed junction with Mulholland Trail, a wide dirt road. Go left (west) on a more level course, pass a junction with Hollyridge Trail (that leads to the closed Beachwood Drive trailhead). Keep right, and wind west to meet Mt. Lee Drive, 2.2 miles from the trailhead.

A 0.4-mile descent on Mt. Lee Drive leads to Hollywood Sign View (great views indeed and photo ops galore from this overlook; see hike description from Innsdale Drive). Ascend the steep paved road about 1 mile to the summit and a view of DOOWYLLOH, those giant white capital letters from above and behind the sign.

A locked gate prevents hikers from reaching the top of Mt. Lee. But do enjoy the views from about 100 feet above the HOLLY-WOOD Sign. Resist the urge to climb over the fence in order to have your picture taken next to the sign; it's strictly illegal.

Hollywood Sign from Innsdale Drive

Innsdale Trail, Mt. Lee Road

From Innsdale Drive to Hollywood Sign Viewpoint is 2 miles round trip with 200-foot elevation gain; to HOLLYWOOD Sign is 4.6 miles round trip with 700-foot gain

This hike does not save the best for last. Great views of the HOLLYWOOD Sign are yours from the beginning of the hike, which makes it highly appealing to the many visitors from across the nation and around the world looking for the easiest way to get photo ops.

A combination of winding streets and dirt fire roads lead a short mile to Hollywood Sign Viewpoint, aka Selfie Heaven. Frame your photos with the flora en route: cactus, California holly, palm trees, bougainvillea and bamboo.

Please be on your best hiker behavior: The classic Hollyridge Trail was closed under pressure from private property owners; no guarantee the route from Innsdale Drive will always be open.

DIRECTIONS: From northbound Highway 101, exit on Barham Drive and drive north 0.3 mile to Lake Hollywood Drive. Turn right and follow the winding road, passing a junction with Wonder View Drive, then Lake Hollywood Reservoir. After 1.5 miles, turn left on Tahoe Drive and continue 0.25 mile to Canyon Lake Drive. Find curbside parking where you can, and the trailhead located 0.1 mile at the end of Canyon Lake Drive at Innsdale Drive.

THE HIKE: Walk up the wide dirt road (Innsdale Trail for lack of a better name) and...wow, there it is, the HOLLYWOOD Sign. Curve around a bend and just 0.25-mile out, you'll find yourself directly below the letters. Wow!

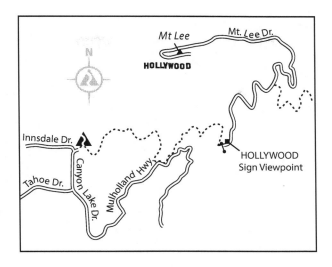

The fire road angles right toward houses and at the 0.5-mile mark, squeeze past a driveway and reach a residential street (Mulholland). Turn left, and make another left at the first junction. March past a thicket of signs, ascend past a last house to reach a dirt road, and wind across a hillside above the HollywoodLand neighborhood.

A short mile from the trailhead, the dirt trail ends at a teal-colored gate. Ascend steps to a paved road located at the crest of Deronda Drive to meet Mt. Lee Drive and a junction. Walk 100 yards up the paved service road (toward a water tank) to Hollywood Sign View. Join visitors from around the world, nearly all taking and posting photos.

Back to business and the route to the Hollywood Sign: 1.3 more miles up paved Mt. Leet Drive. As you ascend get views of Griffith Observatory and Mt. Hollywood to the east, and downtown L.A. to the southeast and, in 0.3 mile, meet a dirt fire road (Mulholland Trail) that leads toward Brush Canyon (see hike description). Keep left on the paved road for the final mile, and get more views: the Verdugo Mountains, San Gabriel Mountains and downtown Burbank.

Just short of the summit, look right and note the signed junction with steep Aileen Getty Ridge Trail that leads to Cahuenga Peak. (A great add-on to this hike!) Minutes later, pass along the chain link fence separating the road from the sign, and reach a vista point above the 'H' in the HOLLYWOOD Sign. Enjoy!

RUNYON CANYON PARK

RUNYON CANYON TRAIL

2.7-mile loop with 700-foot elevation gain

No Man's Canyon was the earliest name given to the deep arroyo that nature sculpted in the Hollywood Hills. A century-and-a-half ago, it was the wild domain of birds and rabbits, coyotes and lizards.

Today Runyon Canyon is the most popular place in L.A. to hike. According to the Friends of Runyon Canyon, some 1.8 million people a year visit the canyon, with about 35,000 coming each week! The park was closed for repairs for four months in 2016 and reopened with more drinking fountains for people and pets and a repaving of the 137-acre park's main trail.

In 1867 Army Camel Corps officer "Greek George" Caralambo acquired the canyon. Coal magnate Carmen Runyon bought it in 1919 and built a hunting lodge and actor/singer John McCormick (hit movie, "Song of My Heart") purchased the canyon in 1929 and built a mansion called San Patrizio. In 1942, wealthy arts patron Huntington Hartford bought the estate and renamed it "The Pines." Later owners tried to develop a subdivision of luxury homes. In 1984, the City of Los Angeles purchased Runyon Canyon and created a park.

Runyon Canyon has three trails, which connect and loop: paved main trail, the most gently sloping and easiest; the west trail, steepest and most challenging; the east trail, which leads to Inspiration Point. Every Runyon regular has a favorite route; for first-timers, I recommend a counterclockwise loop that allows several options.

DIRECTIONS: From the Hollywood Freeway in Hollywood, exit on Highland Avenue and head south past the Hollywood Bowl to Franklin Avenue. Turn west on Franklin and drive 0.3 mile to Fuller

Avenue. Turn right and proceed a short distance to road's end at The Pines entrance gate to Runyon Park. Street parking is where you find it.

THE HIKE:

Enter the park via the wrought iron gate, observe the wide lawn that hosts yoga classes, and soon reach a trail junction. A wide dirt road leads left, but continue straight on the main trail and 0.5 mile from the start reach Inspiration Point. Enjoy metro views and continue on a steeper

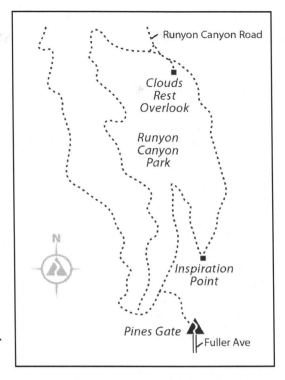

ascent by wooden steps and trail along the park's east ridge 0.3 mile to Cloud's Rest, another vista point. Hike on and soon reach a junction. (Go left, descend to the canyon bottom and loop back to the trailhead to complete a 1.7 mile hike.)

Ascend 0.4 mile to meet a fire road. (To reach park high point Indian Rock (1,325 feet), head right, hike 0.2 mile toward the trailhead on Mulholland Drive, turn left and join a dirt trail that turns south, then take a side trail to the high point. Backtrack, to the junction with the west ridge trail and head south; this adds 0.5 mile to the hike.)

Turn left and soon pass the trail coming down from Indian Rock. Descend along the canyon's west side as the route narrows to a footpath. Enjoy views south of the metropolis but watch your step on the quick and steep drop to the Vista Street Gate. Head back to the center of the canyon and complete the loop.

Brand Park

Brand Trail

From Brand Park to Verdugo Overlook is 6.5 miles round trip with a 1,300-foot elevation gain

"Have you been to Glendale?" This was the question posed in full-page advertisements that ran every Sunday in Los Angeles newspapers during the early 1900s. The man who placed these ads was civic booster and real-estate tycoon Leslie C. Brand, often referred to as "The Father of Glendale."

Born in St. Louis, Brand moved to the Southland in 1898, did well in the insurance business, and by 1902 owned 1,000 acres in the Verdugo Mountains.

At the base of the mountains Brand built El Mirador, a 5,000-square-foot mansion. El Mirador, with its elegant white exterior, horseshoe arches and bulbous domes is a unique example of Saracen architecture—a mixture of Spanish, Moorish and Indian styles.

Brand died in 1925, his widow in 1945, after which, by the terms of his will, Brand's property was deeded to the city of Glendale for use as a park. El Mirador is now Brand Library.

Brand Park, shaped a little like Italy, preserves a portion of the Verdugo Mountains back of Glendale. Brand Trail is a fire road that offers a moderately steep ascent from El Mirador; it extends through Brand Park to the ridgeline of the Verdugos. From Verdugo Overlook (fine valley views), the intrepid can easily extend this hike by joining one of several fire roads that travel the rooftop of the Verdugos.

DIRECTIONS: From the Golden State Freeway (5) in Glendale, exit on Western Avenue and head northeast on the palm-lined avenue 1.5 miles to Brand Library.

THE HIKE: Join the asphalt road to the left of the library that leads past the "Doctor's House," an 1880s Victorian home in the Queen Anne-style that was occupied by a series of four doctors.

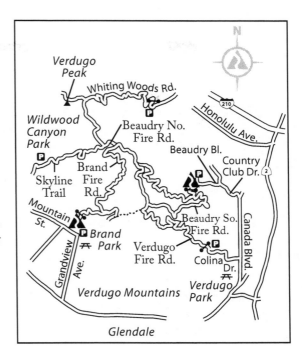

A bit past a pipe gate that closes the road to vehicle traffic, encounter Canary Island pines, palm trees and other tropical vegetation gone wild. These trees and tropical shrubs are what's left of Brand's estate grounds, once a fairyland of waterfalls, fountains and exotic flora.

A half-dozen roads crisscross this area. Stay on the main, widest one. A mile from the trailhead pass a onetime landfill; beyond, the road, now dirt, returns to a more natural setting Pass a sycamore-lined canyon and reach a signed junction. Keep left on "Brand" and don't stray onto "Brand Lat."

The hills are a combo of tilted rock outcroppings and slopes covered with the chaparral and coastal sage communities. Lemonade berry, toyon, ceanothus, sage, buckwheat, manzanita and tree tobacco are among the more common flora.

Two miles of ascent leads to an oak tree, perhaps the only shade en route. Keep climbing another long mile to the overlook. A clear-day view takes in much of the San Fernando Valley and part of the Los Angeles Basin, including downtown. You can see the southeast end of the Santa Monica Mountains, the Hollywood Hills and Griffith Park.

From the overlook, you can travel left (northwest) 2 miles along the ridgetop to 3,126-foot Mt. Verdugo, highest peak in the range.

STOUGH CANYON NATURE CENTER

STOUGH CANYON, VERDUGO FIRE ROAD, VITAL LINK TRAILS

To Fire Warden's Grove with return via Wildwood Canyon is 7.2-mile loop with 1,500-foot elevation gain

Learn about the Verdugo Mountains at Stough Canyon Nature Center and hit the trail with this excellent introductory hike.

Ascend from Stough Canyon and climb eastward to Fire Warden's Grove, a stand of conifers planted by the Los Angeles County Department of Forestry in the 1930s. Many of the grove's mature trees perished in early 21st century wildfires; most trees are replanted young ones. From the ridge above the grove, gain great views of Griffith Park, the Santa Monica Mountains, downtown Los Angeles and the Palos Verdes Peninsula.

Link Trail links the ridge to De Bell Golf Course. I figured it was Links Trail and named for its golf course connection, then discovered its true purpose: to link Wildwood Canyon and Stough parks. *Vital* Link Trail, as it's known now, is an extremely steep path over a sun-scorched south slope. Anyone looking for a rugged conditioning hike will love the 3.6 mile round trip with 1,500 feet (!) in elevation gain on this trail.

Lacking a link trail around the golf course, hikers must walk 1.2 miles on paved roads and sidewalks to complete a loop hike.

DIRECTIONS: From the Golden State Freeway (5) in Burbank, exit on Olive Avenue. Head northeast 1.2 miles to Sunset Canyon Drive. Turn left and drive 0.7 mile to Walnut Drive, turn right, and proceed north another mile to road's end and the parking lot below Stough Canyon Nature Center.

THE HIKE: Walk north on the dirt fire road and climb 0.5 mile along the west wall of Stough Canyon to a junction. The fire road continues north. Take the footpath, which bends west to an overlook of Burbank Airport and the San Fernando Valley. Ascend another 0.5 mile to the foundation and chimney ruins of a 1920s-era youth camp.

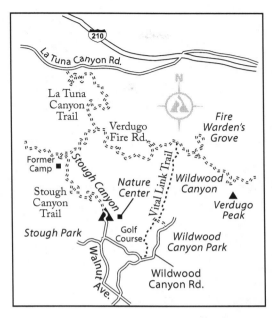

The trail climbs briefly and bends west to meet Verdugo Fire Road. Turn right, and pass a fire road on your right—the east leg of the Stough Canyon loop. (Return to the nature center on this fire road for a 2.5 mile round trip hike.)

Pass a junction with left-branching La Tuna Canyon Trail and ascend another 2 miles to a road split as you approach Fire Warden's Grove. Verdugo Fire Road continues east into the grove. Take the right fork south to the base of a communications facility and signed Vital Link Trail.

Join Vital Link Trail for a 1.5-mile long, knee-jarring descent from the ridgeline via tight switchbacks and stair-steps. Ignore left-branching paths and continue to trail's end in Wildwood Canyon Park near the intersection of Wildwood Canyon Road and Harvard Road. Phew! Amenities here include tree-shaded picnic tables and a drinking fountain.

Walk west on Harvard Road 0.2 mile to De Bell Drive, turn right and walk 0.5 mile past De Bell Golf Course to Walnut Avenue. Turn right and walk the sidewalk north 0.5 mile back to Stough Canyon Nature Center and the trailhead.

O'MELVENY PARK

MISSION POINT TRAIL

From Bee Canyon to Mission Point is 4.5 miles round trip with 1,400-foot gain

O'Melveny Park takes its name from the well-known family of Los Angeles lawyers who once owned a "gentleman's ranch" here. The 672-acre park, features a large developed picnic area and rugged wildland laced with 10 miles of trail.

L.A.'s second-largest city park has two special attractions for the hiker. Mile-long Bee Canyon—a narrow gorge, actually—has a creek that runs most of the year and a surprisingly wild ambiance. Oak and walnut trees line the base of the canyon's high sedimentary rock walls.

The park's Mission Point (2,771 feet) offers great clear-day vistas of the Southland: much of the San Fernando Valley, the San Gabriel Mountains and more. Note the very steep climb (quite the cardio workout) to the point.

I've enjoyed hiking in this park for more than 30 years, and can attest that the trail system has improved over the years. Seems to me, though, the park keeps changing the names of trails (Wasn't O'Melveny Trail once Mission Point Trail? Grotto Trail used to be Grassland Trail, right?) No matter the trail names, you'll find your way just fine up Mission Point and down Bee Canyon.

In spring, a host of wildflowers—California poppies, Indian paintbrush and Mariposa lily—splash color on the hillsides. Inhabiting O'Melveny Park are deer, golden eagle, bobcat, rabbit, raccoon, and coyote. All this flora and fauna next to super-suburban San Fernando Valley!

DIRECTIONS: From the 118/Ronald Reagan Freeway in Granada Hills, exit on Balboa Blvd and go north 2 miles to Sesnon

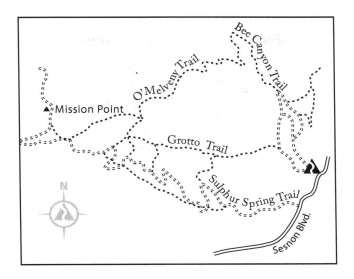

Boulevard. Turn left (west) and drive 0.6 mile to the entrance on the right to O'Melveny Park.

THE HIKE: Head west up the paved park road past the park office (the former O'Melveny ranch house), rising above a walnut tree-lined canyon. Go left on Nature Trail, right on Equestrian Trail to Grotto Trail. Put it in low gear and begin the climb.

As you ascend, notice quite a difference in vegetation between north and south slopes. The canyon's dry north slopes are blanketed with sage and other coastal scrub. To the south, the hills are covered with grasses punctuated with occasional live oak or California walnut.

Hike a long and steep mile to the ridgeline and a meeting with O'Melveny Trail. Head southwest for 0.25 mile on the path, which angles right and switchbacks up to wind-blown Mission Point. A 1932 U.S. Geological Survey marker is atop the point. Two small seasonal ponds are located on the southwest slope.

Enjoy the view of the Santa Susana Mountains, including nearby Oat Mountain, highest peak in the range. The San Gabriel Mountains, Santa Monica Mountains, Santa Clarita Valley, and downtown Los Angeles are also part of the 360-degree panorama.

Retrace your steps on O'Melveny Trail, this time passing by Grotto Trail and continuing your descent into Bee Canyon. Hike through the lovely canyon to a fork in the trail; take either the right or left branch, passing a picnic area and citrus grove and completing the loop.

EAST AND RICE CANYONS

EAST CANYON AND RICE CANYON TRAILS

Through Rice Canyon; is 2.8 miles round trip with 500-foot gain; to Overlook via East Canyon Trail is 7.6 miles round trip with 1,000-foot elevation

The south slopes of the Santa Susana Mountains are pretty enough: a brown, brushy backdrop above the 'burbs of the San Fernando Valley. But this southern exposure offers no clue to what lies on the other side.

The north slopes of the Santa Susana Mountains are green, woodsy and unexpectedly rugged. Some of these north slopes are preserved in the Santa Clarita Woodlands and accessible by footh-path.

Big-cone Douglas fir thrive on the north slopes. The fir are a relict stand from a time (19,000 years ago or so) when the region's climate was considerably wetter and cooler than it is today.

The upper ramparts of the Santa Susana Mountains have temperatures 10 to 15 degrees cooler, and receive about twice as much rain, as the surrounding flatlands. The cold, rain and fog drip help the big-cone Douglas fir prosper and also help sustain healthy populations of valley oak, coast live oak, California bay laurel, big-leaf maple, flowering ash and black walnut.

The hikes to both East and Rice Canyons share a common trailhead and first 0.3 mile of trail. Easy, mile-long, hikers-only up Rice Canyon features several crossings of seasonal Rice Creek, grassy meadows and a vista point at trail's end.

The dirt fire road above East Canyon (it goes by several names) leads hikers on a steady ascent to the ridgeline of the Santa Susana Mountains for grand views of Santa Clarita and San Fernando valleys. (This hike's only downside is noise from the freeway and a nearby shooting range; you need to hike about 2 miles before escaping it.)

DIRECTIONS: From the Golden State Freeway (5) in Santa Clarita, exit on Calgrove Boulevard and go west as Calgrove becomes the Old Road and leads south 0.9 mile to parking (fee). Amenities include a native plant-landscaped picnic ground, water fountain and restroom. The trail begins just down the road from the picnic area.

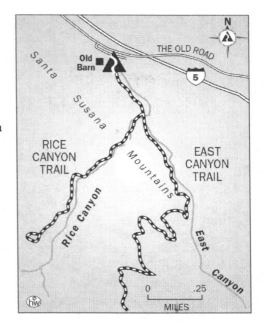

THE HIKE: Head along the fire road 0.3 mile to a signed junction.

Rice Canyon: Branching right is Rice Canyon Trail, which offers a fine little hike for the family. The path meanders along Rice Creek and crosses it several times. Nearly a mile out, it crosses a grassy open slope and ascends to a viewpoint. A large valley oak marks trail's end.

East Canyon: From the junction, East Canyon Trail begins to climb, first among grand old oaks and maples, then over more open slopes that deliver great views of the fir-topped ridgeline above and the Santa Clarita Valley below.

After reaching the first of the Douglas firs continue to the ridge crest, enjoy the views and return. Or the ambitious hiker has options: continue to O'Melveny Park for a 14-mile one-way hike (hope you have a ride waiting). Or traverse the ridge and go down Weldon Canyon and over to the Newhall Pass trailhead (an easier car shuttle to arrange).

Baldwin Hills South

Boy Scout, Ron's, La Brea Loop Trail

2 miles round trip with 200-foot elevation gain

From a distance, the Baldwin Hills appear to have little attraction for the hiker. Oil wells work on slopes scarred by roads and bulldozers. But the oil is petering out, the hillsides are being ecologically rehabilitated, and parkland is being created.

Located in the west/central part of Los Angeles, Kenneth Hahn State Recreation Area was named for the longtime Los Angeles County Supervisor and is operated by Los Angles County. The park encompasses the hills and canyons between La Brea and La Cienega Boulevards.

The clean, well-kept, developed part of the park is no secret to nearby residents, who walk its pathways and enjoy picnics on the expansive lawns. However, the park is unknown to most hikers.

New trails lead through the park's undeveloped "La Brea Extension," a former oil-drilling site on slopes along La Brea Boulevard. Master trail-builder Ron Webster and a trail crew of Sierra Club volunteers built connector trails and linked existing dirt roads to create a two-mile loop.

While the Baldwin Hills are only 500 feet high, park summits offer the hiker dramatic, clear-day vistas of the Santa Monica Mountains, the whole sweep of Santa Monica Bay, the San Gabriel Mountains and much of the metropolis.

DIRECTIONS: From the Santa Monica Freeway (10) in Los Angeles, exit on La Cienega Boulevard and drive south 1.7 miles. Take the right-lane off-ramp exit for Kenneth Hahn State Recreation Area. Follow the park access road to the lot at the top of the park.

THE HIKE: Near Burke Roche Point and opposite exercise stations, join signed Boy Scout Trail on an eastward descent. The path bends north to a three-way junction, where you'll find two sets of benches. (If you continue north, the trail soon makes a 180-degree turn and heads south along La Brea Boulevard.)

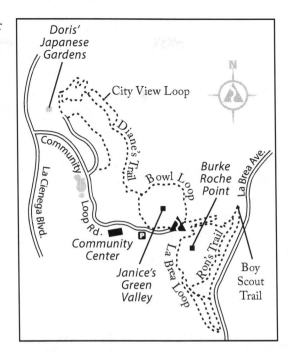

Bear sharply right on Ron Webster Trail (Ron's Trail for short) and hike south with some zigzagging but mostly on a parallel course to La Brea Boulevard. Ron's Trail curves west then east around the head of a minor ravine before heading south again.

A couple of side trails en route allow you to access the main La Brea Loop Trail. Ron's Trail ends at the far south boundary of the park and you go right on the wide dirt road that leads north.

Your route travels terrain that's partly landscaped and partly native brush. Vistas of L.A.'s Westside and the ocean are framed by working oil wells. (Lots of parkland potential from those pumped-out oil fields, if acquired and cleaned up.) Look for sailboats heading out to sea from Marina del Rey and jets zooming in and out of LAX.

Pass a wide green lawn with a fine vista point and helicopter landing spot. Speaking of helicopters, in 1963 when the Baldwin Hills reservoir dam broke, news coverage of the disaster marked the first time in TV history that aerial footage was televised live. The wide path passes a lovely little butterfly garden and returns you to the parking lot and trailhead.

BALDWIN HILLS SCENIC OVERLOOK STATE PARK

HILLSIDE, STAIRS TRAILS

From Jefferson Blvd. to Overlook is 2 miles round trip with 300-foot elevation gain

Even on a foggy morning or smoggy afternoon, vistas from Baldwin Hills Scenic Overlook take in a remarkably wide circle of the metropolis. You can see buildings near and far, from the triangular-shaped Culver City Hotel and Sony Pictures complex in Culver City to the office towers of Century City and downtown L.A. Plus the San Gabriel Mountains, Hollywood Hills and Griffith Observatory, Santa Monica Bay and Catalina Island.

You won't see many nearby parks from the overlook, though; about 3 million people live in the 5-mile area surrounding the Baldwin Hills and there's less than one acre of parkland for every 1,000 people. A decade-long conservation effort and $40 million saved the hills from large-scale development, and Baldwin Hills Scenic Overlook State Park opened in 2009.

More good news: "Baldwin Hills" is back as a place name. The parkland on the east side of La Cienega was known as Baldwin Hills State Recreation Area until 1988 when the state legislature renamed it for longtime County Supervisor Kenneth Hahn. Parks named for predominant geography are typically easier to remember and locate than those named for politicians!

At the top of the 68-acre park is a visitor center (rarely staffed) and a large parking lot (rarely used). Slopes desecrated by dozers have been re-graded to natural contours and replanted with native flora.

This is a park for walkers, hikers and joggers, who begin their workouts at the bottom of the hill and hoof it up to the overlook. Reach the overlook by way of a mile-long trail or 300-plus stone steps that head straight up to the summit. Enjoy this as an early morning nature hike or get a great late afternoon workout with some heart-pounding, stair-climbing cardio.

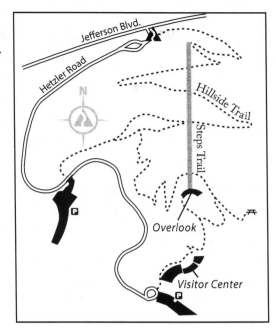

DIRECTIONS: From the Santa Monica Freeway (10) in Los Angeles, exit on La Cienega Boulevard and drive south 0.7 miles to Jefferson Boulevard and turn right. (Continuing another mile south will take you to Kenneth Hahn State Recreation Area. Drive 0.9 mile to Hetzler Road and look for well-signed Baldwin Hills Scenic Overlook State Park, complete with a big and bold TRAILHEAD on the south side of the boulevard. Curbside parking is available on both sides of Jefferson. Yes, you can drive up Hetzler Road to the top of the park, but you're here to hike, right?

THE HIKE: Join the dirt road and soon ascend to the base of the stone staircase. Choose the stairs (and 300-foot vertical gain in 0.2 mile) or continue on the winding path, which offers better and better views. The trail crosses the stairs three more times; at the third crossing, stick with the main trail and avoid right-forking side trails that lead toward the park entry road.

Cross the staircase a fourth and final time and make a fish-hook, nearly 180-degree turn up to the overlook. Partake of the awesome panoramas and note the path leading to the visitor center, restrooms and a native plant garden.

Hacienda Hills

Ahwinga, Native Oak, Schabarum Trails

5-mile loop with 700-foot elevation gain

Hacienda Hills Trailhead is a key entryway to the range and is quite an upgrade from the old Seventh Avenue Trailhead, as it was known to earlier generations of hikers. Restrooms, parking, native plant landscaping, interpretive panels, wrought iron entry gates that are works of art, trail signage—wow!

The trailhead is the gateway to a 225-acre reserve set aside as a mitigation measure after an approved expansion of the nearby mega-landfill. The considerable conservation successes in the Puente Hills have been funded by the Puente Hills Landfill Native Habitat Preservation Authority, which collects "tipping fees" from the Puente Hills Landfill, largest landfill in the U.S. This agency purchased Powder Canyon, Sycamore Canyon and other key parcels in the hills

Fine hiking trails were constructed to link with the pre-existing dirt service roads built by ranchers and oil companies. A loop trail from Hacienda Hills Trailhead offers a great intro to the Puente Hills and excellent vistas.

En route, view typical flora, with coastal sage scrub thriving on south-facing slopes, and oak woodland in the arroyos. This diversity of habitats, woodland and scrubland, attract abundant birds, both resident and migratory. Squirrels and rabbits are commonly sighted, as are coyotes and mule deer.

Millions of years ago, seismic activity thrust these hills upward from the valley floor. Long eroded by wind and water, the hills now stand 400 to 1,400 feet in elevation.

Hike the rugged hills and you'll understand why the precipitous, unstable slopes discouraged several generations of homebuilders.

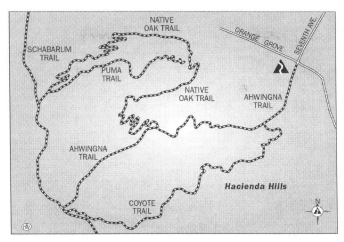

DIRECTIONS: From the Pomona Freeway (60) in Hacienda Heights, exit on Seventh Avenue and head south 4 blocks to the avenue's end at Orange Grove Avenue. Park in the small lot by the signed trailhead.

THE HIKE: Meander into the park on signed Ahwinga Trail alongside a bioswale, an environment you can learn about via strategically posted interpretive signs. The path diverts onto asphalt road for a short distance then switchbacks up the canyon wall, soon offering grand views of the San Gabriel Valley.

Crest a minor ridge and reach a horse tie and trail junction. Join right-forking Native Oak Trail which descends into a lovely woodland, and descends some more nearly back to Orange Avenue and the edge of suburbia.

Next the serious climb starts. Along the way, the hiker experiences both the beauty of the hills on the one hand and the enormity of the Puente Hills Landfill on the other.

Close to the crest, pass a junction with steep Puma Trail and soon thereafter reach a junction with Schabarum Trail. Views from the ridgetop include the San Gabriel Valley to the north and the coastal plain to the south. Look east to observe the range extending to the Orange County line, where the Puente Hills transition into the Chino Hills.

Schabarum Trail follows a fence line to a meeting with Ahwinga Trail, which you'll join on a pleasant mile of downhill hiking back to the junction with Native Oak Trail. From the junction, retrace your steps back to the trailhead.

79

ACROSS THE PUENTE HILLS

PUENTE HILLS SKYLINE TRAIL

From Seventh Avenue to Overlook is 5 miles round trip with 800-foot elevation gain; to Rio Hondo College is 5 miles round trip with 800-foot gain; to Schabarum Park is 12 miles one-way with 1,000- foot gain

The Puente Hills divide the Los Angeles Basin into a northern one-third and a southern two-thirds. North of the hills is the San Gabriel Valley, south is a flat coastal plain tilted gently toward the Pacific.

Puente Hills Skyline Trail extends across the range, offers a variety of hiking options and terrific clear-day views of the metropolis.

DIRECTIONS: Exit the Pomona Freeway (60) on Seventh Avenue and drive 4 blocks south to its end at Orange Avenue. Park near the traffic barrier. (To reach Schabarum Regional Park, end point for one of this day hike's options, exit the Pomona Freeway on Azusa Avenue. Proceed south, turn left on Colima, and right into the park.)

THE HIKE: Ramble up Seventh Avenue Trail, a dirt road. Pass horse corrals, ascend briefly to a water company facility and ascend on dirt trail for a mile amidst thistle and mustard. Atop a long plateau, enjoy vistas of the San Gabriel Valley and intersect Puente Hills Skyline Trail.

Bear right following a fence along the plateau's perimeter overlooking Rose Hills Memorial Park. Hike the length of the plateau to a junction. Bear left here and ascend to an overlook, where a missile facility once stood. View Whittier to the south, San Gabriel Valley to the north and, on clear days, spot the San Gabriel Mountains, the Pacific and Catalina Island. Return the same way, head for Rio Hondo College or continue on the Skyline Trail.

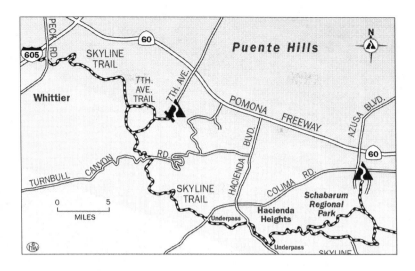

To Rio Hondo College: From the overlook, the trail briefly joins a crumbling road, passes a picnic area, and veers off from the road at a junction. Look down at the gardens of Rose Hills Memorial Park. Civilization grows more evident as you descend toward Workman Mill Road. The trail leads to North Drive at Rio Hondo College.

To Schabarum Park: Bear left on the Skyline Trail, passing a thicket of prickly pear cactus and descend amidst sage and monkeyflowers into Turnbull Canyon. After a short ascent, the trail crosses Turnbull Canyon Road. More climbing leads to an overlook for fine views of downtown Los Angeles, the Westside and the Pacific.

The trail angles toward the suburb of Hacienda Heights, passes behind homes (with swimming pools that look inviting on a hot day), and descends to Colima Road. Follow the pedestrian–equestrian underpass underneath Colima, ascend to Hacienda Boulevard, and hike through another underpass.

Skyline Trail is anything-but for the next half-mile as it turns southeast and follows a culvert alongside Hacienda Boulevard. At Leucadia Road, PHST joins a fire road for an ascent above La Habra Heights. The trail ascends through a eucalyptus grove and passes communication towers.

Civilization—in the form of Puente Hills Mall and the Pomona Freeway—appears close-in to the north. The trail descends a last mile to the wide lawns and picnic areas of Schabarum Park.

81

Bordered by two of the busiest freeways in the world—the Ventura and the San Diego—they remain a near-wilderness. Within easy reach of millions of people, they nevertheless offer solitude and plenty of silent places.

Wildflowers, waterfalls and wonderful scenery that's been the backdrop for hundreds of movies and thousands of episodes of TV shows are highlights for hikers. I grew up hiking in the Santa Monica Mountains and have a particular fondness for my "home mountains." It was a challenge to select a representative sampling of trails to share—there are so many good ones!

CHAPTER 4

SANTA MONICA
MOUNTAINS

HIKE ON.

WILL ROGERS STATE HISTORIC PARK

INSPIRATION POINT LOOP TRAIL

To Inspiration Point is 2 miles round trip with a 300-foot elevation gain

Will Rogers, often called the "Cowboy Philosopher," bought a spread in the Santa Monica Mountains in 1922. He and his family enlarged their weekend cottage to 31 rooms, including 11 baths and 7 fireplaces.

The Oklahoma-born Rogers toured the country as a trick roper, punctuating his act with humorous comments on the news of the day. His roping act led the humorist to later fame as a newspaper columnist, radio commentator and movie star.

Today, the ranch and grounds of the Rogers Ranch is maintained as Will Rogers State Historic Park, set aside in 1944. View a short film on Rogers' life at the park visitor center and tour the ranch house, still filled with his prized possessions.

Come for the history, stay for the hiking; there's a lot here for hikers. Rogers himself designed the riding trails that wind into the hills behind his ranch. The path to Inspiration Point is an easy walk for the whole family.

The park is the eastern terminus for the Backbone Trail that extends some 65 miles across the spine of the Santa Monica Mountains to Point Mugu State Park. Extend the hike to Inspiration Point and get great views by ascending the first mile or so of the Backbone Trail. One of The Trailmaster's favorite lengths of the Backbone connects Topanga and Will Rogers state parks; it's about 11 miles one-way.

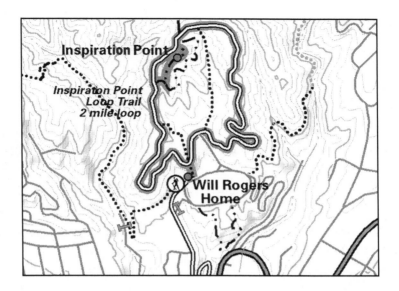

DIRECTIONS: From Sunset Boulevard in Pacific Palisades, 4.5 miles inland from Sunset's junction with Pacific Coast Highway, turn inland on the access road leading to Will Rogers State Historic Park. Park your car near the polo field or near Rogers' house.

THE HIKE: Begin at the Will Rogers home and join the path up the hill to the west of the ranch house and left of the tennis courts. Follow the zigzag path 0.1 mile to meet Inspiration Point Loop Trail (a wide dirt fire road). The trail bends west, offering vistas of Santa Monica Bay, then heads north into the mountains. The path ascends a ridge overlooking nearby Rivas Canyon and leads to a junction, 0.8 mile from the trailhead.

Bear right to Inspiration Point, not really a point at all, it's actually more of a flat-topped knoll. Nevertheless, clear-day views are inspiring: Santa Monica Bay, the metropolis, San Gabriel Mountains, Catalina.

(From the signed junction below Inspiration Point, consider an optional exploration on famed Backbone Trail. Ascend Chicken Ridge (one mile with nearly 500 feet in elevation gain) and enjoy more great views of the mountains, metropolis and wide blue Pacific.)

Return to the main loop and continue your clockwise tour, first continuing northeast, then east and then descending south. The lower length of trail, lined with eucalyptus, leads back to the polo grounds and visitor center.

TEMESCAL CANYON

TEMESCAL CANYON, TEMESCAL RIDGE TRAILS

Canyon loop is 3.8 miles round trip with 900 foot elevation gain

I have a particular fondness for Temescal Gateway Park in Pacific Palisades. Not only does this park have it all (restrooms, picnic grounds, water fountains and more), park pathways quickly leave it all behind.

Temescal Canyon is an ideal Santa Monica Mountains sampler. You get an oak- and sycamore-shaded canyon, a seasonal waterfall and terrific views from the ridge crest.

You'll escape civilization but not other hikers; the canyon is a very popular place to hike.

Sidewalks, picnic grounds, and an intermittent greenbelt along Temescal Canyon Road might tempt intrepid hikers to stride the mile from the beach to the trailhead.

Temescal has long been a canyon that inspired nature lovers and enlightenment-seekers. During the 1920s and 1930s, the canyon hosted Chautauqua assemblies—large educational and recreational gatherings that featured lectures, concerts and stage performances. The canyon was purchased by the Presbyterian Synod in 1943 and used as a retreat center until 1995 when the Santa Monica Mountains Conservancy acquired it.

Check out the SMMC's nature-themed presentations held in Temescal Canyon—very much in keeping with the Chautauqua tradition.

DIRECTIONS: From Los Angeles, head west on the Santa Monica Freeway (10) to its end and continue up-coast on Pacific Coast Highway. Turn north (right) on Temescal Canyon Road and drive 1.1 miles. Just after the intersection with Sunset Boulevard, turn left into the lower parking area (fee) for Temescal Gateway Park. You can also locate free parking along Sunset Boulevard or along Temescal Canyon Road and walk into Temescal Gateway Park.

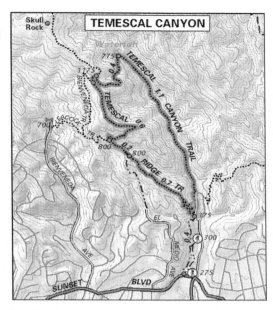

THE HIKE: Walk up-canyon on the landscaped path past the restrooms. The footpath takes on a wilder appearance and soon crosses a branch of Temescal Creek via a wooden footbridge.

At a signed junction, save Temescal Ridge Trail for your return route and continue through the canyon on Temescal Canyon Trail. Travel among graceful old oaks, maples and sycamores to the "doggie turnaround" (no dogs beyond this point) and enter Topanga State Park.

The path ascends moderately to another footbridge and a close-up view of the small waterfall, tumbling over some large boulders. Leaving the canyon behind, the path steepens and climbs westward up Temescal Ridge to a signed junction with Temescal Ridge Trail.

(I always enjoy heading uphill on this trail a half mile or so to distinctly shaped Skull Rock, a good place to rest, cool off, and admire the view.)

As you return to the trailhead down Temescal Ridge Trail, you'll get excellent views of Santa Monica Bay, Palos Verdes Peninsula, Catalina Island, and downtown Los Angeles.

The path descends steeply and tunnels into tall chaparral. Continue past junctions with Bienveneda and Leacock trails and follow the narrow ridgeline back to a junction with Temescal Canyon Trail. Retrace your steps back to the trailhead.

TOPANGA STATE PARK

EAGLE SPRINGS FIRE ROAD
(BACKBONE TRAIL)

To Eagle Rock via Eagle Rock/Eagle Springs Loop is 6.5 miles round trip with 800-foot elevation gain

Topanga Canyon is a quiet retreat, surrounded by L.A. sprawl but retaining its rural character. The state park is sometimes billed as "the largest state park within a city limit in the U.S."

The name Topanga is from the Shoshonean Indian dialect. Until the 1880s, there was little permanent habitation in the canyon. Early settlers tended vineyards, orchards, and cattle ranches.

In the 1920s, the canyon became a popular weekend destination for Los Angeles residents. Summer cabins were built along Topanga Creek and in surrounding hills. For $1 round trip fare, tourists could board a Packard auto stage in Santa Monica and be driven up Pacific Coast Highway and Topanga Canyon Road to the canyon's scenic spots.

Most Topanga trails are good fire roads. In the heart of the state park, the hiker will discover Eagle Rock, Eagle Spring and get topographically oriented to Topanga.

I have a particular fondness for Topanga Canyon, having resided there and hiked there often during my grad school days. The park definitely offers four-season hiking: On a blustery winter day, city and canyon views are superb, in springtime, the hillsides are colored with wildflowers, and autumn offers great hiking weather and clear-day vistas.

Summer, too, has its charms. It's doubtful any poets will rhapsodize about such summer bloomers as bur-sage, mugwort, Indian

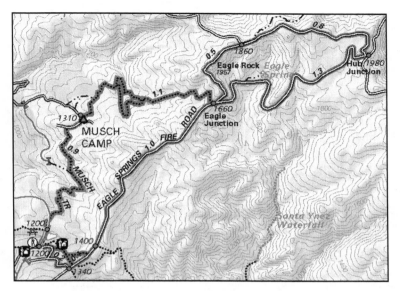

milkweed, chaparral pea or ashyleaf buckwheat, though the scarlet petals of the California fuchsia and the tiny pink petals of the slim aster do have a certain charm. Just get an early start!

DIRECTIONS: From Topanga Canyon Boulevard, turn east on Entrada Road; that's to the right if you're coming from Pacific Coast Highway. Follow Entrada Road by turning left at every opportunity until you arrive at Topanga State Park. The trailhead is at the end of the parking lot.

THE HIKE: From the Topanga State Park parking lot, follow the distinct trail eastward to a signed junction, where you'll begin hiking on Eagle Springs Road. You'll pass through an oak woodland and through chaparral country. The trail slowly and steadily gains about 800 feet in elevation on the way to Eagle Rock. When you reach a junction, bear left on the north loop of Eagle Springs Road to Eagle Rock. A short detour will bring you to the top of the rock.

To complete the loop, bear sharply right (southwest) at the next junction, following the fire road as it winds down to Eagle Spring. Past the spring, you return to Eagle Spring Road and retrace your steps back to the trailhead.

Three-mile long Musch Ranch Trail, which passes from hot chaparral to shady oak woodland, crosses a bridge and passes the park pond, is another fine way to return to the trailhead.

MALIBU CREEK

CRAGS ROAD, HIGH ROAD TRAILS

From Main Parking Area to Century Lake is 2.8 miles round trip with 100-foot elevation gain; to M*A*S*H site is 6 miles round trip with 200-foot gain

Before land for Malibu Creek State Park was acquired in 1974, it was divided into three parcels belonging to Bob Hope, Ronald Reagan and 20th Century Fox. Although the park is still used for moviemaking, it's primarily a haven for day hikers and picnickers.

Today the state park preserves more than 7,000 acres of rugged country in the middle of the Santa Monica Mountains.

The trail along Malibu Creek explores the heart of the state park. It's an easy, nearly level walk that visits a dramatic rock gorge, Century Lake and several locales popular with moviemakers.

Fans of the long-running TV show, M*A*S*H, will enjoy making the pilgrimage to the site where so many episodes were filmed. Some rusted vehicles, interpretive panels, a picnic table and helicopter pad are at the site. The prominent Goat Buttes that tower above Malibu Creek were featured in the opening shot of each episode.

DIRECTIONS: From Pacific Coast Highway, turn inland on Malibu Canyon Road and proceed 6.5 miles to the park entrance, 0.25 mile south of Mulholland Highway. If you're coming from the San Fernando Valley, exit the Ventura Freeway (101) on Las Virgenes Road and continue four miles to the park entrance.

THE HIKE: From the parking area, descend a staircase near the restrooms at the western edge of the parking lot. Cross a small bridge, passing signs marked "Backcountry Trails." Crags Road soon forks into a high road and a low road. Go right and walk along the oak-shaded high road, which makes a long, lazy left

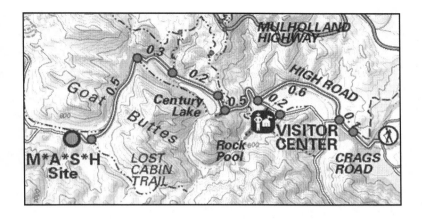

arc as it follows the north bank of Malibu Creek. You'll reach an intersection and turn left on a short road that crosses a bridge over Malibu Creek.

Gorge Trail is well worth a detour; follow it upstream a short distance to the gorge, one of the most dramatic sights in the Santa Monica Mountains. Malibu Creek makes a hairpin turn through 400-foot volcanic rock cliffs and cascades into aptly named Rock Pool. The Swiss Family Robinson television series and some Tarzan movies were filmed here, as were a number of scenes from the "Planet of the Apes" series of flicks.

Retrace your steps back to the high road and bear left toward Century Lake. As the road ascends you'll be treated to a fine view of Las Virgenes Valley. When you gain the crest of the hill, you'll look down on Century Lake. Near the lake are hills of porous lava and topsy-turvy sedimentary rock layers that tell of the violent geologic upheaval that formed Malibu Canyon. A side trail leads down to the lake which was scooped out by members of Crag's Country Club, a group of wealthy, turn-of-the-20th century businessmen who had a nearby lodge.

The road follows a (usually) dry creek bed though, after a good rain, it can be wet and wild going. Soon after passing a junction with the Lost Cabin Trail, you'll reach the M*A*S*H site.

CALABASAS PEAK & RED ROCK CANYON

CALABASAS PEAK, RED ROCK CANYON TRAILS

From Stunt Road to Calabasas Peak is 3.8 miles round trip with 900-foot elevation gain; to Red Rock Canyon Park is 4.4 miles round trip with 600-foot gain

Towering red rocks, along with floral clouds of white and blue-hued ceanothus are among the attractions of Red Rock Canyon Park near Topanga Canyon. The rocks are joined by colorful wildflowers in the spring, including cliff aster, clarkia, golden bush and many more blooms.

Check out red sandstone outcroppings reminiscent of the American Southwest and ascend Calabasas Peak (2,163 feet) for great clear-day views of the Santa Monica Mountains, San Fernando Valley and the San Gabriel Mountains. And/or hike to Red Rock Canyon Park, which offers drinking water and a small picnic area but is otherwise undeveloped.

DIRECTIONS: From the Ventura Freeway (Highway 101) in Calabasas, exit on Las Virgenes Road and travel 3.25 miles south to Mulholland Highway. Turn left (east) and proceed 4 miles to Stunt Road, bear right and drive exactly a mile to the parking area on the right side of Stunt Road. The trailhead is on the left side of Stunt Road by road paddle "1.0"

THE HIKE: Ascend north on the Calabasas Peak Motorway Trail. Behind you is a view of Cold Creek Canyon, one of the treasures of the Santa Monica Mountains. Trail-side geology is fascinating: large, tilted slabs and fins of sandstone have been sculpted by erosion into weird shapes.

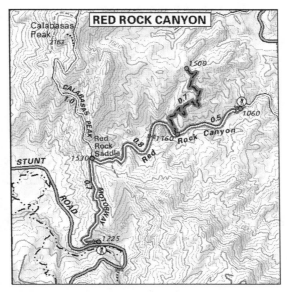

Bordering the fire road are chaparral-blanketed slopes dominated by toyon, laurel sumac, mountain mahogany and ceanothus. These larger shrubs are joined by a host of smaller ones including buckwheat, black sage, bush sunflowers and sagebrush.

About 0.7 mile from the trailhead is a saddle, where powerlines cross the road, sometimes known as Red Rock Saddle, and a junction.

(The left-forking road is a continuation of Calabasas Peak Motorway and leads another mile to the top of a ridge. A left-branching path leads directly to the peak.)

Rest a while at the bench at the saddle, then take the right fork and begin a 0.7-mile long descent to the bottom of Red Rock Canyon. The canyon narrows and appears more and more intriguing as you near the bottom.

At the 1.5-mile mark, signed Red Rock Canyon Trail offers an intriguing option. The northbound footpath crosses a trickle of a creek and climbs among the rock formations on the north wall of the canyon. Trail's end is at an overlook.

The major trail continues along the canyon bottom another 0.5 mile to the heart of Red Rock Canyon Park. It's worth extending your hike with a short stroll among the impressive red-rock formations stacked up along the dirt segment of this road that leads to the park entry road.

ZUMA CANYON

ZUMA CANYON TRAIL

**To trail's end is 3 miles round trip with 100-foot elevation gain;
to Zuma-Edison Road is 6.8 miles round trip with 600-foot gain;
return via Zuma Ridge Trail is 8.2-mile loop with 1,800-foot gain**

Zuma Canyon is a living illustration of the Santa Monica Mountains of a century ago: a creek cascading over magnificent sandstone boulders, a jungle of willow and lush streamside flora, fern-fringed pools and towering rock walls.

The canyon is one of the gems of the Santa Monica Mountains. National Park Service staff improved trails, but wisely left well enough alone, preserving the wild and remote flavor of this rugged country.

Partake of Zuma Canyon's grandeur with a mellow walk to the end of the trail and by two miles of trail-less creek-crossing and boulder-hopping—one of the most challenging hikes in the Santa Monicas. Return via Zuma Ridge Trail and enjoy grand ocean and mountain views.

In winter, the canyon can be inaccessible because of high water levels. In spring, the lovely creek is energetic, but crossings manageable. In summer—well, it's not the heat it's the humidity; the canyon's tight confines and jungle-like vegetation combine to make uncomfortable hiking. Autumn months are great for hiking because the creek is low and the weather mild.

DIRECTIONS: From Pacific Coast Highway in Malibu, head up-coast one mile past an intersection with Kanan-Dume Road and turn right on Bonsall Drive (this turn is just before the turnoff for Zuma Beach). Drive a mile to road's end at a parking lot.

THE HIKE: From the parking area, head north on the main trail 0.2 mile to a three-way junction. Continue past junctions with

Canyon View Trail and Ocean View Trail north into Zuma Canyon.

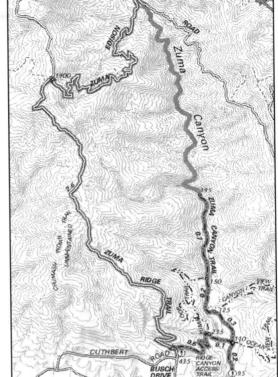

Nearly a mile from the trailhead, the canyon narrows and a half mile later the trail peters out in a cluster of boulders. Should you decide to continue up-canyon, boulders will be very much in your picture. Expect to boulder-hop small and mid-sized boulders and navigate around compact car and mid-size truck-sized boulders.

Also expect slow progress—one mile an hour or less. The only intrusions into the wilderness scene are sky-high powerlines over the canyon, about three miles from the trailhead, and Zuma-Edison Road that crosses the canyon another mile north.

Turn left on this road and ascend very steeply, gaining a thousand feet in elevation in less than a mile and a half by the time you reach Zuma Ridge Trail (a fire road). Turn left (south).

Enjoy the coastal and mountain views as you descend rapidly on this popular mountain bike route, dropping 1,500 feet in elevation over the course of 2.6 miles to the Busch Drive Trailhead and parking area. Here you'll join the signed trail and travel east 0.6 miles to the main trail network for Zuma Canyon and then another 0.3 mile back to where you began this hike.

SOLSTICE CANYON PARK

SOLSTICE CANYON, RISING SUN TRAILS

To waterfall and Roberts Ranch house ruins is 3 miles round trip with 400-foot elevation gain

At least some of the serenity and scenery offered by Solstice Canyon has returned. The 2007 Corral Fire scorched the canyon's hillsides and thereafter vast amounts of soil and rock debris were later dislodged and fell into the canyon.

However, some of the chaparral plants and grasses quickly re-colonized and Solstice Canyon is once more becoming a favorite of hikers.

Several historic buildings were lost in the fire, including the 1865 Mathew Keller House. The fire damaged Solstice Canyon's strangest structure sometimes compared to a futurist farm house with a silo attached. From 1961 to 1973 Space Tech Labs, a subsidiary of TRW used the building to conduct tests to determine the magnetic sensitivity of satellite instrumentation.

Solstice Canyon Park opened on summer solstice, 1988. The Santa Monica Mountains Conservancy purchased the land from the Roberts family and transformed the 550-acre Roberts Ranch into a park. Today National Park Service rangers are the stewards of Solstice Canyon.

NPS officials are working to regenerate native plant species lost in the blaze and attempting to prevent invasive non-native species from returning to an area with a long history of human presence. Hikers will observe much progress toward the habitat restoration of Solstice Canyon.

The main canyon path is a narrow country road—suitable for strollers and wheelchairs—and offers an easy family hike in the shade of grand old oaks and towering sycamores. In autumn, enjoy the fall color display of the sycamores and in winter, from the park's upper slopes, look for gray whales migrating past Point Dume.

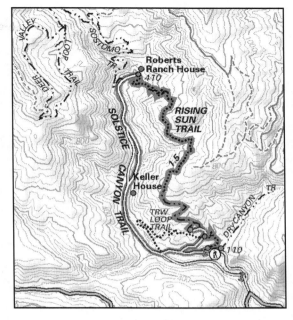

DIRECTIONS: From Pacific Coast Highway, about 17 miles up-coast from Santa Monica and 3.5 miles up-coast from Malibu Canyon Road, turn inland on Corral Canyon Road. At the first bend in the road, you'll leave the road and proceed straight to the parking lot, where there are restrooms and a shelter used for educational programs.

THE HIKE: Walk up the wide road. About halfway along, you'll pass what's left of the 1865 Mathew Keller House and in a few more minutes—Fern Grotto. The road travels under the shade of oak and sycamore to its end at the remains of the old Roberts Ranch House.

Palms, agave, bamboo, bird of paradise and many more tropical plants once thrived in the Roberts' family garden gone wild.

A waterfall, fountain and an old dam were some of the other special features found in this paradisiacal setting known as Tropical Terrace. It's no paradise these days, but the waterfall still tumbles with sufficient rainfall.

Across the creek from Tropical Terrace is signed Rising Sun Trail, which climbs a ridge for rewarding canyon and ocean views. The two-mile trail offers an excellent, but more difficult, return route to the trailhead.

CHARMLEE WILDERNESS PARK

MEADOW RANCH, FIRE ECOLOGY, BOTANY TRAILS

2-mile loop around the park

Charmlee, perched on the blufftops above Malibu, often has outstanding spring wildflower displays. Most of the park is a large open meadow; the flower display, given timely rainfall, can be quite colorful. Lupine, paintbrush, larkspur, mariposa lily, penstemon and California peony bust out all over.

Stop at Charmlee's small nature center and inquire about what's blooming where. Also pick up a copy of a brochure that interprets the park's Fire Ecology Trail. This nature trail interprets the important role of fire in Southern California's chaparral communities.

Good views are another reason to visit Charmlee, operated by the City of Malibu Department of Parks and Recreation. The Santa Monica Mountains spread east to west, with the Simi Hills and Santa Susana Mountains rising to the north. Down-coast you can see Zuma Beach and Point Dume and up-coast Sequit Point in Leo Carrillo State Park.

Beginning in the early 1800s, this Malibu meadowland was part of Rancho Topanga-Malibu-Sequit and was used to pasture cattle. For a century and a half, various ranchers held the property. Last of these private landholders—Charmain and Leonard Swartz—combined their first names to give Charmlee its euphonious name.

For the hiker, 530-acre Charmlee is one of the few parks, perhaps the only park, offering a surplus of trails. Quite a few paths and old ranch roads—nine miles worth no less—wind through the park, which is shaped like a big grassy bowl.

Because the park is mostly one big meadow fringed with oak trees, it's easy to see where you're going and improvise your own circle tour of Charmlee.

DIRECTIONS: From Pacific Coast Highway, about 12 miles up-coast from the community of Malibu, take Encinal Canyon Road 4.5 miles to Charmlee Wilderness Park.

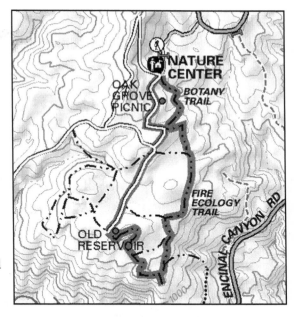

THE HIKE: From the parking lot, walk past the restrooms, and visit the native plant garden. Next stroll through the park's Oak Grove Picnic Area on a dirt road. Travel under the shade of coast live oaks on the road, which crests a low rise, offers a couple of side trails to the left to explore, and soon arrives at a more distinct junction with a fire road leading downhill along the eastern edge of the meadow. This is a good route to take because it leads to fine ocean views.

Take this to the Old Reservoir, then travel down-coast along the tall bluffs to a couple of ocean overlooks, including one rocky outcropping that offers particularly terrific views. Circle back inland by a trail leading toward an oak grove, one of the park's many picturesque picnic spots.

Join Fire Ecology Trail for a close-up look at how Southern California's Mediterranean flora has adapted to fire and aptly named Botany Trail to loop back to Oak Grove Picnic Area and the trailhead.

NICHOLAS FLAT

NICHOLAS FLAT TRAIL

From Leo Carrillo State Park entry road to Nicholas Flat is 6.6 miles round trip with 1,600-foot elevation gain

Leo Carrillo State Park's Nicholas Flat area is one of the best spots in the Santa Monica Mountains for spring wildflowers because it's a meeting place for four plant communities: chaparral, grassland, coastal scrub and oak woodland.

Another reason for the remarkable plant diversity is the park's elevation, which varies from sea level to nearly 2,000 feet. Along park trails, look for shooting star, hedge nettle, sugar bush, purple sage, chamise, blue dick, deer weed, burr clover, bush lupine, golden yarrow, fuschia-flowered gooseberry, and many more flowering plants.

Nicholas Flat's charms also include a big meadow, a pond, and Malibu coast views.

DIRECTIONS: From the west end of the Santa Monica Freeway in Santa Monica, head up-coast on Pacific Coast Highway about 25 miles to Leo Carrillo State Beach. There's free parking along Coast Highway, and fee parking in the park's day use area.

THE HIKE: Locate the trailhead a short distance past the park entry kiosk, opposite the day use parking area. Join signed Camp 13 Trail, which almost immediately splits. The right branch (Willow Creek Trail) circles the hill, climbs above Willow Creek, and after a mile, rejoins the main Nicholas Flat Trail. Enjoy this interesting option on your return from Nicholas Flat.

Take the left branch, which immediately begins a moderate to steep ascent of the grassy slopes above the park campground. The trail switchbacks through a coastal scrub community up to a saddle on the ridgeline. Here you'll meet Willow Creek, the alternate

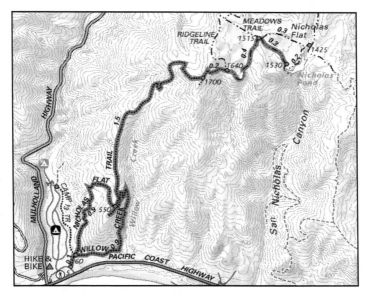

branch of Nicholas Flat Trail. From the saddle, a short side trail leads south to a hilltop, where there's a fine coastal view. From the viewpoint, observe Point Dume and the Malibu coastline.

Following the ridgeline, Nicholas Flat Trail climbs inland over a chaparral-covered slope. Enjoy increasingly grand coastal views and survey the open slopes, browsed by nimble deer.

After a good deal of climbing, the trail levels atop the ridgeline and, about 2.6 miles from the trailhead, intersects Ridgeline Trail coming in from the north. Keep right and continue another 0.4 mile to another junction, a four-way. Meadows Trail heads west while two trails head east 0.3 mile to Nicholas Pond—one to the north end of the pond, and one to the south end. (A 0.2-mile long trail leads along the pond shore and connects the two trails.)

Picnic beneath the shady oaks or in the meadow. The man-made pond is backed by handsome boulders. From the south end of the pond, a sketchy path leads up to a rocky perch that offers commanding coastal views.

Return the way you came until reaching the junction located 0.9 mile from the trailhead. Bear left at the fork and hike Willow Creek Trail as it descends into the canyon cut by Willow Creek, contours around an ocean-facing slope, and returns you to the trailhead.

SANDSTONE PEAK

BACKBONE TRAIL, MISHE MOKWA TRAIL

6 miles round trip with 900-foot elevation gain.

Sandstone Peak, highest peak in the Santa Monica Mountains, is one of the highlights of a visit to Circle X Ranch, 1,655 acres of National Park Service land on the border of Los Angeles and Ventura counties. The parkland boasts more than 30 miles of trail.

The ranch once belonged to movie actor Donald Crisp, who starred in "How Green was My Valley." The Exchange Club purchased the nucleus of the park in 1949 and gave it to the Boy Scouts. The emblem for the Exchange Club was a circled X—hence the name of the ranch.

Sandstone Peak offers outstanding views from its 3,111-foot summit, though "Sandstone" is certainly a misnomer; the peak is a large mass of volcanic rock.

DIRECTIONS: Drive up-coast on Pacific Coast Highway past Malibu, a mile past the Los Angeles County line. Turn inland on Yerba Buena Road and proceed five miles to Circle X Ranch. Pass the park's headquarters building and continue one more mile to the signed trailhead on your left and plenty of parking.

THE HIKE: From the signed trailhead, walk up the fire road 0.3 mile to a signed junction with Mishe Mokwa Trail. Leave the fire road here and join the trail, which climbs and contours over the brushy slopes of Boney Mountain.

Breaks in the brush offer good views to the right of historic Triunfo Pass, used by the Chumash to travel from inland to the coast. Mishe Mokwa Trail levels and tunnels through chaparral.

The path then descends into Carlisle Canyon. Across the canyon are striking red volcanic formations, among them well-named

Balanced Rock. The path, shaded by oak and laurel, drops into the canyon at another aptly named rock formation—Split Rock, 1.8 miles from the trailhead. Here you'll find a picnic area, shaded by oak and sycamore. An all-year creek and a spring add to the site's charm.

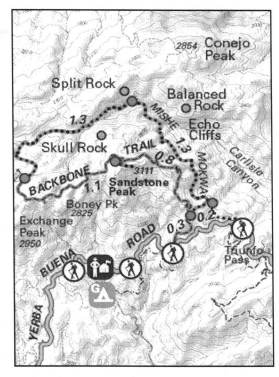

From Split Rock, ascend out of Carlisle Canyon. From the road's high point, look straight-ahead up at a pyramid-like volcanic rock formation known as Egyptian Rock.

About 1.3 miles from Split Rock, Mishe Mokwa Trail meets the Backbone Trail. West fork of the trail leads toward Point Mugu State Park, but you head south and before long bend east on the fire road.

Look sharply to the right for the short, unsigned spur trail to Inspiration Point. Mount Baldy and Catalina are among the inspiring sights pointed out by a geographical locator monument.

Keep climbing with the fire road. After a few switchbacks, look for a well-signed trail and steps on the right. Follow this trail to the top of Sandstone Peak.

Enjoy commanding, clear-day views: the Topatopa Mountains, haunt of the condors, the Oxnard Plain, the Channel Islands, and the wide blue Pacific. After enjoying the view, return to the wide Backbone Trail and descend a bit more than a mile back to the trailhead.

RANCHO SIERRA VISTA

SYCAMORE CANYON ROAD, SATWIWA LOOP TRAIL

To Sycamore Canyon Falls is 3 miles round trip with 300-foot elevation gain; return via Satwiwa Loop Trail is 4 miles round trip

Take a hike to Sycamore Canyon Falls, comprised of a half a dozen waterfalls cascading into pools bordered by handsome sandstone canyon walls. Oaks, sycamores, big-leaf maples, woodwardia and sword ferns grace the canyon bottom nearby.

Rancho Sierra Vista/Satwiwa, located on the north boundary of Point Mugu State Park, offers the opportunity explore a place where Chumash walked for thousands of years before Europeans arrived on the scene. A visitor center and guest speakers help moderns learn the habits of birds and animals, the changes the seasons bring, and gain insight into the ceremonies that kept—and still keep—the Chumash bonded to the earth.

For hunter-gatherers, as anthropologists call them, this land on the wild west end of the Santa Monica Mountains was truly bountiful: seeds, roots, bulbs, berries, acorns and black walnuts. Birds, deer and squirrel were plentiful, as were fish and shellfish from nearby Mugu Lagoon. This abundant food supply helped the Chumash become the largest tribal group in California.

DIRECTIONS: From the Ventura Freeway (Highway 101) in Newbury Park, exit on Wendy Drive and head south a mile to Borchard Road. Turn right and travel 0.5 mile to Reino Road. Turn left and proceed 1.2 miles to Lynn Road, turn right and continue another 1.2 miles to the park entrance road (Via Goleta) on the south side of the road. The paved park road passes equestrian parking on the

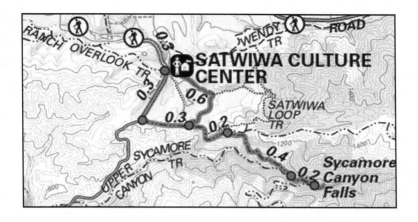

right and a small day use parking lot on the left before dead-ending at a large parking lot 0.7 miles from Lynn Road.

THE HIKE: From the parking lot, follow the wide service road 0.3 mile to signed Satwiwa Native American Indian Culture Center, then continue another 0.3 mile to the crest of a low ridge and the boundary with Point Mugu State Park. Gaze down at Big Sycamore Canyon, then go left (east) on Old Boney Trail.

Ascend briefly, pass a branch of Satwiwa Loop Trail and continue to a fork. Take the right fork, descending 0.4 mile to a junction with Upper Sycamore Canyon Trail, and continuing past this junction another 0.2 mile to a tight bend and the side trail on your left leading to Sycamore Canyon Falls. Hike along the creek, crossing it, and boulder-hopping to the falls, which spills into a quiet grotto.

Retrace your steps back to the Satwiwa Loop Trail and bend north to junction a connector trail leading to Wendy Drive, then west toward an old cattle pond, now a haven for waterfowl and wildlife and to a Chumash village exhibit. From Satwiwa Culture Center, retrace your steps 0.3 mile on the service road back to the trailhead.

Sycamore Canyon

Sycamore Canyon Trail

From Big Sycamore Canyon to Deer Camp Junction is 7.6 miles round trip with 200-foot elevation gain; return via Overlook Trail is 9.7 miles round trip with 700-foot gain

Sycamore Canyon Trail takes you through a peaceful wooded canyon, where a multitude of monarch butterflies dwell in the fall, and past some magnificent sycamores. By some accounts, it's the finest example of a sycamore grove in the entire California State Parks system.

The trail follows the canyon on a gentle northern traverse across Point Mugu State Park, largest preserved area in the Santa Monica Mountains. This trail, combined with Overlook Trail, gives the hiker quite a tour of the park. The canyon offers flat, family-friendly outings as well.

DIRECTIONS: Drive up-coast on Highway 1, 32 miles from Santa Monica, to Big Sycamore Canyon Campground in Point Mugu State Park. Park in the day-use area (fee) or along Pacific Coast Highway (free). Walk through the campground to a locked yellow gate at the end of the campground loop and the trailhead for the Sycamore Canyon Fire Road.

THE HIKE: Take the trail up-canyon, following the creek. (Note Scenic Trail, leading westward; this could be an optional return route.) Winter rains cause the creek to rise, and sometimes keeping your feet dry while crossing is difficult. Underground water keeps much of the creekside vegetation green year-round.

About 0.4 from the campground, look for Overlook Trail, which switchbacks to the west up a ridge and then heads north toward the native tall grass prairie in La Jolla Valley. Make note of this trail, an optional return route.

Another 0.7 mile of nearly level canyon trail leads to a trail that branches right—Serrano Canyon Trail, an absolute gem. A mile more of easy walking beneath the sycamores brings you to an ideal picnic table shaded by a grove of large oak trees; this might be a good turnaround spot. Total round trip distance would be a bit more than 4 miles.

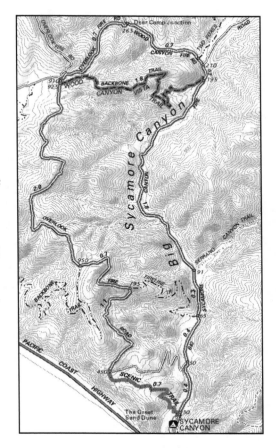

Continue up the canyon, pass beneath more giant sycamores, and soon arrive at a junction with the Backbone Trail, a.k.a. Wood Canyon Vista Trail. Join this path ascending west 1.8 miles to meet the Overlook Fire Road. Or continue on Sycamore Canyon Trail another 0.2 mile and then bend northwest 0.7 mile to Deer Camp Junction, a fine lunch stop. Oaks predominate over sycamores along Wood Canyon Creek.

Call it a day here and return the way you came. Or return via Overlook Trail: Climb 0.7 mile on Overlook Fire Road to the divide between Sycamore Canyon and La Jolla Valley. Upon reaching a junction, head south on the Overlook Trail, staying on the La Jolla Canyon side of the ridge. True to its name, Overlook Trail offers good views of grassy mountainsides, Boney Peak and Big Sycamore Canyon as it travels 3.8 miles to a junction with Scenic Trail. Take this trail, scenic and a shortcut, too, 0.7 mile southeast back to the trailhead.

MUGU PEAK

CHUMASH, MUGU PEAK TRAILS

To Mugu Peak is 3 miles round trip with 1,250-foot elevation gain; loop via La Jolla Valley is 4.5 miles round trip

Mugu Peak anchors the wild west end of the Santa Monica Mountains. From the summit, the hiker gains grand mountain, ocean and island views. Ascending the peak, though, is quite the aerobic workout!

At the base of Mugu Peak lies La Jolla Valley, ringed by ridges and home to a native grassland, a rarity in Southern California. In taking a circle tour around the peak, you gaze over ocean waves, as well as waves of grass. And a lot of burned park!

The May 2013 Springs Fire burned 12,000 of the 14,000 acres of Point Mugu State Park and a majority of the park's 70 miles of hiking trails. The park's chaparral and native grassland communities recovered quickly. And the hiking these days is as good or better than ever.

Super-steep Chumash Trail aggressively tackles a coastal slope dotted with cactus, yucca and yellow coreopsis, the so-called tree sunflower. Make a beeline for Mugu Peak if you wish, but I prefer rounding the peak by trail and enjoying the natural attractions before heading up the peak for the panoramic views.

DIRECTIONS: Head up-coast on Pacific Coast Highway some 35 miles from Santa Monica and about 3.5 miles past the Sycamore Canyon entrance to Point Mugu State Park. Look on the inland side a parking lot and signed Chumash Trail.

THE HIKE: Chumash Trail ascends relentlessly up the coastal scrub- and cactus-dotted slopes. Look behind you to mark your progress and to behold grand ocean views.

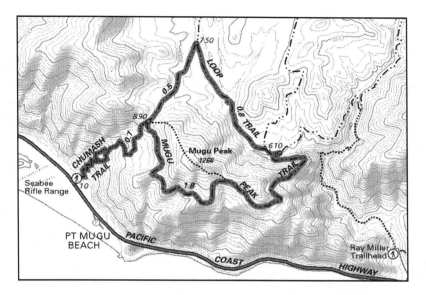

After 0.7 mile and a 900-foot elevation gain, the trail reaches a saddle and a junction. (Mugu Peak Trail on your right is the one to take if time is short and you want to get right to the top of the peak.)

Head north a half mile and gaze over the waves of native grassland. La Jolla Valley really looks like a valley from this perspective because you can see that it's surrounded by peaks and ridges: La Jolla Peak to the north, Boney Mountain to the northeast, and Laguna Peak (topped by Navy radar and communication apparatus and looking like something from another planet) to the west.

Intersecting La Jolla Valley Loop Trail, go right and make a gentle descent southeast across the grasslands. You'll pass an oak grove, cross a creek, and pass a junction with a left forking trail that extends north across La Jolla Valley. Stay right and soon reach the junction with Mugu Peak Trail.

Mugu Peak Trail travels a ridge above La Jolla Canyon then soon contours around the south slope of the peak. As for reaching the summit of the peak, a trail rounds the west side of Mugu Peak and another makes some tight aggressive switchbacks up to the peak. Keep your eyes on the prize—the flagpole atop Mugu Peak—and you'll get there just fine.

After enjoying the view, return to the main trail and back to Chumash Trail for the knee-jarring descent to the trailhead.

Most of the San Gabriel Mountains lie just north of metro Los Angeles and within Angeles National Forest, one of the nation's most popular national forests for hiking. For more than a century the range has delighted Southland residents seeking quiet retreats and tranquil trails.

Enjoy classic trails through Big Santa Anita Canyon and to Mt, Wilson, Mt. Lukens and Mt. Lowe. The range's front country offers the hiker inviting arroyos, fine vista points and easy-to-access trailheads from metropolitan flatlands. Angeles Crest Highway offers a scenic byway to the high country, grand mountain peaks and a wealth of taller trees.

CHAPTER 5

SAN GABRIEL MOUNTAINS

HIKE ON.

PLACERITA CANYON

CANYON, WATERFALL TRAILS

From Nature Center to Walker Ranch Picnic Area is 3.8 miles round trip with 250-foot elevation gain; to Los Pinetos Waterfall is 5.3 miles round trip with 500-foot gain

Placerita Canyon has a gentleness that is rare in the steep, severely faulted San Gabriel Mountains. A superb nature center, plus a walk through the oak- and sycamore-shaded canyon adds up to a nice outing for the whole family.

In 1842, seven years before the '49ers rushed to Sutter's Mill, California's first gold rush occurred in Placerita Canyon. Miners from all over California, the San Fernando Placers, as they became known, poured into canyon. The tree shading the spot where herdsman Francisco Lopez first discovered gold is now called the Oak of the Golden Dream.

Placerita Canyon has been the outdoor set for many movies, plus such 1950s TV westerns as "The Cisco Kid" and "Hopalong Cassidy." Movie companies often used the cabin built in 1920 by Frank Walker. Walker, wife Hortense and 12 children raised cows and pigs, and panned for gold in the then remote canyon.

The park nature center features excellent exhibits and live animal displays, and offers guided walks and family-friendly programs. Short nature trails include Hillside Trail, which serves up views of Placerita Canyon, and Heritage Trail that leads to the Oak of the Golden Dream. My favorite is Ecology Trail (0.65 mile one way), which highlights a wide variety of native flora in the oak woodland, canyon bottom, and chaparral communities.

Canyon Trail meanders through Placerita Canyon to the park's group campground. From here, Waterfall Trail ascends along Los

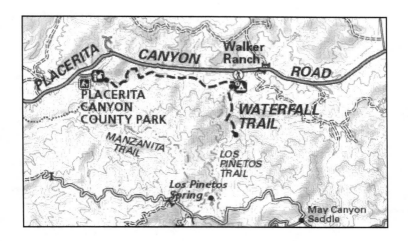

Pinetos Canyon's west wall, then drops into the canyon for an up-close look at the 25-foot fall.

DIRECTIONS: From Interstate 5 at Newhall Pass, take Highway 14 (Antelope Valley Freeway) 2.5 miles north and exit on Placerita Canyon Road. Turn right (east) and drive 1.5 miles to Placerita Canyon County Park. Park in the large lot near the Nature Center.

THE HIKE: From the signed Main Trailhead, cross a bridge and follow Canyon Trail east up-canyon. Willows, alders, oaks and sycamores shade the creek banks.

The canyon narrows; it's gorge-like appearance is the result of thousands of years of natural erosion as well as a very destructive period of hydraulic mining in the 19th century.

About a mile out, the trail splits. The right branch stays on the brushy south side of the canyon while the left branch intersects a side trail ascending to a parking area on Placerita Canyon Road and then continues up-creek along the canyon bottom.

The two intersect a little short of the Walker Ranch Group Campground, where the hiker will find tables, water and restrooms.

Join Waterfall Trail (not to be confused with Los Pinetos Trail) and ascend into narrow Los Pinetos Canyon. Big-cone spruce, coastal live oak and a few stray big-leaf maples shade the canyon walls. The waterfall, sometimes an impressive flow after a good rain, splashes into a grotto at trail's end.

MT. LUKENS

STONE CANYON TRAIL

From Vogel Flats to Mt. Lukens is 8 miles round trip with 3,200-foot elevation gain

Mt. Lukens, a gray whale of a mountain beached on the eastern boundary of Los Angeles, is the highest peak within the city limits. A hike up this mile-high mountain offers a challenging workout and terrific clear-day views of the metropolis.

Theodore P. Lukens, for whom the mountain is named, was a Pasadena civic and business leader, and an early supporter of the first scientific reforestation effort in California. A self-taught botanist, Lukens believed that burnt-over mountainsides could be successfully replanted. During 1899 alone, Lukens and fellow mountaineers planted some 65,000 seeds in the mountains above Pasadena.

After the death of Lukens in 1918, a 5,074-foot peak was named to honor the one-time Angeles National Forest Supervisor and Southern California's "Father of Forestry." Stone Canyon Trail is by far the nicest way to ascend Mt. Lukens. (Other routes are via long wearisome fire roads.) The trail climbs very steeply from Big Tujunga Canyon over the north slope of Lukens to the peak.

Carry plenty of water on this trail; none is available en route. A city map, paper or digital, will assist you in identifying the diverse geography and many points of interest visible from the summit of Mt. Lukens.

One warning: In order to reach the beginning of Stone Canyon Trail, you must cross the creek flowing through Big Tujunga Canyon. During times of high water, this creek crossing can be difficult and dangerous—even impossible. Use your very best judgment when approaching this creek at high water.

DIRECTIONS:
From Foothill Boulevard in Sunland, turn north on Mt. Gleason Avenue and drive 1.5 miles to Big Tujunga Canyon Road. Turn right and proceed 6 miles to Doske Road and make another right. Descend to Stonyvale Road, then left and drive 0.5 mile to a parking area at road's end.

THE HIKE:
After carefully crossing the creek, begin the vigorous ascent, which first parallels Stone

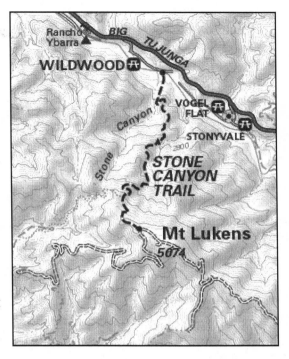

Canyon, then switchbacks to the east above it. Pausing now and then to catch your breath, enjoy the view of Big Tujunga Canyon.

The trail leads through chamise, ceanothus and high chaparral. Fires have scorched the slopes of Mt. Lukens. Stone Canyon Trail could use a few more shady conifers and a little less brush. Theodore Lukens and his band of tree planters would today be most welcome on the mountain's north slopes!

About 3.5 miles from the trailhead, intersect an old fire road and bear left toward the summit. Atop the peak is a forest of antennae. Old maps called the summit "Sister Elsie" before the peak was renamed for Lukens. As the story goes, Sister Elsie Peak honored a beloved Roman Catholic nun who was in charge of an orphanage for Native American children located in the La Crescenta area.

Enjoy the sweeping panorama of the Santa Monica and Verdugo mountains, Santa Monica Bay and the Palos Verdes Peninsula, and the huge city spreading from the San Gabriel Mountains to the sea.

ARROYO SECO

GABRIELINO NATIONAL RECREATION TRAIL

From Windsor Avenue to Teddy's Outpost is 3 miles round trip; to Gould Mesa is 4 miles round trip; to Paul Little Picnic Area is 6.5 miles round trip with a 400-foot elevation gain

Before the November 2009 Station Fire devastated the Arroyo Seco, the only warning I gave hikers was about the smog that occasionally collects in the arroyo. Wow, times have changed and so has the terrain!

Perhaps the best way to approach the Arroyo Seco these days is as a quaint artifact from another era; nevertheless, I'm an optimist and hope one day for a return of the sylvan scene.

During the early decades of the 20th century, Arroyo Seco was an extremely popular place for a weekend outing. About halfway up the trail stood Camp Oak Wilde, a rustic resort constructed in 1911. Hikers stayed a night or two or used the hostelry as a rest stop on the way up to Mt. Wilson. During the 1920s, a road was constructed and visitors drove the arroyo to Camp Oak Wilde.

Southern California's "flood of the century" wiped out Oak Wilde in 1938, along with the road leading to it. For the next 60 years, hikers walked the old 1920s auto road and newer Forest Service trails to quiet picnic areas. Until the fire, the path up the Arroyo Seco (part of the Gabrielino National Recreation Trail) was usually kept in good condition.

While overgrown and ugly, eroded by flood and covered by muddy debris, the trail is hike-able. Oaks on the arroyo banks appear to have survived far better than the creekside alders. More stone steps, walls, foundations and other remains are visible now than in pre-fire days; however, my memory could be faulty and I might just be struggling to find something positive to say.

Oakwilde Trail Camp was destroyed by the Station Fire and has not been rebuilt. The 1.7 miles of trail leading from Paul Little Picnic Area to Oakwilde is in poor shape.

DIRECTIONS: From the Foothill Freeway (210) in Pasadena, take the Arroyo Boulevard/Windsor Avenue exit. Head north on Arroyo, which almost immediately becomes Windsor, and travel 0.75 mile. Just before

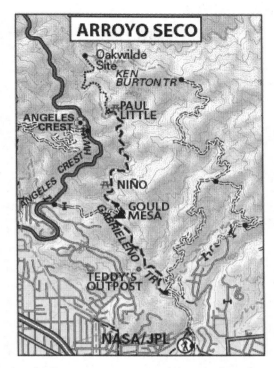

Windsor's intersection with Ventura Street, turn into the small parking lot on your left.

THE HIKE: Walk up Windsor to two roads. The leftward road descends to JPL. Head right on a narrow asphalt road (closed to vehicles), pass fenced-off areas and facilities belonging to the Pasadena Water Department and a junction with Lower Brown Mountain Road. The road transitions to dirt and enters (what used to be) a more sylvan scene, shaded by oaks and sycamores.

At the 1.5-mile mark, reach Teddy's Outpost Picnic Area. Hike another 0.5 mile to another picnic area at Gould Mesa. Next stop, a short distance past the campground, is a small picnic area called Nino. A mile beyond Gould Mesa Campground is Paul Little Picnic Area.

The trail (when passable) ascends from the arroyo to the east wall of the canyon, curves along, then drops back into the arroyo and visits the former site of Oakwilde Camp.

Echo Mountain

Sam Merrill Trail

From Cobb Estate to Echo Mountain is 5.6 miles round trip with 1,400-foot elevation gain

Professor Thaddeus Sobieski Coulincourt Lowe's Echo Mountain Resort area can be visited not only by retracing the tracks of his "Railway to the Clouds" (See Mt. Lowe Railway hike), but also by way of a fine urban edge trail that ascends from the outskirts of Altadena.

From Pasadena, visitors rode a trolley up Rubio Canyon, where a pavilion and hotel were located. Then they boarded the "airships" of the great cable incline, which carried them 3,000 feet (gaining 1,300 feet) straight up to the Echo Mountain Resort Area. "Breathtaking" and "hair-raising" were the most frequent descriptions of ride that thrilled tourists from the 1890s to the 1930s. Atop Echo Mountain was a hotel and observatory.

This historic hike visits the ruins of the one-time "White City" atop Echo Mountain. From the steps of the old Echo Mountain House are great clear-day views of the megalopolis.

Pasadena and Altadena citizens have been proud to share their fascination with the front range of the San Gabriels. This pride has extended to the trails ascending from these municipalities into the mountains. Local citizens, under the auspices of the Forest Conservation Club, built a trail from the outskirts of Altadena to Echo Mountain during the 1930s. During the next decade, retired Los Angeles Superior Court clerk Samuel Merrill overhauled and maintained the path. When Merrill died in 1948, the trail was named for him.

Sam Merrill Trail begins at the former Cobb Estate, now a part of Angeles National Forest. A plaque placed by the Altadena

Historical Society dedicates the estate ground as "a quiet place for people and wildlife forever."

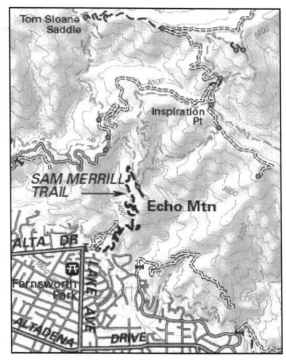

DIRECTIONS: From the Foothill Freeway (210) in Pasadena, exit on Lake Avenue and travel north 3.5 miles to its end at Loma Alta Drive. Park along Lake Avenue.

THE HIKE: From the great iron gate of the old Cobb Estate, follow the trail along the chain-link fence. The path dips into Las Flores Canyon, crosses a seasonal creek in the canyon bottom, and begins to climb. With the earnest, but well-graded ascent, enjoy good vistas of the San Gabriel Valley and downtown Los Angeles.

After 2.6 miles of, steep and mostly shadeless travel, arrive at a signed junction with Mt. Lowe Railway Trail (see hike description). Bear right and walk 100 yards along the bed of the old Mt. Lowe Railway to the Echo Mountain ruins. Just before the ruins is a very welcome drinking fountain.

Up top, spot the railway's huge bull wheel, now embedded in cement, and just below a pile of concrete rubble, all that remains of the railway depot. The steps and foundation of the Echo Mountain House are great places to take a break and enjoy the view straight down precipitous Rubio Canyon, the route of Lowe's railway.

Echo Mountain takes its name from the echo that supposedly bounces around the semicircle of mountain walls. You can try shouting into the strategically placed "megaphone" to get an echo but perhaps even echoes fade with time.

MT. LOWE

MT. LOWE HISTORIC RAILWAY TRAIL

To Echo Mountain, Mt. Lowe Trail Camp and Inspiration Point is 11-mile loop with 2,800-foot elevation gain

Professor Thaddeus Lowe, man of fame and fortune, was the quintessential California dreamer. His dream was to build a railway into—and a resort complex atop—the San Gabriel Mountains high above Pasadena. In the 1890s, his dream became a reality.

During the height of its popularity, millions took Professor Lowe's "Railway to the Clouds" to fine hotels and spectacular views of Southern California. Until it was abandoned in the 1930s, it was the Southland's most popular tourist attraction.

From Pasadena, visitors rode a trolley up Rubio Canyon, where a pavilion and hotel were located. Then they boarded the "airships" of the great cable incline, which carried them 3,000 feet (gaining 1,300 feet) straight up to the Echo Mountain Resort Area. From Echo Mountain, tourists could board a trolley and ride another few miles to Mt. Lowe Tavern at the end of the line.

Begin this journey back into history with a 2.6-mile hike to Echo Mountain (see hike description) to meet the Mt. Lowe Historic Railway Trail. The old railway bed has a gentle 7 percent grade for easy walking. You'll pass attractions that impressed an earlier generation of travelers: Granite Gate, Horseshoe Curve, and the site of the Great Circular Bridge. Ten stations mark the route and interpret the highlights.

DIRECTIONS: From the Foothill Freeway (210) in Pasadena, exit on Lake Avenue and travel north 3.5 miles to its end at Loma Alta Drive. Park along Lake Avenue.

THE HIKE:
(See Echo Mountain hike description) After 2.6 miles of ascent, arrive at a signed junction with Mt. Lowe Railway Trail (Echo Mountain Trail). Begin the self-guiding interpretive hike over railroad ties still half-buried in the ground.

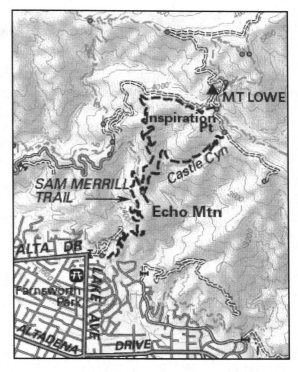

Here are the 10 stations along the railway trail with the hiking distances: Station 1 Echo Mountain; Station 2 View of Circular Bridge (0.5); Station 3 Cape of Good Hope (0.8); Station 4 Dawn Station/Devil's Slide (1.0); Station 5 Horseshoe Curve (1.2); Station 6 Circular Bridge (1.6); Station 7 Horseshoe Curve View (2.0); Station 8 Granite Gate (2.4); Station 9 Ye Alpine Tavern (3.4); Station 10 Inspiration Point (3.9).

Little remains at the site of Ye Alpine Tavern, but near this peaceful spot under oaks and big cone spruce is Mt. Lowe Trail Camp, with shade, water, restrooms and picnic tables.

From the camp, follow the fire road east and south for 0.5 mile to Inspiration Point, where there's a pavilion. Where the fire road makes a hairpin left to Mt. Wilson, go right. At Inspiration Point, gaze through several telescope-like sighting tubes aimed at Santa Monica, Hollywood, the Rose Bowl and more LA-area sights.

Return the way you came, but a faster way down is via Castle Canyon Trail, which begins below Inspiration Point and descends 2 miles to meet the railway trail just north of Echo Mountain. Hike Sam Merrill Trail back to the trailhead.

EATON CANYON

EATON CANYON TRAIL

From the Nature Center to Eaton Falls is 3 miles round trip with 200-foot gain

Late one August afternoon in 1877, John Muir set out from Pasadena to begin his exploration of the San Gabriel Mountains. The great naturalist was very impressed with Eaton Falls, as he wrote in his book, *The Mountains of California*: "It is a charming little thing, with a low, sweet voice, singing like a bird, as it pours from a notch in a short ledge, some thirty-five or forty feet into a round mirror-pool."

Judge Benjamin Eaton channeled and piped the canyon's waters to nearby ranches. The judge's neighbors laughed when he planted grapevines, but the vines were quite successful and commanded a high price. Soon many other San Gabriel Valley farmers planted vineyards.

Much of the canyon named for Judge Eaton is now part of Eaton Canyon Natural Area. The park's nature center has exhibits that emphasize Southern California flora and fauna. Nature trails explore a variety of native plant communities—chaparral, coastal sage, and oak-sycamore woodland.

Eaton Canyon is a busy place on weekends. Family nature walks are conducted by docent naturalists; the park also has birdwalks, natural history classes and children's programs.

The walk up Eaton Canyon to the falls is an easy one, suitable for the whole family. Eaton Canyon Trail leads through a wide wash along the east side of the canyon to a junction with Mt. Wilson Toll Road; ambitious hikers can join the road for a steep ascent of Mt. Wilson.

DIRECTIONS: From the Foothill Freeway (210) in Pasadena, exit on Altadena Drive. Proceed north 1.7 miles to the signed entrance of

Eaton Canyon Natural Area. Turn right into the park and leave your car in the large lot near the nature center.

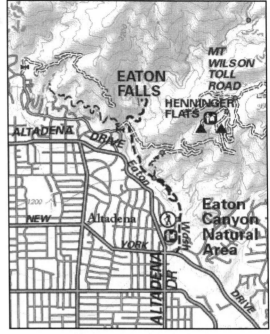

THE HIKE: From the parking lot, hike through the attractive grounds of the nature center. Cross the creek, then meander beneath the boughs of large oak trees and pass a junction with a connector trail that leads to the Mt. Wilson Toll Road.

The trail leads along the wide arroyo. Eaton Canyon has been widened considerably by repeated floods that have washed away canyon walls floods and spread alluvium, or water-transported sand and rock, across the canyon floor. It takes a hearty group of drought-resistant plants to survive in this soil. Notice the steepness of the canyon's walls. Early Spanish settlers called the canyon "El Precipio."

After a mile's travel from the nature center, reach the Mt. Wilson Toll Road bridge. A right turn on the toll road will take you on a long, steep ascent to the top of Mt. Wilson. A left turn on Mt. Wilson Toll Road leads a very short distance to the unsigned junction with Altadena Crest Trail. Walking 0.5 mile on Altadena Crest Trail to a vista point rewards the hiker with great clear-day views of the Los Angeles Basin.

To reach Eaton Falls, continue straight up Eaton Canyon wash. Rock-hop across the creek several times as you walk to trail's end at the falls. (Don't climb the falls; people have recently been injured and killed doing this.)

Henninger Flats

Mt. Wilson Toll Road

From Altadena to Henninger Flats is 7 miles round trip with 1,400-foot elevation gain

Fortunately for California's cone-bearing tree population—and tree lovers—there is a place where trees, more than 120,000 a year, are grown to replace those lost to the capriciousness of nature and the carelessness of humans. The place is Henninger Flats, home of the Los Angeles County Experimental Nursery.

Perched halfway between Altadena and Mt. Wilson, Henninger Flats is the site of Southern California's finest tree plantation. On the flats you'll find reforestation exhibits and be able to view trees in all shapes and sizes, from seedlings to mature stands.

After careers as a gold miner, Indian fighter and first Sheriff of Santa Clara County, Captain William Henninger came to Los Angeles to retire in the early 1880s. While prospecting, Henninger discovered the little mesa that would soon bear his name.

Atop the flats he built a cabin, planted fruit trees, raised hay and corn. His solitude ended in 1890 when the Mt. Wilson Toll Road was constructed for the purpose of carrying the great telescope up to the new observatory. Henninger's Flats soon became a water and rest stop for hikers, riders and fishermen who trooped into the mountains.

After Henninger's death in 1895, the flats became a U.S. Forest Service tree nursery. Foresters emphasized the nurturing of fire- and drought-resistant varieties of conifers. Many thousands of seedlings were transplanted to fire- and flood-ravaged slopes all over the Southland. Since 1928, Los Angeles County foresters have continued the good work at Henninger Flats.

A moderate outing on good fire road, the trail to Henninger Flats is suitable for the whole family. The flats offer a large picnic area and fine clear-day city views.

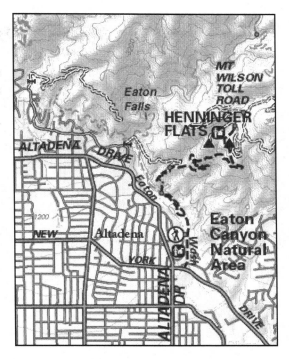

DIRECTIONS: From the Foothill Freeway (210) in Pasadena, exit on Altadena Drive. Proceed north 1.7 miles to the signed entrance of Eaton Canyon Natural Area. Turn right into the and park in the large lot near the nature center.

THE HIKE: Cross the creek and bear left, following the well-traveled path meandering beneath the boughs of large oak trees to a junction with the signed connector trail (often called the "equestrian trail") leading to Mt. Wilson Toll Road. Turn right and ascend this steep, long footpath to the toll road and turn right. The road begins a series of switchbacks up chaparral-covered slopes. Occasional painted pipes mark your progress.

Henninger Flats welcomes the hiker with water, shade, and two campgrounds. At the visitor center, view a huge pinecone display and learn about the natural and social history of the San Gabriel Mountains. Growing on the flats are some of Califonia's more common cone-bearing trees including knobcone, Coulter, sugar, gray and Jeffrey pine, as well as such exotics as Japanese black pine and Himalayan white pine.

After your tree tour, return the same way. Ultra-energetic hikers will continue up the old toll road to Mt. Wilson; the journey from Altadena to the summit is 9 miles one-way with an elevation gain of 4,500 feet.

Mount Wilson

Mt. Wilson Trail

From Sierra Madre to Orchard Camp is 7 miles round trip with a 2,000-foot elevation gain; to Mt. Wilson is 15 miles round trip with a 4,500-foot gain

The tale of Mt. Wilson Trail begins with Benjamin Davis Wilson, who gazed up at the commanding peak located high above his San Gabriel Valley vineyard and figured those stands of pine and cedar on the mountain's shoulders would be an ideal source of timber. He built the first trail to "Wilson's Peak" in 1864.

The old trail was hugely popular when a hiking fervor known as the "Great Hiking Era" swept the Southland. In 1905 the Pacific Electric Railway extended its trolley service to Sierra Madre, reaching within 0.25 mile of the trailhead. Some 40,000 travelers passed through trail mid-point, Orchard Camp, in 1911.

Near the trailhead stands Lizzie's Trail Inn, built in 1895 and long known as an eatery for hikers. It's now a historical museum.

This hike leads up Little Santa Anita Canyon, visits Orchard Camp, and climbs to the top of Mt. Wilson. It's a classic climb, and one of SoCal's nicest all-day hikes.

DIRECTIONS: From the Foothill Freeway (210) in Arcadia, exit on Baldwin Avenue and head north 1.5 miles. Turn right on East Miramonte Avenue and travel 0.2 mile near to Mt. Wilson Trail Road, which is on your left. Park on Miramonte or along Mt. Wilson Trail Road. The trail begins 150 yards up this road and is marked by a large wooden sign. After passing some homes, the trail shortly intersects the main trail.

THE HIKE: The path ascends the west side of Little Santa Anita Canyon. A mile from the trailhead, the path reaches a switchback that

begins a half-mile
section of pathway
re-routed around a
frequently washed out
and eroded length of
trail.

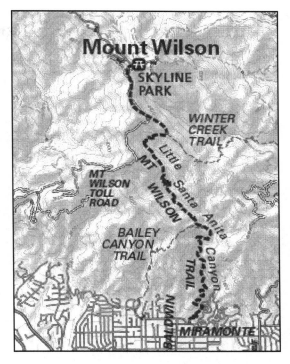

At 1.5 miles, the
trail splits and an
older branch de-
scends to the bottom
of the canyon to a
locale named First
Water. Stay left and
take the trail into the
increasingly narrow
canyon.

The trail angles
westward into Lost
Canyon, crosses a
creek and ascends
past oak to a junction with a connector trail that ascends north to
meet Bailey Canyon Trail. Soon thereafter, where Mt. Wilson Trail
bends left, a path continues straight 100 feet to a clearing (helipad)
that offers fine vistas.

At about the three-mile mark, the path descends to Decker
Spring, returns to the main canyon, then continues another 0.5-mile
to Orchard Camp, a shady glen dotted with oak and spruce trees.
Homesteaders tried their hands at planting apple and cherry trees—
hence the name Orchard Camp.

The trail continues through thick chaparral up Santa Anita
Canyon to its head. It contours on the shelf-like trail, heads east on
a firebreak, and crosses over a steep manzanita-covered ridge. At the
intersection with Winter Creek Trail, turn left (west) and ascend
steeply to Mt. Wilson Toll Road, 2 miles from Orchard Camp.

Turn right on the Toll Road and ascend a mile to Mt. Wilson
Road, just outside Skyline Park.

BIG SANTA ANITA CANYON
GABRIELINO NATIONAL RECREATION TRAIL

**From Chantry Flat to Sturtevant Falls is 3.5 miles round trip
with 500-foot gain; to Spruce Grove Camp is 8 miles round trip
with 1,400-foot gain; to Mt. Wilson is 8 miles one-way with
4,000-foot gain**

Cascades, a waterfall and giant woodwardia ferns are a few of
the many delights of historic Big Santa Anita Canyon. The bucolic
canyon has been popular with hikers for more than a hundred years.

Burro-packer William Sturtevant pioneered many miles of San
Gabriel Mountains trails.

"Sturde" hewed out a trail over the ridge from Winter Creek to
the top of the canyon and in 1898 opened Sturtevant Camp; it was a
popular trail resort well into the 1930s.

Sturtevant's trail is now a section of 28-mile long Gabrielino
National Recreation Trail.

Hikers may continue past the falls to Spruce Grove Camp and to
the top of Mt. Wilson.

DIRECTIONS: From the Foothill Freeway (210) in Arcadia,
exit on Santa Anita Avenue and drive six miles north to its end
at Chantry Flat. The trail begins across the road from the often
jammed parking area. A tiny store at the edge of the parking lot sells
maps, refreshments and parking passes.

THE HIKE: Descend on the paved fire road, part of Gabrielino
Trail, into Big Santa Anita Canyon. At the bottom of the canyon,
cross a footbridge near the confluence of Big Santa Anita and Winter
Creeks. Here a small sign commemorates Roberts Camp, a resort
camp founded in 1912.

Thanks to 1960s-era check-dams, the creek flows in well-organ-
ized fashion, lingering in tranquil pools, and then spilling over the

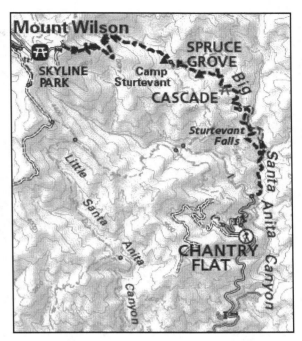

dams in 15-foot cascades. Moss, ferns, alders and other creekside flora have softened the appearance of the dams and they now fit much better into the lovely surroundings.

The trail passes private cabins and reaches a three-way trail junction. To visit Sturtevant Falls, continue straight ahead. Cross Big Santa Anita Creek, then re-cross where the creek veers leftward. Pick your way along the boulder-strewn creek bank a final hundred yards to the falls. The falls drops in a silver stream 50 feet to a natural rock bowl.

Two signed trails lead toward Spruce Grove Trail Camp. The leftward one zigzags high up on the canyon wall; the other passes above the falls. The left trail is easier hiking while the right trail heads through the heart of the canyon and is prettier.

After a mile, the trails rejoin. Continue along the spruce-shaded path to Cascade Picnic Area. Call it a day here or ascend another mile to Spruce Grove Trail Camp. Both locales offer picnic tables and shade.

Hikers in top condition will charge up the trail to Mt. Wilson—an 8-mile (one way) journey from Chantry Flat. Continue on the trail up-canyon a short distance and cross the creek to a trail junction. A left brings you to historic Sturtevant Camp, now owned by the Methodist Church. The trail to Mt. Wilson soon departs Big Santa Anita Canyon and travels many a switchback through the thick forest to Mt. Wilson Skyline Park.

WINTER CREEK

WINTER CREEK TRAIL

From Chantry Flat to Hoegees Camp is 5.1 miles round trip with 1,000-foot total elevation gain; return via Mt. Zion Trail and Gabrielino Trails is 9 miles round trip with 1,500-foot gain

Before the dawn of the 20th century, packer/entrepreneur William Sturtevant set up a trail camp in one of the woodsy canyons on the south-facing slope of Mt. Wilson. This peaceful creekside refuge from city life was called Sturtevant's Winter Camp.

In later years the name Winter was given to the creek whose headwaters arise from the shoulder of Mt. Wilson and tumble southeasterly into Big Santa Anita Canyon. The hike along the creek is one of my favorites of the half-dozen that depart from the popular Chantry Flat Trailhead.

In 1908, Arie Hoegee and his family built a resort here that soon became a popular destination for Mt. Wilson-bound hikers; it remained so until battered by the great flood of 1938. A trail camp named for the Hoegees now stands on the site of the old resort.

DIRECTIONS: From the Foothill Freeway (210) in Arcadia, exit on Santa Anita Avenue and drive six miles north to its end at Chantry Flat. The trail begins across the road from the parking area. A tiny store at the edge of the parking lot sells maps and refreshments.

THE HIKE: Descend 0.75 mile on the paved fire road, part of signed Gabrielino Trail, into Big Santa Anita Canyon. At the bottom of the canyon, cross a footbridge near the confluence of Big Santa Anita and Winter Creeks.

After crossing the bridge, look leftward for the signed Lower Winter Creek Trail. Following the bubbling creek, the trail tunnels beneath the boughs of oak and alder, willow and bay.

Pass some cabins, built early in the 20th century and reached only by trail. The needs of the cabin owners have long been supplied by pack train. When you see man and beast moving through the forest, it's easy to imagine that you've stepped a century back in time, back into Southern California's Great Hiking and Trail Resort Era.

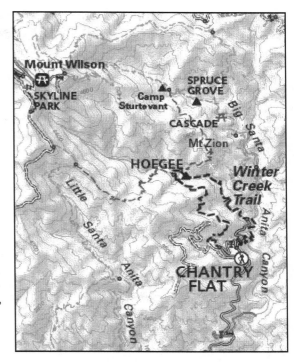

After crossing Winter Creek, arrive at Hoegees Camp. Tables beneath the big-cone spruce offer fine picnicking. Most signs of the original Hoegees Camp are gone, with the exception of flourishing patches of ivy. (In later years, Hoegees was renamed Camp Ivy.)

Walk through the campground until you spot a trail sign. Cross Winter Creek here and bear left on the trail. Soon you'll pass a junction with Mt. Zion Trail, a steep trail that climbs over the mountain to Sturtevant Camp and Big Santa Anita Canyon.

After re-crossing the creek, pass a junction with a trail leading to Mt. Wilson and join Upper Winter Creek Trail. This trail contours around a ridge onto open chaparral-covered slopes and offers fine clear-day views of Sierra Madre and Arcadia. The trail joins a fire road just above Chantry Flat and you follow this road through the picnic area back to the parking lot.

SAN GABRIEL RIVER EAST FORK

EAST FORK TRAIL

From East Fork Station to the "Bridge to Nowhere" is 9 miles round trip with 1,000-foot elevation gain

Sometimes a weekend gold miner finds a flash in the pan, but the real treasure of this section of the San Gabriel River lies in its beauty, its alders and tumbling waters. It's wet going; expect do a lot of wading, boulder-hopping and stream-crossing.

This hike leads through the monumental middle section of the East Fork of the San Gabriel River, and into Sheep Mountain Wilderness. The dizzy chasm of the Narrows is awesome, the steepest river gorge in Southern California.

Road builders of the 1930s envisioned a highway through the East Fork to connect the San Gabriel Valley with Wrightwood and the desert beyond. The great flood of 1938 interrupted these plans, leaving a handsome highway bridge stranded far up-river, the so-called "Bridge to Nowhere."

You'll pass the cracked asphalt remains of the old East Fork Road and gain access to the well-named Narrows. Intermittent trail leads to a junction with the main river and Iron Fork where, in the early years of the 20th century, miner George Trogden had a home and angler's headquarters.

The lower portion of the river is heavily visited on the weekends. Please use extra caution in times of high water.

DIRECTIONS: From the San Bernardino Freeway (10) exit on Azusa Avenue (Highway 39) and head north. Ten miles up Highway 39, turn right (east) on East Fork Road and continue eight more miles to the East Fork Ranger Station. Park in the lot below the station.

THE HIKE:

Follow the service road above the east side of the river 0.5 mile. Next, descend to the canyon floor and begin crossing and re-crossing the river. A bit more than two miles from the trailhead is Swan Rock, a mighty wall west of the river with the faint outline of a gargantuan swan.

As the canyon floor widens and twists northward, you'll climb up the right side of the canyon and continue up-river on the remains of East Fork Road, high above the rushing

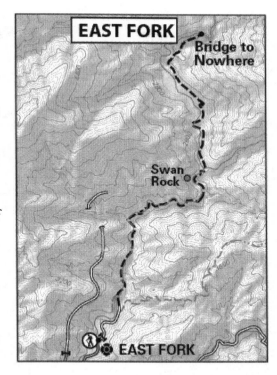

water. After ascending north a ways, you'll reach the "Bridge to Nowhere." No road meets this bridge at either end; the highway washed away in the flood of 1938.

Cross the bridge and join a slim trail that soon drops you into The Narrows. A quarter-mile from the bridge, Narrows Trail Camp (just a wide spot on the bank) is a fine place to picnic and view the handsome gorge.

Hardy hikers will boulder-hop along between towering granite walls. Iron Fork joins the river from the left, six miles from the trailhead.

Up-river another mile from Iron Fork is Fish Fork, whose waters cascade from the shoulders of Mt. Baldy. It, too, has been a popular fishing spot for generations of anglers. You can slosh up Fish Fork for another mile before a falls and the sheer canyon walls halt your progress.

San Gabriel River West Fork

West Fork National Scenic Trail

From Highway 39 to Glenn Camp is 14 miles round trip, but (much) shorter trips are possible

The San Gabriel River has two major forks, each with a claim to fame. East Fork is known for its gold, West Fork for its trout.

Early West Fork fishing camps catered to men looking for camaraderie, rustic accommodations and good fishing. The 1890s were a particularly grand time to cast a line. While most anglers caught no more than the limit—50(!) fish—others were greedy and some even used dynamite to "fish" for trout. California Governor Henry H. Markham was hardly an example of the conservation-minded sportsman; he landed 98 fish in six hours of fishing the West Fork.

Finally, the California Department of Fish and Game stepped in to enforce limits and replenish the West Fork with fingerlings and trout brought in from Lake Tahoe.

West Fork is even today one of the Southland's best fishing rivers. Most of the West Fork has been set aside as a wild trout preserve. Fishing is of the "catch and release" variety. Barbless hooks must be used and the daily limit is zero. Fishing for keeps is permitted along a portion of the West Fork—a 1.5-mile length near the trailhead.

The river can be reached from a couple different directions, but most anglers, as well as hikers and bicyclists, join the West Fork Scenic Trail which departs from Highway 39. The trail, actually an asphalt road, meanders 7 miles with the river to shady Glenn Camp. (The road continues another 1.5 miles past Glenn Camp to Cogswell Reservoir, which is closed to the public, and connects with forest service fire roads heading west.) Walk the whole way to Glenn Camp or pick a picnic or fishing spot anywhere you choose.

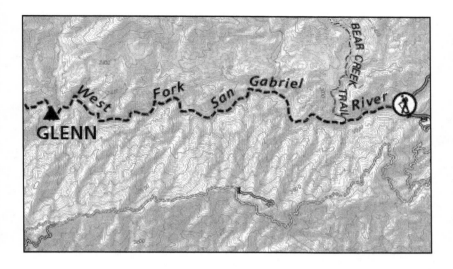

DIRECTIONS: From the Foothill Freeway (210) in Azusa, exit on Azusa Avenue (Highway 39) and head north. Fourteen miles later, and 0.5 mile past the Forest Service's San Gabriel Canyon Off-Highway Vehicle Area and Rincon Fire Station, look for a parking lot and locked gate on your left. Signed West Fork National Scenic Trail is the asphalt road descending into the canyon.

THE HIKE: Head past the locked gate and down the road into the canyon. On the weekends, expect plenty of company along the first mile of trail. Many canyon visitors will be toting coolers, lawn chairs and fishing poles.

After a mile, intersect Bear Creek Trail that leads north into the San Gabriel Wilderness. Pioneers had many an encounter with a grizzly along this creek, which is how this tributary of the San Gabriel River got its name. After another 0.5 mile of travel, re-cross the river and enter the designated wild trout preserve.

The road, which climbs very slowly, but steadily, upriver leads past many, tranquil, oak- and sycamore-shaded pools. Seven miles from the trailhead reach Glenn Camp, set on a shady flat right by the river. It's a peaceful place with tables that invite a picnic.

ICEHOUSE CANYON

ICEHOUSE CANYON TRAIL

From Icehouse Canyon to Icehouse Saddle is 8 miles round trip with 2,600-foot gain

Icehouse Canyon Trail, leading from Icehouse Canyon to several 8,000-foot peaks, is an ideal introduction to the high-country delights of Cucamonga Wilderness. The precipitous subalpine slopes of the wilderness, thickly forested with sugar pine, ponderosa pine and incense cedar, offer fresh mountain air and a network of good footpaths.

The 12,781-acre wilderness includes the Three T's—Timber Mountain, Telegraph Peak and Thunder Mountain—as well as 8,859-foot Cucamonga Peak, easternmost sentinel of the San Gabriel Mountains.

Icehouse Canyon is the hiker's only easy entry into the Cucamonga high country. The saddle and nearby peaks offer fine views to the hiker. Peak-baggers like this trail because several peaks are within "bagging distance" of Icehouse Saddle.

Icehouse Canyon was long known as Cedar Canyon because, as the story goes, the great cedar beams for Mission San Gabriel were logged here. The name Icehouse originated in the 1860s when ice was cut in the lower canyon and shipped to San Gabriel Valley residents.

Well-constructed Chapman Trail, named for the family that built the Icehouse Canyon resort in the 1920s, heads up Cedar Canyon to Cedar Glen, climbs out of Cedar Canyon, then contours on a steady grade back over to Icehouse Canyon.

DIRECTIONS: From the Foothill Freeway (210) in Claremont, exit on Baseline Road and head west one block to Padua

Avenue. Turn right and drive north 1.7 miles to a stop sign and an intersection with Mt. Baldy Road. Turn right and drive 7.2 miles to the Angeles National Forest's Mt. Baldy Visitor Center in Mt. Baldy Village. Proceed another 1.5 miles past the village to Icehouse Canyon parking area.

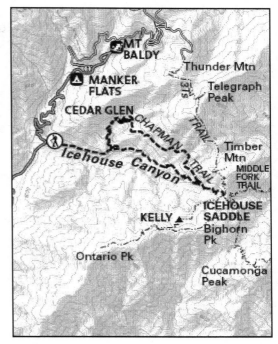

THE HIKE: The trail leads east along the floor of the canyon. The path stays close to the oak- and spruce-shaded creek and passes some cabins. After 1.5 miles, the trail forks. Take the "high route," the Chapman Trail, 1 mile to Cedar Flats and then 3 miles up to Icehouse Saddle, or continue straight ahead on the shorter and steeper Icehouse Canyon Trail directly up the canyon.

Icehouse Canyon Trail leads past more cabins and climbs up the north slope of the canyon, before dropping down again and crossing the creek. The trail switchbacks steeply through pine and spruce, which frame fine vistas of Old Baldy. Chapman Trail and Icehouse Canyon Trail intersect and a single trail ascends a steep 0.75 mile to the top of Icehouse Saddle.

Enjoy the view and return the same way, or choose among the fine trails that lead from Icehouse Saddle. You can continue eastward and drop down the Middle Fork Trail to Lytle Creek. A right (southeast) turn puts you on a trail that climbs two miles to Cucamonga Peak. A sharp right southwest leads 2.5 miles to Kelly's Camp and Ontario Peak. And a left on the Three T's Trail takes you past Timber Mountain, Telegraph Peak and Thunder Mountain, and then drops to Baldy Notch.

SAN ANTONIO CANYON

SKI HUT TRAIL

To San Antonio Falls is 2.5 miles round trip with 200-foot elevation gain; to San Antonio Canyon Overlook is 6.5 miles round trip with 2,600-foot gain; to Mt. Baldy summit is 8.5 miles round trip with 3,800-foot gain

The attractive trail leading up San Antonio Canyon to the top of Baldy is a Trailmaster favorite. Hikers of all ages and abilities will enjoy the short excursion to three-tiered, 60-foot San Antonio Falls.

Two more destinations beckon: the Sierra Club ski hut, where there's a cool spring, and a high ridge overlooking San Antonio Canyon. Hikers in top form will relish the challenge of the climb to the top and summit views: a panorama of desert and ocean, the sprawling Southland and the southern High Sierra.

DIRECTIONS: From the Foothill Freeway (210) in Claremont, exit on Baseline Road and head west one block to Padua Avenue. Turn right and drive north 1.7 miles to a stop sign and an intersection with Mt. Baldy Road. Turn right and drive 7.2 miles to the Angeles National Forest's Mt. Baldy Visitor Center in Mt. Baldy Village, then a few more miles to Manker Flats. Drive to the upper end of the campground and look for Falls Road on the north side of the street.

THE HIKE: Walk up the fire road (closed to public traffic). After modest ascent, behold San Antonio Falls. (You can descend to the base of the falls on rough trail.) Continue walking along the road (unpaved beyond the falls) and look sharply left for an unsigned trail.

The trail ascends very steeply along the side of San Antonio Canyon. Appreciate this steep path: it has a hand-hewn, unobtrusive

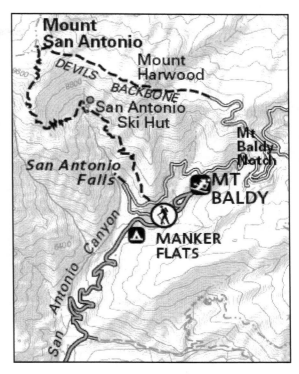

look and follows the natural contours of the land. Jeffrey pine, ponderosa pine and fir shade the path.

From the ski lift road it's 1.75 miles by trail to Sierra Club ski hut. Near the hut, constructed in 1935, is a cool and refreshing spring. Just past the ski hut, the trail crosses a tiny creek, and snakes through a boulder field. Beyond the boulders the trail ascends via a 0.5-mile series of steep switchbacks to a ridgetop overlooking the headwaters of San Antonio Canyon. Enjoy great views from the tree-shaded ridgetop.

Peak-baggers will continue up the extremely rugged trail for another mile to the summit. The trail is rough and tentative in places, but rocks piled in cairns help you stay on course. Take in good views of Devil's Backbone, the sharp ridge that connects the east slope of Mt. Harwood with the top of the ski slope, coming up from Baldy Notch.

Atop Baldy's crown, rock windbreaks offer shelter. Enjoy vistas view of San Gabriel and San Bernardino mountain range peaks, the Mojave and the metropolis.

Return the same way or take Devil's Backbone Trail to Mt. Baldy Notch. From the Notch, follow the fire road down Manker Canyon back to the trailhead or ride down the ski lift.

Mount Baldy

Devil's Backbone Trail

From Baldy Notch via ski lift, then to Mt. Baldy summit is 6.4 miles round trip with 2,200-foot gain; (without ski lift) 13 miles round trip with 3,800-foot gain

Mt. San Antonio, more commonly known as Mt. Baldy, is the highest peak (10,068 feet) in the mountains and visible from much of the Southland. Its summit gleams white in winter and early spring, gray in summer and fall. Old Baldy is so big and bare that it seems to be snow-covered even when it's not.

Baldy is a bit austere from afar, but up-close, the white granite shoulders of the mountain are softened by a forest of pine and fir. Padres of Mission San Gabriel, circa 1790, named the massive stone bulwark after Saint Anthony, a 13th-century friar from Padua, Italy. In the 1870s, gold-seekers dubbed the massive peak a more earthly "Old Baldy."

From Baldy Notch, Devil's Backbone Trail offers a moderately challenging route to the summit. This popular trail is the one most hikers associate with Baldy. Clear-day views from the top offer a panorama of desert and ocean, the sprawling Southland and the Southern High Sierra.

An alternative is to walk up a fire road to Baldy Notch. This option adds 3 miles each way and a 1,300-foot gain to the hike. The fire road switchbacks up the west side of steep San Antonio Canyon, offers a good view of San Antonio Falls, then climbs northward to the top.

DIRECTIONS: From the Foothill Freeway (210) in Claremont, exit on Baseline Road and head west one block to Padua Avenue. Turn right and drive north 1.7 miles to a stop sign and an intersection with

Mt. Baldy Road. Turn right and drive 7.2 miles to the national forest's Mt. Baldy Visitor Center in Mt. Baldy Village, then a few more miles up to Manker Flats. To walk up the fire road, drive to the upper end of the Manker Flats Campground. Look for a vehicle gate and a paved road.

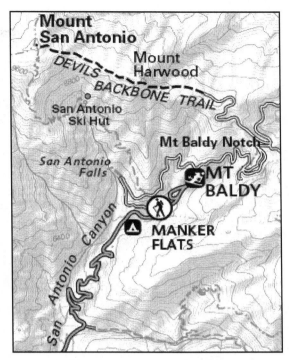

Those riding the ski lift will continue 0.25 mile past the campground to the Baldy Ski Lifts and free parking. Purchase a ticket and ride the ski lift up to Baldy Notch. (The lift is operated weekends and holidays all year.)

THE HIKE: From Baldy Notch, a wide gravel path leads to a commanding view of the desert. Join a chair lift access/fire road, and ascend a broad slope forested in Jeffrey pine and incense cedar. The road ends in about 1.25 miles at the top of a ski lift.

From here, a trail leads onto a sharp ridge, the Devil's Backbone. Look north down into the deep gorge of Lytle Creek, and south into San Antonio Canyon. Pass around the south side of Mt. Harwood, "Little Baldy," and up through scattered stands of lodgepole pine.

Reach a tempestuous saddle (Hold onto your hat!) and continue on a steep rock-strewn pathway that zigzags past wind-bowed limber pine to the summit. Atop Baldy's crown, rock windbreaks offer shelter. Enjoy vistas of San Gabriel and San Bernardino mountain peaks, the Mojave and the metropolis.

MOUNT WILLIAMSON

PACIFIC CREST TRAIL

From Islip Saddle to Mt. Williamson is 5 miles round trip with 1,600-foot elevation gain

Mt. Williamson stands head and shoulders above other crests along Angeles Crest Highway. The 8,214-foot peak offers grand views of earthquake country—the Devil's Punchbowl, San Andreas Fault and the fractured northern edges of the San Gabriel Mountains.

Desert views this peak may offer, but Mt. Williamson is anything but a desert peak. It's plenty green and bristling with pine and fir.

The summit of Mt. Williamson is the high point and culmination of well-named Pleasant View Ridge, a chain of peaks that rises from the desert floor to Angeles Crest Highway. It's quite a contrast to stand atop the piney peak, which is snow-covered in winter, and look down upon Joshua trees and the vast sandscape of the Mojave Desert. Pleasant View Ridge Wilderness, 26,757 acres located north of the Angeles Crest Highway where the San Gabriel Mountains slope north to meet the Mojave Desert, was designated in 2009.

Hot and cold, desert and alpine environments—these are the contrasts that make hiking in Southern California so very special.

Mountain namesake Major Robert Stockton Williamson first explored the desert side of the San Gabriels in 1853. Williamson, a U.S. Army mapmaker led an expedition in a successful search for a railroad route around or through the mountains. Williamson's report to Congress detailed two routes: Cajon Pass on the east end of the San Gabriels and Soledad Canyon on northwest.

Two fine segments of Pacific Crest Trail ascend Mt. Williamson from Angeles Crest Highway. One trail leads from Islip Saddle, the other from a saddle 1.5 miles farther west. With a car shuttle, you could hike both. However, don't even think about walking Angeles Crest Highway to make a loop trip; it's unsafe to walk the highway and through two tunnels en route.

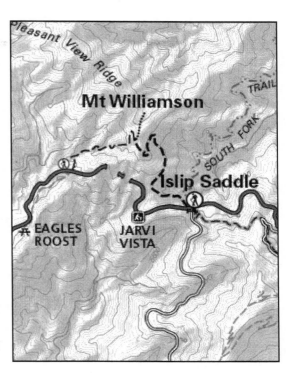

DIRECTIONS: From the Foothill Freeway in La Canada, follow Angeles Crest Highway (2) 41 miles to the parking area at Islip Saddle on the left (north) side of the highway.

THE HIKE: At Islip Saddle, note South Fork Trail (descending northeast toward Devil's Punchbowl County Park.) From the north side of the parking lot, join signed Pacific Crest Trail as it ascends somewhat aggressively along the eastern shoulder of Mt. Williamson and through a forest of Jeffrey and ponderosa pine.

A bit more than 2 miles out, near 8,000 feet in elevation, reach a junction. PCT continues west. Take the fainter path north on a steep ascent passing scattered white fir. Enjoy over-the-shoulder views south into the heart of the rugged San Gabriel Wilderness. Keep hiking north on the trail, which gets increasingly sketchy as it passes over a few bumps and reaches the summit of Mt. Williamson.

Enjoy dramatic views of the desert. Gaze out at the many playas (dry lake beds), buttes and mountain ridges of the dry lands below. At the base of Mt. Williamson lies that greatest of earthquake faults—the San Andreas Rift Zone. Most striking of all is the view of Devil's Punchbowl and its jumbled sedimentary strata.

MT. ISLIP

MT. ISLIP TRAIL

From Angeles Crest Highway to Little Jimmy Trail Camp is 3 miles round trip with 500-foot elevation gain; to Mt. Islip is 5 miles round trip with 1,100-foot gain

Mt. Islip (pronounced eye-slip) is by no means one of the tallest San Gabriel mountain peaks, but its relatively isolated position on the spine of the range makes it stand out. The summit offers the hiker fine views of the middle portion of the Angeles National Forest high country and of the metropolis.

Mt. Islip has long been a popular destination for hikers. Occidental College students built a huge cairn (heap of boulders), dubbed "Occidental Monument," atop the summit in 1909. The monument, which had the name Occidental on top, stood about two decades, until the Forest Service cleared the summit to make room for a fire lookout tower. The monument and fire lookout are long gone, but the stone foundation of the fire lookout's living quarters still remains.

One early visitor to the slopes of Mt. Islip was popular newspaper cartoonist Jimmy Swinnerton (1875-1974), well known in the early years of the 20th century for his comic strip "Little Jimmy." By the time he was in his thirties, hard-working, hard-drinking Swinnerton was suffering from the effects of exhaustion, booze, and tuberculosis. His employer and benefactor, William Randolph Hearst, sent him to the desert to dry out, but Swinnerton opted for the mountains.

During the summers of 1908 and 1909 Swinnerton often set up camp near Gooseberry Spring, which soon became known as Little Jimmy Spring, and entertained passing hikers with sketches of his

Little Jimmy character. His campsite now bears the name of Little Jimmy Trail Camp.

DIRECTIONS: From the Foothill Freeway (210) in La Canada, exit on Angeles Crest Highway (2) and proceed some 41 miles to signed Islip Saddle. On the north side of the highway, is a large parking area.

THE HIKE: The trail begins as a dirt road shaded by Jeffrey and sugar pine.

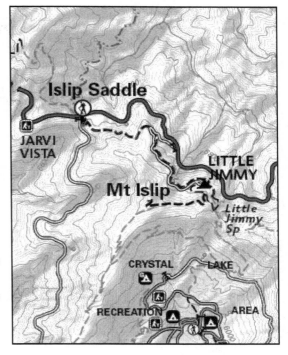

A half-mile ascent leads to a three-way junction. To the right is the old crest trail coming up from Islip Saddle. The forest road continues to Little Jimmy Trail Camp.

Bear left on the signed trail to Little Jimmy. The trail stays just below and parallel to the road as it ascends a mile over forested slopes to Little Jimmy Trail Camp. The camp, popular with youth groups, has tables, stoves and restrooms. A side trail leads 0.25 mile southeast to all-year Little Jimmy Spring.

At the west end of camp, join the signed trail to Mt. Islip. Ascend 0.5 mile of switchbacks through piney woods to a sharp ridgeline. From atop the ridge, enjoy great views of Crystal Lake, the San Gabriel Wilderness, and canyons cut by Bear Creek and the San Gabriel River.

The trail turns east and follows the ridge for another 0.5 mile to the 8,250-foot peak. Summit views include ski areas and Mt. Waterman to the west and Mt. Baden-Powell to the east.

MT. BADEN-POWELL

MT. BADEN-POWELL TRAIL

From Vincent Gap to summit is 8 miles round trip with 2,800-foot elevation gain

This trail and peak honor Lord Baden-Powell, a British Army officer who founded the Boy Scout movement in 1907. The well-engineered trail, grooved into the side of the mountain by the Civilian Conservation Corps in the mid-1930s, switchbacks up the northeast ridge to the peak.

The peak was once known as North Baldy, before Southern California Boy Scouts lobbied the Forest Service for a name change. Mt. Baden-Powell is the terminus of the scouts' 53-mile Silver Moccasin Trail, a rugged week-long backpack through the San Gabriels.

The trail follows a moderate, steady grade to the top of the mountain, where there's a monument honoring Powell. On the summit, you'll meet those ancient survivors, the limber pines, and be treated to superb views across the Mojave Desert and down into the Iron Fork of the San Gabriel River.

DIRECTIONS: Take the Angeles Crest Highway (2) for 53 miles from La Cañada to the Vincent Gap Parking Area. The signed trailhead is at the northwest edge of the parking area. If you're coming from the east, take Interstate 15 to the Wrightwood exit, three miles south of Cajon Pass. Proceed 8 miles west on Highway 138 to its intersection with Highway 2. Turn left on Highway 2 and drive 14 miles to the trailhead.

THE HIKE: Begin the ascent from Vincent Gulch Divide, a gap separating the upper tributaries of the San Gabriel River to the south from Big Rock Creek to the northwest. The trail switchbacks southwest through Jeffrey pine and fir. The trail numbers more than three dozen of these switchbacks; however, so many inspiring scenes compete for the hiker's attention it's hard to get an accurate count.

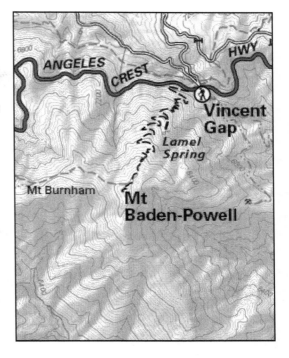

In 1.5 miles, a side trail (unmarked) leads a hundred yards to Lamel Spring, an inviting resting place and the only dependable water en route.

With increased elevation, the switchbacks grow shorter and steeper and the vegetation changes from fir to lodgepole pine. Soon, even the altitude-loving lodgepoles give way to the heartiest of pines, the limber pine. A half-mile from the summit, around 9,000 feet in elevation, the first of these squat, thick-trunked limber pines come into view.

To Limber Pine Forest: A tiny sign points right (southwest) to the limber pine stand, 0.125 mile. These wind-loving, subalpine dwellers are one of the few living things that can cope with the rarefied atmosphere. *Pinus flexilis*, botanists call the species, for its long, droopy, flexible branches. They bow and scrape like hyperextended dancers and appear to gather all their nourishment from the wind.

Back on the main trail, a few more switchbacks bring you atop the ridge where Mt. Baldy can be glimpsed. Walk along the barren crest and intersect the Pacific Crest Trail. PCT swoops off to Little Jimmy Spring.

Continue past the limber pines to the summit. A concrete monument pays homage to Lord Baden-Powell. Enjoy the superb view out across the Mojave to the southern Sierra and east to Baldy, San Gorgonio and San Jacinto.

Old stereotypes die hard, and the prevailing opinion of far too many Southlanders, hikers and not, is that there is nowhere to hike in Orange County. Nothing could be farther from the truth. While California's most densely populated county, Orange is also its second-most biologically diverse and boasts an excellent regional park system and a fine trail network.

The county's wilderness parks, including Caspers, Laguna Coast, Aliso and Wood Canyons, are particularly compelling places to take a hike, and the Santa Ana Mountains, extending the length of OC's perimeter, offer plenty of room to roam.

CHAPTER 6

ORANGE COUNTY

HIKE ON.

Santiago Oaks Regional Park

Santiago Creek, Oak, Anaheim Hills Trails

To Robbers Peak is 3 miles round trip with 700-foot elevation gain

Santiago Oaks Regional Park preserves 350 acres of pastoral Orange County, including a splendid oak woodland, groupings of mature ornamental trees and even grove of Valencia oranges.

For great views of the Anaheim Hills, Chino Hills and a whole lot of OC, hike up to the 1,152-foot rocky knob known as Robbers Peak. As the story goes, such infamous outlaws as Joaquin Murietta and Three-Finger Jack prowled Orange County; they rode down from the hills to rob stagecoaches and back into the hills to escape the sheriff's posse.

Stop at the engaging nature center before hitting the trail—lots of park trails, in fact. Sure bets are aptly named Santiago Creek Trail and other footpaths that meander near the creek.

Historic Dam Trail leads to…an old dam. With the aid of Chinese laborers, the Serrano and Carpenter Water Company built a clay dam here in 1879. This dam was destroyed by floods, and replaced in 1892 with a more substantial structure of river rock and cement. The dam looks particularly tiny when compared to the huge Villa Park Flood Control dam a short distance upstream.

Sample the park's ecosystems with Windes Nature Trail. The 0.75-mile trail and its Pacifica Loop offer clear-day glimpses of the county's coastline. As nature trails go, this one is definitely on the steep side. Reward for following the trail on the ascent up 770-foot Rattlesnake Ridge are good views of the park and beyond.

For a longer (2.5 mile) loop of the park, in a counterclock-wise direction, begin with Santiago Creek Trail and follow it to the

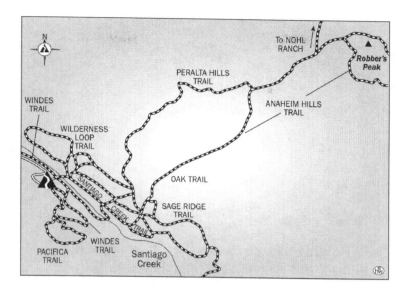

eastern boundary of the park. Take Sage Ridge Trail and Wilderness Loop Trail westbound back to reconnect with Santiago Creek Trail.

DIRECTIONS: From the Costa Mesa Freeway (55) in Orange, exit on Katella Avenue and head east. Katella undergoes name changes to Villa Park Road, then to Santiago Canyon Road. About 3 miles from the freeway, turn left on Windes Drive and drive 0.75 mile to Santiago Oaks Regional Park.

THE HIKE: From the parking lot, cross Santiago Creek and follow Santiago Creek Trail amongst the oaks along the north side of the creek. At a signed junction with Oak Trail, turn left (northeast).

As you ascend, pass a couple of right-forking side trails. Pass a junction with Peralta Hills Trail and leave the regional park behind. At a point on the ridge about 1,000 feet in elevation, enjoy a grand view from suburbia to the Pacific.

Nearing the sandstone peak, Anaheim Hills Trail peels off to the right but you keep following the ridge, curving north then west to the summit. From atop the peak, you can look over the Peralta Hills and trace the path of Santiago Creek. Once upon a time the view would have taken in hundreds of cattle, orange groves and barley fields. Nowadays the panorama is considerably less pastoral.

WEIR CANYON
WILDERNESS PARK

WEIR CANYON LOOP TRAIL

From Hidden Canyon: a 4-mile loop with 300-foot elevation gain.

From the trail high on the west wall of Weir Canyon, the hiker gets a view of Orange County that's both stereotypical and surprising. The view westward is that of Orange County to the max: houses perched everywhere on the slopes of the Anaheim Hills, several freeways, the city of Anaheim, plus many more cities sprawling toward the coast.

In contrast to this 21st-century vista, the view east is minimalist Orange County; that is to say, mostly parkland, a pastoral landscape of hills and canyons that in the right light looks like a plein-air painting made during the late 19th century.

Weir Canyon Wilderness Park ("wilderness" is stretching the definition a bit, but it's certainly a wilderness compared to developed areas of the Anaheim Hills) and is one of those great so-near-yet-so-faraway places in Orange County to take a hike.

It's a pleasure to report it's the park—not nearby subdivisions—that's been extending its boundaries farther into the hills toward the toll road (Highway 241).

Weir Canyon is ideal for a family hike, as a training trail for those hiking for health and fitness, and as a quiet getaway from OC's fast pace and freeways. I'm not sure why some folks call Weir the "Secret Park," but they do. Mountain bikers have discovered it. And so have hikers. Definitely it has a peaceful vibe and I like that it doesn't have any towers or power lines crossing the park—unlike like neighboring Santiago Oaks Regional Park.

Geographers say the Anaheim Hills comprise a long, low ridge extending west from the Santa Ana Mountains and rising above

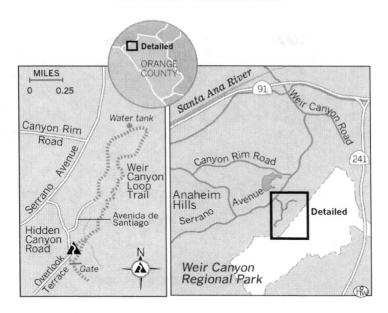

Santa Ana Canyon and the Santa Ana River. Weir Canyon Trail offers a gentle introduction to the considerable pleasures of these hills.

DIRECTIONS: From the Riverside Freeway (91) in Anaheim Hills, exit on Weir Canyon Road. Head south 0.7 mile to Serrano Avenue. Turn right (west) and proceed 2 miles to Hidden Canyon Road. Turn left (south) and follow it a half-mile to its end at Overlook Terrace and the signed trailhead. Park along Hidden Canyon Road.

THE HIKE: From the park sign, walk the wide dirt trail northeast about 0.1 mile to a junction. Anaheim Hills Trail forks left leading to Robbers Peak and Santiago Oaks Regional Park. Go left along a fence line, enjoying eastward views into Weir Canyon and westward ones of some intriguing sandstone outcroppings.

The path dips into and climbs out of some minor side canyons, skirts some residences at about the 2.5 mile mark, then U-turns and begins heading south. When the trail bends left and ascends, you'll be getting in some good cardio. Reward for the climb are clear-day vistas from the Anaheim Hills to downtown L.A.

After leading you a mile along the western rim of Weir Canyon, the path drops to the end of Avenida de Santiago. Walk down the steep residential street to Hidden Canyon Road, turn left, and return to the trailhead.

IRVINE REGIONAL PARK

HORSESHOE LOOP TRAIL

Loop around park is 4 miles round trip with 200-foot elevation gain; longer options available

Irvine Park is a classic: stately groves of oak and sycamore, lovely picnic areas and a boat pond ringed with handsome stonework. It also boasts ball fields and playgrounds, as well as the Orange County Zoo and the Irvine Park Railroad.

Rolling foothills with accompanying trails border the central part of the park and offer the hiker a chance to get both then and now looks at Orange County.

Irvine Park is a lot of things but one thing it's not: it's not in Irvine! It's located in Santiago Canyon about six miles east of the City of Orange.

Irvine is Orange County's largest (traditional as opposed to wilderness) county park, and now encompasses 477 acres. And Irvine is the county's oldest park, too. In 1897, James Irvine donated a 160-acre oak grove with the stipulation that the trees should always have the best of care. (Learn more about the park's colorful history at the interpretive center and check out native California flora on a 0.25-mile trail leading across William Harding Nature Area.)

Horseshoe Trail offers a loop around the historic core of the park. Parallel paths to the north and south of Horseshoe Trail ascend ridges for fine panoramic views. I prefer a counter-clockwise tour of the park and I like to take the ridge route wherever possible. Add the Roadrunner Loop to this hike or put it on your "To Hike" list for next time.

DIRECTIONS: From the Newport Freeway (55), exit on Chapman Avenue (East) and head east 5 miles to Jamboree. Turn left and proceed north 0.25 mile to the park entry road and turn right. At a fork, bear left to pay admission at the park entry station

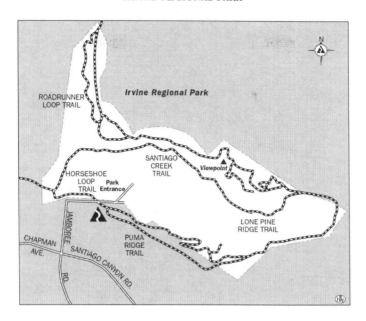

but note that the right fork (a dead-end road) is where you'll find the start of this hike.

THE HIKE: From the park entry road, join eastbound Horseshoe Loop Trail. If you continue with this path be sure to explore the short Cactus Canyon Trail.

An (almost immediate) alternative is Puma Ridge Trail, a rather steep, rough and often eroded path that ascends the park's southern ridgeline and travels parallel to Horseshoe Trail. Take in the good views, and descend to rejoin Horseshoe Loop Trail.

The trail makes a horseshoe bend north and west before reaching a junction. Choose between two westbound paths (the upper or northern trail goes to a viewpoint and connects with Roadrunner Loop Trail. Keep in mind, there aren't many places to cross Santiago Creek, easily forded at times of low water levels and a risky venture at times of high water.

The northern trail leads to a developed viewpoint and descends to meet Roadrunner Loop Trail. The eastern leg of the 1.5-mile loop is better defined than the western one, which travels among willows and other riparian growth closer to the creek.

Return to Santiago Creek, cross it, and finish your loop, by trail and park walkway.

PETERS CANYON

LAKE VIEW, LOWER CANYON, EAST RIDGE TRAILS

2.6-mile Lake Loop; 6-mile Canyon Loop with 300-foot elevation gain

In 1899, "green space" had an entirely different meaning around here than it does today. In a remote canyon, local golfers laid out a golf course—Orange County's first.

Today Golf Canyon is the site of 340-acre Peters Canyon Park. Its convenient mid-OC location, variety of terrain and excellent trail network make the park a very popular one with hikers.

Lake View Trail loops around Peters Canyon Reservoir, gathering place for migratory and resident waterfowl. Watch for herons and egrets along shores lined with black willow, sycamore and cottonwood.

A longer hike travels Peters Canyon to the park's south end and returns atop East Ridge, which offers excellent vistas.

DIRECTIONS: From Highway 55 in Orange, exit on Chapman Avenue and head east 4.5 miles to Jamboree Road. Turn right, proceed 0.5 mile to Canyon View Avenue, and turn right again. Main entrance to the park (parking fee) is a short distance up the road on your left. Limited free parking is available off Skylark Place.

THE HIKE: From the park ranger station hike east on wide Lake View Trail that traces the northern edge of the reservoir and soon bends southwest to parallel Skylark Drive.

About 0.4 mile out, intersect Skyline Trail, but stay left with Lake View Loop continuing another 0.4 mile to a junction with Cactus Point Trail. Oddly, to stay with the Lake View Loop route, abandon Lake View Trail and join Cactus Point Trail, which leads 0.25 mile to a vista point overlooking the reservoir.

Continue on Cactus Point Trail as it makes an almost 180-degree turn and backtracks to Lake View Trail. Go left and ascend to a vista point with a bench. The path dips and rises and passes a short path leading to a viewpoint of the dam and reservoir.

Lake View Trail ends at a junction with Peters Canyon Trail, part of the 22-mile Mountains to Sea Trail extending from Irvine Regional Park to Newport Bay. To close the loop and return to the trailhead, head north (left) then bend west with Lake View Trail or with scenic alternative Willow Trail (closed in spring and summer to protect bird habitat).

For a longer outing, turn right and soon reach a junction. Save left-forking East Ridge View Trail for the return trip and continue along Peters Canyon Trail. Pass two left-forking connector trails going up to East Ridge before reaching a 1940s-era reservoir; it's dry these days, and serves as an emergency flood control basin.

Near the basin, leave Peters Canyon Trail and fork left . Watch the skies for hawks circling above the eucalyptus groves located in lower Peters Canyon and connect with East Ridge View Trail, a wide dirt road that extends north.

Near trail's end the path reaches a vista point. Take in clear day views of the San Bernardino Mountains to the east and the Pacific and Catalina Island to the west, then descend steeply 0.2 mile to meet Peters Canyon Trail.

O'NEILL PARK

LIVE OAK TRAIL

From Trabuco Canyon to Ocean Vista Point is 3 miles round trip with 600-foot elevation gain

The soldier marching with Captain Gaspar de Portola's 1769 expedition who lost his firearm in this hilly region would no doubt be astonished at the number of Orange County place-names inspired by his loss. Trabuco, which means "blunderbuss" in Spanish, now names a canyon, a creek, a plain, a trail, a road and much more in OC.

If that soldier marched this way again he'd be even more amazed at the land itself, so drastically has it changed. He might recognize Trabuco Canyon, though, at least that part of it preserved by O'Neill Regional Park.

After six decades of conservation activity, O'Neill Park now encompasses more than 4,000 acres, taking in Trabuco Canyon and neighboring Live Oak Canyon. From the park's ridges, the hiker gets vistas of two scenes typical of rural Orange County: hawks circling over classic ranch country and brand new suburbs—indeed whole communities. O'Neill Park has changed almost unbelievably since my Boy Scout troop enjoyed camping here, but it still offers a place to reconnect with nature.

Park pathways include nature trails, short loops into the hills, and links to lengthy Arroyo Trabuco Trail that extends to Whiting Ranch Wilderness Park. Edna Spaulding Nature Trail (0.8 mile) offers a fine intro to the park's oak woodland and coastal sage environments. This hike rises above wooded canyons and ascends to Ocean Vista Point for views of nearby peaks, canyons, and the Pacific.

DIRECTIONS: From the San Diego Freeway (5) in Lake Forest, exit on El Toro Road and head 7.5 miles east to the junction known as Cooks Corner. Santiago Canyon Road angles left (north) but you veer right on Live Oak Canyon Road (S19) and follow Live Oak Canyon Road east then south 3 miles to the O'Neill Regional Park entrance on the right. Past the park entry station, make a right to reach the parking area and signed Live Oak Trail and Spaulding Nature Trail trailhead in 0.25 mile.

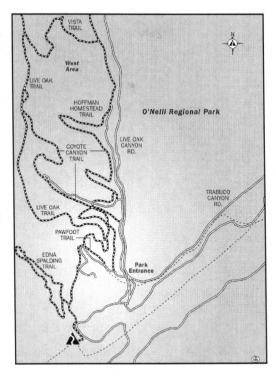

THE HIKE: Continue past the junction with Edna Spaulding Trail on your left and head north. At some hillside water tanks, the trail very briefly joins the water tank road, and then you'll resume with Live Oak Trail on the climb up the west wall of the canyon.

Pass junctions with Pawfoot Trail, Homestead Trail and Coyote Canyon trail as you ascend along a ridge. From the 1,492-foot summit, enjoy clear-day coastal views from Santa Monica Bay to San Clemente, with Catalina Island floating on the horizon.

After enjoying the views, choose between two or more return routes. One way back is by retracing your steps on Live Oak Trail, then joining Coyote Trail to Homestead Trail and back to Live Oak Trail. Another way to go is by way of Valley Vista Trail which drops steeply into Live Oak Canyon. An old park service road paralleling the highways returns you to the heart of the park.

LIMESTONE-WHITING RANCH WILDERNESS PARK

BORREGO CANYON, WHITING, VISTA POINT TRAILS

From 4 to 6 miles round trip

Oak-shaded canyons, grassy hills and handsome, rose-color-ed sandstone cliffs are some of the attractions of Orange County's Limestone-Whiting Ranch Wilderness Park. The 2,500-acre park, crisscrossed by 17 miles of trails, is a hiker's delight.

First-time visitors are amazed to find a lush oak woodland and rugged hills in such close proximity to suburban developments. Park highlights include handsome rock formations, particularly beautiful Red Rock Canyon, plus 3 seasonal creeks: Borrego, Serrano and Aliso. About 90% of the park burned in the Santiago Fire of 2007, but the land has recovered fairly well.

While the park is indeed a wild land as its name suggests, the trailhead is anything but. A shopping center is located across Portola Parkway. Near the trailhead is a sculpture entitled "California Song," a windmill-topped tower that depicts native birds and wildlife.

With so many named and unnamed trails, the park lends itself to improvisational hiking. Put Red Rock Canyon Trail, a rare hik-ers-only path on the "must hike" list.

If you're up for a challenge consider the ascent of Dreaded Hill. According to local hikers, the park's highest hill had a lot of names, but "Dreaded" was the only one that could be printed on a map and repeated in public. The brutal climb required to reach the top of this hill, which looms to the south of the park's popular Four Corners area, has been known to prompt trail users to describe it with some colorful—and quite off-color—words.

DIRECTIONS:
From Interstate 5
in the El Toro area,
exit on Lake Forest
Drive and proceed
east 4.8 miles to
Portola Parkway.
Turn left and drive
0.5 mile to the
entrance and park-
ing lot of Whiting
Ranch Wilderness
Park.

THE HIKE:
Borrego Trail leads
a mile through
oak-studded
Borrego Canyon,
a peninsula of park-

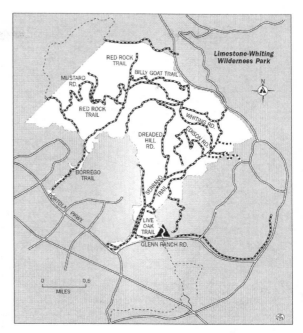

land surrounded on three sides by residential and commercial development. The path up Borrego Canyon leads to junctions with other
trails that lead to more remote sections of the park. Three popular
hikes (mileage calculated from Portola Parkway trailhead) include:

Vista Point Trail (4 miles round trip) leads from Borrego Canyon
to a high ridge for excellent views of south Orange County.

Red Rock Trail (4 miles round trip) explores what some rock
connoisseurs consider to be one of Orange County's finest formations. It's a 1.5-mile hike to reach Red Rock Trail, a 0.5-mile pathway into the strangely eroded sandstone.

The Borrego Trail-Mustard Road-Whiting Road Loop is a grand
6-mile tour of the park. The route climbs through heavily wooded
Borrego Canyon, tops out at a junction called Four Corners, and descends Serrano Canyon to Portola Parkway. A mile of walking along
the road brings you back to the trailhead.

Still, climbing Dreaded Hill has its rewards apart from its test of
one's physical fitness. Like the great views from the 1,624-foot crest:
Orange County near and far, Catalina Island and the wide, blue
Pacific.

Caspers Wilderness Park
Nature, Oak, Bell Canyon Trails

2- to 4-mile loops

At 7,600 acres, Caspers Wilderness Park is the largest park in Orange County's regional park system and, to date, the park most removed from major OC population centers. With its size, scope wildness and wildlife, the park is worthy of the "wilderness" in its name.

Crisscrossing Casper are 30 miles of trail, which explore grassy valleys, chaparral-cloaked ridges and splendid groves of coastal live oak and sycamore. Best hiking in the park is through the two major oak-lined canyons—Bell and San Juan—and along the brushy ridges, which offer grand clear-day views from the Santa Ana Mountains to the Pacific. The mostly level, Nature Trail-Oak Trail-Bell Canyon Trail-loop I describe is only one of many possible day hikes you can fashion from the park's extensive trail network.

Centerpiece of the park is oak-lined Bell Canyon. Acorns from the oaks were an important food source for the native Juaneno Indians who lived in the canyon. As the legend goes, the Juaneno would strike a large granite boulder with a small rock to make it ring. You can learn more about the region's human and natural history at the park's visitor center.

DIRECTIONS: From Interstate 5 in San Juan Capistrano, take the Highway 74 (Ortega Highway) exit. Drive 8 miles inland to the entrance to Caspers Wilderness Park. There is a vehicle entrance fee. From the entry kiosk, take the park road 1.5 miles to its end at the corral and windmill. There's plenty of parking near the signed trailhead for Nature Trail.

THE HIKE: Nature Trail loops through a handsome grove of antiquarian oak. Look for woodpeckers checking their store of acorns, which the birds have stuffed in hidey-holes in the nearby sycamores. Beneath the oaks are substantial patches of poison oak, but the trail steers clear of them.

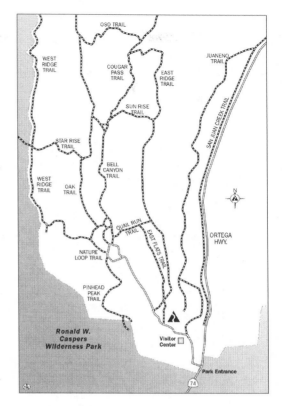

Pass a junction with a left-branching trail that leads to Gunsight Pass and West Ridge Trail, and soon arrive at a second junction. (If you want a really short hike, keep right at this junction and loop back to the trailhead via Nature Trail.)

Head north on signed Oak Trail, which meanders beneath the oak and sycamore that shade the west wall of Bell Canyon. The trail never strays far from Bell Creek, its streambed, or sandy washes. During drought years, it's difficult to imagine that in the 19th century, black bears used to catch spawning steelhead trout in Bell Creek. Fragrant sages perfume the trail, which is also lined with lemonade berry and prickly pear cactus.

Oak Trail reaches a junction at Post "12." You may take a short connector trail east to Bell Canyon or head north on another short trail, Star Rise, and join Bell Canyon Trail. A wide dirt road, Bell Canyon Trail travels the canyon floor.

To return to the trailhead, head south on Bell Canyon Trail, which passes through open oak-dotted meadows. Red-tailed hawks roost atop spreading sycamores. The trail returns to the parking area, within sight of the beginning of Nature Trail, where you began your walk.

CRYSTAL COVE STATE PARK

MORO CANYON TRAIL

From Park Headquarters to the top of Moro Canyon is 7 miles round trip with 700-foot elevation gain

Extending three miles along the coast between Laguna Beach and Corona del Mar, and inland over the San Joaquin Hills, 3,000-acre Crystal Cove State Park attracts bird-watchers, beachcombers and hikers.

The backcountry of Crystal Cove State Park is part of the San Joaquin Hills, first used by Mission San Juan Capistrano for grazing land. In 1864, James Irvine and partners bought the land and it became part of Irvine Ranch. Grazing continued until shortly after the state purchased the property as parkland in 1979.

Former Irvine Ranch roads form a network of hiking trails that loop through the state park. An especially nice trail travels the length of Moro Canyon, main watershed of the park. Oak woodland, a seasonal stream and sandstone caves are some attractions of a walk through this canyon.

After exploring inland portions of the state park, visit the park's coastline, highlighted by grassy bluffs, sandy beaches, tidepools and coves.

DIRECTIONS: Crystal Cove State Park is located off Pacific Coast Highway, about 2 miles south of the town of Corona del Mar or 1 mile north of Laguna Beach. Turn inland on the park road, signed "El Moro Canyon." Drinking water, restrooms, interpretive displays and plenty of parking is available at the ranger station.

THE HIKE: Below the ranger station, near the park entry kiosk, join Moro Canyon Trail, which crosses the grassy slopes behind a school and leads down into Moro Canyon. At the canyon bottom, meet a fire road and head left, up-canyon.

The hiker may observe such native plants as black sage, prickly pear cactus, monkeyflowers, golden bush, lemonade berry and deer weed. The abundance of edible plants in the area, combined with the mild climate and easy access to the bounty of the sea, contributed to the success of a Native American population, whom anthropologists believe lived off this land for more than 4,000 years.

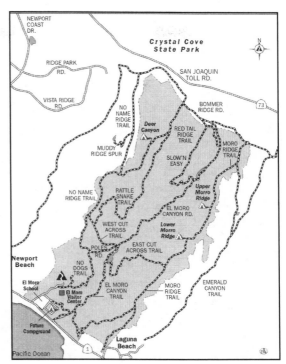

The canyon narrows, and you ignore fire roads joining Moro Canyon from the right and left. Stay in the canyon bottom and proceed through an oak woodland, which shades a trickling stream. You'll pass a shallow sandstone cave just off the trail to the right.

About 2.5 miles from the trailhead, reach the unsigned junction with a fire road. If you wish to make a loop trip, bear left on this road, which climbs steeply west, then northeast toward the ridgetop that forms a kind of inland wall for Muddy, Moro, Emerald and other coastal canyons.

When you reach the ridgetop, enjoy far-reaching views of the San Joaquin Hills and Orange County coast, Catalina and San Clemente Islands. You'll also have a raven's-eye view of Moro Canyon and the route back to the trailhead.

After catching your breath, bear right (east) along the ridgetop and quickly descend back into Moro Canyon. A 0.75-mile walk leads to the junction where you earlier ascended out of the canyon. This time continue straight down-canyon, retracing your steps to the trailhead.

Emerald Bay Viewpoint

Emerald Ridge Trail

From Park Visitor Center to Emerald Bay Viewpoint is 3.5 miles round trip with 500-foot elevation gain; return via Moro Canyon is 5 miles round trip

All of Crystal Cove State Park's ridgelines offer inspiring Pacific views, but surely the grandest of panoramas are to be found from a perch atop Moro Ridge. Emerald Bay and Laguna Beach are the most obvious sights to see from this little lookout located less than a 0.5 mile as the seagull flies from the Pacific breakers.

That's just a start. Down-coast lie Dana Point, Point Loma and, south of the border, Mexico's Coronado Islands. Santa Clemente floats gently on the seas to the southwest while Catalina, looking quite rugged and mountainous, rises boldly in your face in the west. Up-coast, the Palos Verdes Peninsula, too, rises dramatically above the shoreline. On particularly clear days the Santa Monica Mountains and the Ventura County coastline are visible.

You might expect a considerable trek to a high elevation peak to get such a view, but no, the hiker gains this awesome vista with a very modest climb to a promontory that measures but 594 feet above sea level. Sea is certainly an operative word here because you see so much of it, as well as some 200 miles of coastline, from the vista point.

The point has two distinctly utilitarian functions—as an antennae site (small, low ones) and as a reservoir site with some 400 thousand gallons of water stored underground.

DIRECTIONS: Crystal Cove State Park is located off Pacific Coast Highway, about 2 miles south of the town of Corona del Mar or one mile north of Laguna Beach. Turn inland on the park road, signed El Moro Canyon. Drinking water, restrooms, interpretive displays, park maps, a picnic area and plenty of parking are available at the visitor center. Check out the park's schedule of guided interpretive walks and hikes.

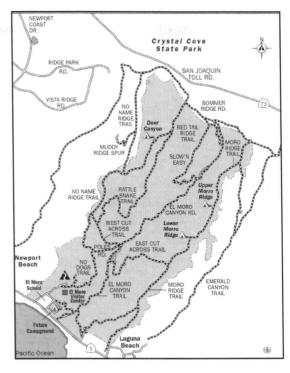

THE HIKE: From the visitor center, head down to the coastward side of the parking lot, join the fire road and file south past the El Morro School. At a junction you meet a connector trail, long called BFI, and now referred to more lyrical Emerald Ridge Trail, which continues south, climbing steeply at first, then leveling and serving up good coastal views.

The path intersects Moro Ridge Trail at a spot, very low on the ridge (scarcely 0.1 mile above Pacific Coast Highway). Hike uphill on the steep road, which alternates between pavement and gravel, eventually de-evolving into eroded dirt.

When you reach Moro Ridge, travel to an unsigned road (paved for a short distance, then dirt) and then head coastward. Disbelieving that you're traveling downhill to get a good view, but that's the case. Savor the terrific views

Extend the hike to a 5-mile or so loop by continuing another 0.8 mile up Moro Ridge to the East Cut Across Trail, descending to El Moro Canyon Trail and following this major route down-canyon and back to the trailhead parking lot.

NO NAME RIDGE

NO NAME RIDGE TRAIL

Loop from El Moro Visitor Center to Moro Canyon is 3.5 miles round trip with 300-foot elevation gain; to Deer Canyon Campground is 7 miles round trip with 600-foot gain

A great intro to the park and popular interpretive walk led by park rangers, this jaunt from the visitor center ascends No Name Ridge and returns via the park's main thoroughfare, Moro Canyon. It offers a sampling of the park's natural attractions and great views. A longer loop option rewards hikers with even better views.

A distinct ridgetop on the San Joaquin Hills marks the northern boundary, the ocean the south boundary. Moro Ridge is on the east and No Name Ridge on the west. I guess they could have called the ridges East Moro Ridge and West Moro Ridge, but then again, there are already too many park features with Moro in the name.

Odd that no-name ridge has no name considering other park features have colorful names. Poles Road is lined with poles. Easy and Mach One are no doubt suggestive of the speeds realized by the mountain bikers who use them.

DIRECTIONS: Crystal Cove State Park (day use fee) is located off Pacific Coast Highway, about 2 miles south of the town of Corona del Mar or 1 mile north of Laguna Beach. Turn inland on the short park road, signed "El Moro Canyon."

THE HIKE: Head up No Name Ridge Trail, the first part of which is still popularly referred to as No Dogs Trail. Enjoy the views from the ridge up and down Moro Canyon as well as over your shoulder back to the coast. The path wastes no time climbing to a junction with Poles Road.

Those opting for the short loop, should descend this absurdly steep road down to Moro Canyon. Enjoy tramping El Moro Canyon Trail on a gentle descent to a connector trail that in turn leads back to El Moro Visitor Center and the trailhead parking lot.

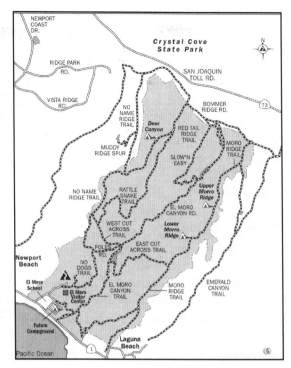

Those bound for the park's upper heights will continue the brisk ascent up No Name Ridge. Rising in French Riviera-fashion on the eastern park boundary is the new community of Newport Coast.

At a signed junction, a narrow path descends steeply to the bottom of Deer Canyon, then heads north, up-canyon to pleasant Deer Canyon Campground. Relax at one of the picnic tables, and rise steeply, but briefly, on the connector path leading to Red Tail Ridge Trail. Turn right, south, on the narrow ridgetop path, which offers grand vistas of the parks, and the hills and canyons up and down the coast.

Red Trail Ridge Trail merges into Rattlesnake Trail, which descends the ridge into Deer Canyon, then rises again to meet West Cut Across Trail. Turn left, southeast for the brief descent into Moro Canyon. Follow the park's main thoroughfare (as described above) back to the visitor center or ascend the very steep, but mercifully brief, Poles Road to regain No Name Ridge Trail. Enjoy great coastal vistas as you retrace your steps down No Name Ridge back to the trailhead.

Aliso and Wood Canyons Wilderness Park

Aliso Creek, Wood Canyon Trails

To Wood Canyon is 3 miles round trip; through Wood Canyon to Sycamore Grove is 6 miles round trip; loop of Wood Canyon is 9 miles round trip

Aliso and Wood Canyons Wilderness Park, largest park in the hills above Laguna Beach, preserves 3,400 acres of pastoral OC.

Most locals and other hikers refer to the low hills that back the Orange County coast from Corona del Mar to Dana Point as the Laguna Hills or "the mountains behind Laguna Beach." Actually, the northerly hills are the San Joaquin Hills—their cousins to the south are the Sheep Hills.

Nature writer Joseph Smeaton Chase described an outing in the Sheep Hills in his classic 1913 book, *California Coastal Trails*: "A few miles along a road that wound and dipped over the cliffs brought us by sundown to Aliso Canyon. The walls of the canyon are high hills sprinkled with lichened rock, sprinkled with brush… Our camp was so attractive that we remained for several days."

Aliso and Wood Canyons Wilderness Park is a great place to hike, but it does present a minor access problem: From the parking area to the mouth of Wood Canyon is a less-than-scintillating 1.5-mile walk alongside a road. Some hikers avoid this road walk by bringing their bikes—either mountain bike or standard bicycle will do—and cycling to the "true" trailhead. Cyclists can leave their bikes at conveniently placed racks and walk the narrower, hikers-only paths.

DIRECTIONS: From the San Diego Freeway (5) in Laguna Hills/ Mission Viejo, exit on Alicia Parkway and drive 4 miles south. Trailhead parking for Aliso and Wood Canyons Wilderness Park is

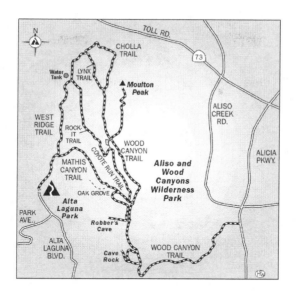

located a quarter-mile south of Aliso Creek Road. Take a right into the parking lot, which is opposite Laguna Niguel Regional Park.

THE HIKE: From the parking area, hike along the paved road into Aliso Canyon. The road, and a parallel dirt path for hikers, heads southeast, and meanders just west of Aliso Creek.

After 1.5 miles of walking, arrive at a signed junction (complete with restrooms no less). Join Wood Canyon Trail Trail (a dirt road) and begin a gentle ascent through Wood Canyon. Look left for the side trail leading to Cave Rock, where you'll find a number of caves, wind-sculpted into a substantial sandstone formation.

Continue up-canyon on Wood Canyon Trail to another left-branching side trail that leads to Dripping Cave, aka Robbers Cave, where 19th-century cattle rustlers and stagecoach robbers supposedly hid out. The "Dripping," much of the year anyway, refers to water seeping above the cave.

Wood Canyon Trail continues to meet Mathis Canyon Trail. A short distance farther is an old sheep corral. Turn around here or push on.

If you want to leg it just a little more, head up Mathis Canyon, then north on Coyote Run Trail. Next, fork right to reconnect with Wood Canyon Trail. For a longer loop, bear left on northbound Rock-It Trail and connect with West Ridge Trail.

LAGUNA COAST WILDERNESS PARK

LAUREL CANYON, WILLOW CANYON TRAILS

Laurel-Willow canyons loop is 3.5 miles with 600-foot elevation gain; to Bommer Ridge Overlook is 7 miles round trip

Laguna Coast Wilderness Park is the Orange County of the 19th century, a lovely diversity of landscapes highlighted by woodlands, grasslands and scenic ridgelines with handsome sandstone outcroppings. The 6,5000-acre park also contains Orange County's only natural lakes, which provide habitat for fish as well as for such waterfowl as geese, grebes, coots, cormorants and kingfishers.

James Irvine and his partners purchased the one-time Rancho San Joaquin in 1865 and the company grazed cattle on it for more than a century. With the Irvine Company's cooperation, substantial acreage in and around Laguna Canyon became parkland

That these hills and canyons don't resemble the developed Orange County of the 21st century is a tribute to four decades of exemplary work by local conservationists, park agencies and municipalities. In 1989, 8,000 people marched along Laguna Canyon Road to show their commitment to preserving the Laguna Hills. A year later citizens of Laguna Beach voted overwhelmingly to tax themselves $20 million in order to purchase land alongside Laguna Canyon Road and far up into the hills. Additional preservation efforts spearheaded by the Laguna Canyon Foundation took place during the 1990s and into the 21st century.

Laurel Canyon is a hiking-only trail, in contrast to the park's many multi-use trails, including Willow Canyon Road, return route for this hike. The canyon has plenty of laurel sumac that inspired its name, lots of intriguing rock formations, and even a seasonal waterfall.

DIRECTIONS: From the San Diego Freeway (405) in Irvine, a few miles north of this freeway's junction with the Santa Ana Freeway (5), exit on Laguna Canyon Road (133) and head south toward the coast and Laguna Beach. Look for the main (Laurel Canyon) entrance to the park on the right (west) side of the road.

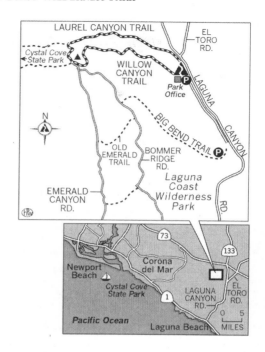

THE HIKE: Join the path leading north parallel to Laguna Canyon Road and soon pass a sandstone boulder sculpted by wind and water into a very small cave. Keep an eye out for more such caves and rock formations crowning the park's ridges.

The trail traverses an open slope that, with an end to cattle grazing, is making the environmental transition from annual grassland to coastal sage scrub. Buckwheat and sage line the path, which turns away from Laguna Canyon Road and enters the quiet of Laurel Canyon.

Begin a westward ascent among live oaks and sycamores. The path leads by a seasonal creek (look for an ephemeral waterfall during the rainy season) and ascends to meet a dirt road. Turn left on this road and begin an ascent to a saddle on Willow Ridge and another junction. Go left again and descend Willow Canyon Road.

Most of the view on your descent east is of parkland, with the major exception of the San Joaquin Hills Toll Road which, alas, bisects Laguna Coast Wilderness Park. Your journey ends at the park office, a short walk from the trailhead and parking area.

MODJESKA CANYON

HARDING TRAIL

From Tucker Wildlife Sanctuary to Laurel Spring is 10 miles round trip with 2,300-foot gain

The story of Modjeska Peak and Modjeska Canyon in Orange County began in Warsaw, Poland in the 1870s. Actor/director "Count" Karol Bozenta Chlapowski and his wife, acclaimed actress Helena Modrzejewski, yearned for the freedom of America.

Helena mastered English, shortened her name to Modjeska, and under the Count's management, began a tremendously popular stage career. The two bought a ranch in Santiago Canyon and called it "Arden" after the enchanted forest in Shakespeare's "As You Like It." New York architect Stanford White designed them a dream home, where the couple rested after 9-month-long tours with their theater company.

The natural history of Modjeska Canyon is as intriguing as its human history. Tucker Wildlife Sanctuary was created in 1939 and ever since has been a haven for birds and bird-watchers. Birds may be viewed from an observation porch. The sanctuary attracts a diversity of birdlife—nearly 200 species have been spotted in the canyon, chaparral and oak woodland environments. The sanctuary is operated by CSUF, which uses it as a research center.

"The Tuck," as its sometimes known, includes a compact nature museum and interpretive center, ponds and picnic areas. Two short nature trails wind through the preserve. One trail interprets chaparral flora, and the other leads along the banks of Santiago Creek.

The sanctuary is the trailhead for Harding Trail, a dirt road ascending 10 miles to Old Saddleback, comprised of 5,687-foot Santiago Peak and 5,496-foot Modjeska Peak. Halfway up the mountain is Laurel Spring, tucked under the boughs of giant bay laurel. On

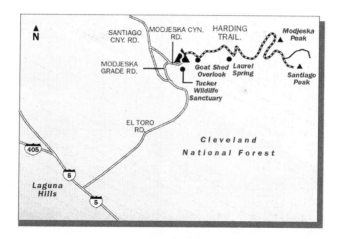

the hike to the spring, you'll get great views of Madame Modjeska's peak and canyon, and much of rural OC.

DIRECTIONS: From the San Diego Freeway (5) in El Toro, exit on El Toro Road (S-18). Drive inland on the road, which after about 7 miles bends north and continues as Santiago Canyon Road. About 8.5 miles from the freeway, veer right onto Modjeska Grade Road, travel a bit more than a mile, turn right and follow Modjeska Canyon Road a mile to its end at Tucker Wildlife Sanctuary to free parking and the trailhead.

THE HIKE: Harding Trail immediately begins a no-nonsense ascent above Modjeska Canyon. To the northwest is Flores Peak, named for outlaw Juan Flores.

Notice the lumpy, pudding-like clumps of conglomerate rock revealed by road cuts. After a mile, the trail descends a short distance, rounds the head of a canyon, and delivers a fine view of Modjeska Canyon. If you're time-short, this is a good turnaround point for a 3-mile round trip jaunt.

Chaparral-lined Harding Trail continues climbing east along a sharp ridgeline. About 4.5 miles from the trailhead, the path offers clear-day views of the southern end of the L.A. Basin, the San Joaquin Hills, the central Orange County coastal plain, the Pacific and Catalina Island.

A narrow trail descends 50 yards from the right side of the road to the spring. The spring, often overgrown, waters an oasis of toyon, ferns and wonderfully aromatic bay laurel.

175

BEAR CANYON & SITTON PEAK

BEAR CANYON, BEAR RIDGE, SITTON PEAK TRAILS

From Ortega Highway to Pigeon Springs is 5.5 miles round trip with 700-foot elevation gain; return via Bear Ridge Trail is a 6.5-mile loop; to Sitton Peak is 9.8 miles round trip with 1,300-foot gain

Bear Canyon Trail offers a pleasant introduction to the Santa Ana Mountains. The trail climbs through gentle brush and meadow country, visits Pigeon Springs, and arrives at Four Corners, the intersection of several major hiking trails through the southern Santa Anas.

One of these trails takes you to Sitton Peak (3,273 feet) for splendid, far-reaching views from the Cleveland National Forest to Catalina Island. Along the trail, refreshing Pigeon Springs welcomes hot and dusty hikers to a handsome glen. Bear Ridge Trail offers an alternate return route and a way to make a loop trip out of this jaunt around Bear Canyon.

DIRECTIONS: Take the Ortega Highway (California 74) turnoff from the San Diego Freeway (Interstate 5) at San Juan Capistrano. Drive east 20 miles to the paved parking area across from the Ortega Oaks store. Bear Canyon Trail starts just west of the store on Ortega Highway.

THE HIKE: From the signed trailhead, the broad, well-graded trail climbs slowly up brushy hillsides. The trail crosses a seasonal creek, which runs through a tiny oak woodland.

A half mile from the trailhead, the path enters San Mateo Canyon Wilderness and after a mile, a fork appears on the left (Morgan

Trail). Bear Canyon Trail climbs on, skirts the periphery of a meadow and crests a chaparral-covered slope.

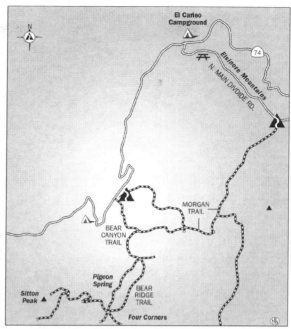

Two miles of travel from the trailhead brings you to a signed intersection with Bear Ridge Trail (return route for this hike). Stick with Bear Canyon Trail, formerly known as the Verdugo Truck Trail, and head right (south) 0.75 to Pigeon Springs. The springs, including a horse trough, are located among oaks on the left of the trail.

From the springs, continue another half mile south, and past a gate to Four Corners and a meeting of five trails (fire roads), among them, Tenaja Trail, that descends to San Mateo Creek.

From Four Corners, bear right on Sitton Peak Trail, which begins to climb and contour around the peak. In about 1.2 miles you'll be at the high point of Sitton Peak Trail, a saddle perched over San Juan Canyon. From this saddle, wend your way 0.4 mile on a somewhat sketchy use trail past rocky outcroppings to the summit. Enjoy superb clear-day views of the twin peaks of Old Saddleback (Mt. Modjeska and Mt. Santiago), Mt. San Gorgonio and Mt. San Jacinto, and the wide blue Pacific.

Meanwhile, back at Four Corners…head northeast on Bear Ridge Trail for an alternate return to the trailhead. The narrow pathway follows a ridge north, overlooking Bear Canyon. After bending west, the trail meets up again with Bear Canyon Trail.

Holy Jim Waterfall

Holy Jim Trail

From Trabuco Creek Road to Holy Jim Waterfall is 2.5 miles round trip with 200-foot elevation gain

Holy Jim Trail, creek, waterfall and canyon take their names from "Cussin'" Jim Smith, an early Santa Ana Mountain settler who, when displeased, unleashed a string of unholy epithets. Early 20th century mapmakers were unwilling to geographically honor such a blasphemer, so they changed his name to "Holy."

The trail is one of the most popular in the Santa Anas, though many hikers go only as far as the falls. Something of a Santa Ana Mountains sampler, the trail offers the hiker a creek, a lush canyon, a waterfall, a hike into history and, with the optional trek to Santiago Peak, a chance to conquer OC's highest summit.

Smith was a beekeeper by profession (perhaps explaining his proclivity toward profanity). His operation and those of neighboring beekeepers were targets of a grizzly bear dubbed "Honey Thief." Believed to be the last grizzly in the Santa Ana Mountains, the bear was shot near the mouth of Trabuco Canyon in 1907.

Strictly by the tape measure, Holy Jim Falls at 20 feet high does not wow the hiker with its stature. Ah, but the "wow factor" is the waterfall's setting—a lovely grotto with ferns springing from the rock walls around it.

Some hikers think getting to the trailhead is half the fun. It's definitely a bumpy ride along Trabuco Canyon Road to the trailhead. Passenger cars with good ground clearance can make it over the wash-boarded, pot-holed road.

You'll spot a number of cabins, privately owned but on land leased from the Forest Service, in the Holy Jim-Trabuco Canyon

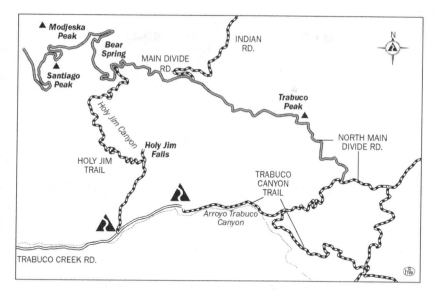

area. During the 1930s, it was Forest Service policy to encourage city dwellers to experience the great outdoors and overnight in a vacation cabin.

DIRECTIONS: From the San Diego Freeway (5) in Lake Forest, exit on El Toro Road and drive east 7 miles. Turn right on Live Oak Canyon Road and proceed 4.2 miles (a mile past O'Neill Regional Park) to Trabuco Creek Road. Make a left and follow this rough dirt road 4.6 miles to the trailhead parking area just past the volunteer fire station.

THE HIKE: From the trailhead parking lot, hike up the canyon road 0.5 mile to the beginning of the trail. Head up the vine- and oak-filled canyon. The trail stays near Holy Jim Creek, crossing and re-crossing the bubbling waters several times.

You'll spot stone check dams, built in the 1950s by the California Department of Fish and Game in order to create deep pools for fish. A clearing allows a glimpse at Santiago Peak and, while tramping creekside, look for aptly named Picnic Rock.

The trail crosses the creek a final time and comes to a fork. Holy Jim Trail embarks on a climb up Holy Jim Canyon on the way to Santiago Peak, but you take the right fork and head up-creek. A quarter mile of boulder-hopping and creek-crossing brings you face to face with Holy Jim Falls.

Santiago Peak

Holy Jim Trail

From Trabuco Creek Road to Main Divide Road is 10 miles round trip with 2,200-foot gain; to Santiago Peak is 15 miles round trip with 4,000-foot gain

Looking up at Santiago Peak from various points near the trailhead has a way of prompting hikers to examine their plans: Do we really want to climb way up there?

Well, yes you do. Admit it, Orange County's 5,687-foot landmark peak calls to you. Well, I was referring to a kind of spiritual beckoning to the hiker, but now that we're discussing calling, I should mention that Santiago Peak is topped with transmitting stations and thickets of antennae, so crucial these days to microwave relays and cell phone signals.

The northern Santa Anas were once known as Sierra de Santiago for this dominant peak. Santiago is the higher of the two neighboring summits (Modjeska Peak is the other) comprising Old Saddleback. You can get a 360-degree view from the top of Santiago Peak, but not from any one place, crowded as it is by dense clusters of telecommunications apparatus. The view includes five counties worth of urban-suburban sprawl, as well as east to Mount San Jacinto and Mount San Gorgonio, south to Mt. Palomar, and Catalina Island and San Clemente Island way out in the Pacific Ocean.

Trails and fire roads approach Orange County's highest peak from all directions, but Holy Jim Trail is the most scenic route to the summit of Santiago. Don't underestimate the challenge of this hike: It's pretty good trail, but the gain is substantial.

DIRECTIONS: (See Holy Jim Falls hike description.)

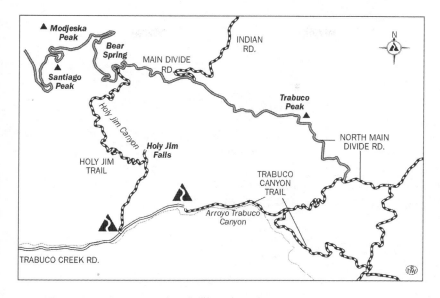

THE HIKE: From the trailhead parking lot, hike up the canyon road 0.5 mile to the beginning of the trail. Head up the vine- and oak-filled canyon. The trail stays near Holy Jim Creek, crossing and re-crossing the bubbling waters several times.

You'll spot stone check dams, built in the 1950s by the California Department of Fish and Game in order to create deep pools for fish. A clearing allows a glimpse at Santiago Peak and, while tramping creekside, look for aptly named Picnic Rock.

The trail crosses the creek a final time and comes to a fork. The right fork leads to the waterfall, while Holy Jim Trail embarks on the climb up the west side of the canyon toward Santiago Peak. The path presents some hearty switchbacks and begins a lengthy contour along the canyon wall.

About 3.5 miles into the hike, the trail gets less brushy, and there is some flora you can look up to: oaks, sycamores and an occasional big-cone Douglas fir. At the 4.5 mile-mark, the trail meets Main Divide Road by Bear Spring, a tank and water trough built by the Forest Service.

Hit the road for another 3 miles of hiking on the Main Divide (gaining 1,800 feet) to Santiago Peak. Enjoy the grand vista of most of the Southland's mountain ranges including the Palomars, the San Bernardinos, the San Gabriels and Santa Monicas.

181

LOS PIÑOS PEAK

NORTH MAIN DIVIDE, LOS PIÑOS TRAILS

From Main Divide Road to Los Piños Peak is 4.5 miles round trip with 900-foot elevation gain.

Q: What are the four highest peaks in Orange County?

A: 1. Santiago Peak (5,687 feet) 2. Modjeska Peak (5,496 feet) 3. Trabuco Peak (4,604 feet) 4. Los Piños Peak (4,510 feet)

Experienced hikers may have guessed numbers one and two—the peaks comprising the landmark Old Saddleback. OC's number 3 and number 4 peaks are much more obscure.

Los Piños Peak, located about 3 miles as the hawk flies from the southeast corner of Orange County where it meets both San Diego and Riverside counties, offers terrific clear-day vistas. From the summit, look down to Lake Elsinore and up at snow-capped Mt. Baldy and the high peaks of the San Gabriel Mountains, the San Bernardino Mountains and San Jacinto Mountains. Gaze west over miles of hills and valleys to the great blue Pacific.

Happily only a modest effort is required to earn this rewarding panorama. Another positive aspect of this hike is that the trailhead is accessible by paved roads.

Scale Los Piños in the springtime when lupine, bush poppy and ceanothus splash color on the mountain. Crisp, clear autumn days are good ones to head for the peak, too. Winter storms sometimes dust the crest of Los Piños with a bit of snow. Stay away in summer; it's way too hot for hiking.

DIRECTIONS: From Interstate 5 in San Juan Capistrano, exit on Highway 74 and follow it 22 miles northeast to Long Canyon Road. Turn left (northwest) and follow this paved road 2.5 miles to Blue Jay Campground, then another mile to a pullout on your left. The gated road is signed "North Main." Park in the pullout.

Another way to go: From Interstate 15 in Lake Elsinore, exit on Highway 74 and drive 11 miles southwest to Long Canyon Road, then follow the above directions. From Highway 74 you can also turn west on Main Divide Road (signed "To Blue Jay Campground") and follow this paved road 4 miles to the trailhead.

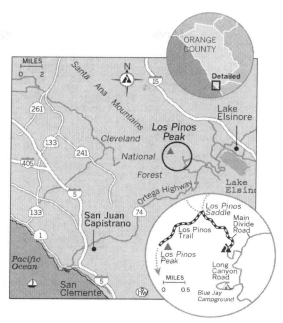

THE HIKE: From the gate, follow the wide dirt road, which soon gains elevation and good views. A mile out, look for a particularly good vista of Lake Elsinore and out to high mountain peaks to the north and east.

About 1.25 mile from the start, the road brings you to Los Piños Saddle, where you'll spot a convergence of trails. Leave Main Divide Road, which goes right, and step onto signed Trabuco Trail. Almost immediately look left and fork left onto signed Los Piños Trail. The path soon gains the top of the ridge and you quickly learn why Los Piños Trail is often called Los Piños Ridge Trail.

The steep path gains a high point that is only 20 feet lower in elevation than your goal, then dips, climbs again, dips some more, and finally climbs steeply to the top of Los Piños Peak. Savor the great views and retrace your steps to the trailhead.

Tenaja Falls

Tenaja Falls Trail

To Tenaja Falls 1.5 miles round trip with 300-foot elevation gain.

When the Southland is blessed with a rainy, rainy season, Tenaja Falls spills over granite ramparts with great vigor. With five tiers and a drop of some 150 feet, it's a large waterfall, particularly in comparison to other falls in the Santa Ana Mountains.

Tenaja's size is all the more a delightful surprise considering its locale: a rather dry section of the Cleveland National Forest near the boundary of Orange and Riverside counties. Some hikers claim Tenaja Falls is the most intriguing natural highlight of the national forest, and even in that crown jewel of the mountains—the San Mateo Canyon Wilderness.

For Tenaja Falls-bound hikers, there's good news and bad news. Good news: the trail is a wide dirt road, easy enough for the whole family. Bad news: the drive to the trailhead is circuitous to say the least.

For nature photographers, there's one more minor bit of bad news: No viewpoint allows an angle of the whole of Tenaja Falls, that is to say, all five cascades at once. Two tiers at a time is the usual view from the trail.

For those looking for a longer hike in the area, an adventure awaits: an exploration of the San Mateo Canyon Wilderness. I recommend a 5-mile loop that begins just 1.5 miles down the road from the Tenaja Falls trailhead.

DIRECTIONS: From I-15 (Temecula Valley Freeway) in Murietta, exit on Clinton Keith Road and drive 5 miles south into Santa Rosa Plateau Ecological Reserve. After a sharp right bend, continue on what is now Tenaja Road for 2 more miles and turn right again

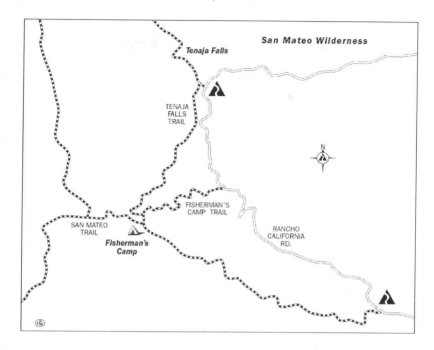

to stick with Tenaja Road. Proceed another 4.3 miles to Cleveland Forest Road, turn right and follow this narrow, one-lane pave road to the signed trailhead and parking area on the left.

THE HIKE: Meander over to the fence that bars motorized entry to the San Mateo Canyon Wilderness. Cross the creek on the concrete vehicle ford. If the creek is high, you'll have to wade carefully across, though skilled rock-hoppers can sometimes cross without getting their boots wet. Another creek-crossing option is to walk along the creek until you find a narrower place to cross.

The trail/road ascends northward over brush-clad slopes and before long serves up distant vistas of Tenaja Falls. Just keep walking toward the falls.

The trail leads right to Tenaja's top tier. Exploration of the lower cascades is tricky, and for experienced rock-climbers only. Those granite boulders are darn slippery.

If you're bound and determined to reach the lower falls, a somewhat safer and saner way to go is retrace your steps back down the trail, then bushwhack through the brush to the banks of the creek.

SAN MATEO CANYON WILDERNESS

FISHERMAN'S CAMP, SAN MATEO CANYON TRAILS

From Tenaja Road to Fisherman's Camp is 3 miles round trip with 300-foot loss; loop via Tenaja Road is 5 miles round trip with 400-foot elevation gain; to Lunch Rock is 8 miles round trip with 400-foot loss

Two-hundred-year-old oaks, tangles of ferns, nettles and wild grape, and the quiet pools of San Mateo Creek make the bottom of San Mateo Canyon a wild and delightful place.

San Mateo Canyon Wilderness protects 40,000 acres of the Cleveland National Forest, including the headwaters and watershed of San Mateo Creek. Crown jewel of the Santa Ana Mountains, it's a relatively untouched wilderness of oaks, potreros and cattail-lined ponds.

The canyon drops from 3,500 feet to the coastal plain at Camp Pendleton. It's nine miles from Fisherman's Camp to the Marine base, with a hundred ideal picnic spots along the way.

San Mateo Canyon Trail and other trails in the wilderness have been in use for more than a century. Volunteers work on the trail, but it's often in rough shape. Creek crossings are sometimes difficult to spot.

DIRECTIONS: From I-15 (Temecula Valley Freeway) in Murietta, exit on Clinton Keith Road and drive 5 miles south into Santa Rosa Plateau Ecological Reserve. After a sharp right bend, continue on what is now Tenaja Road for 2 more miles and turn right again to stick with Tenaja Road. Proceed another 4.3 miles to Cleveland Forest Road, turn right and follow this narrow, one-lane paved road for a mile to the signed Tenaja Trailhead. Proceed another 2.5 miles to the small parking area on the left side of the road.

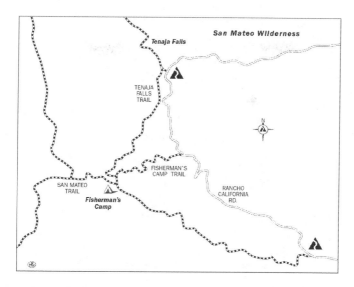

THE HIKE: Walk down an old fire road, now a footpath, often lined with wildflowers in spring. About 1.5 miles of travel brings you to Fisherman's Camp, once a drive-in campground and now an oak- and sycamore-shaded trail camp. From the camp, the path angles north toward San Mateo Canyon and a junction with San Mateo Canyon Trail on the west side of the creek.

Hikers heading down San Mateo Canyon will follow the trail that climbs among ceanothus to a ridge that offers a view of the canyon. After 0.5 mile, the path switchbacks down to San Mateo Creek and follows it along the heavily vegetated canyon bottom.

Along the creek, the trail may be indistinct; simply continue down-creek. About a mile after reaching the creek, reach a small potrero dotted with oaks and sycamore. Here Bluewater Creek flows into San Mateo Creek and the Bluewater Trail leads off three miles to the Clark Trail and Oak Flat. Picnic under the oaks near the trail junction and return, or continue down the canyon.

Resume down-creek passage on San Mateo Canyon Trail, which follows the right side of the canyon, now and then dropping to wide sandy beaches along bends in the creek. The boulders get bigger, the swimming holes and sunning spots nicer. One flat rock, popular with hikers, has been nicknamed "Lunch Rock." A cluster of massive boulders form pools and cascades in the creek. It's a nice place to linger.

In addition to huge desert recreation areas such as Joshua Tree National Park and Palm Springs, Riverside County also entices the hiker with parks and preserves close to population centers. In recent decades, the county has witnessed phenomenal Inland Empire-style growth; so creating more parks and trails is crucial to residents and visitors alike.

Hike to the top of Mt. Rubidoux, located in Riverside for a 360-degree panorama of the county—one very different from the view of a century ago. Put Santa Rosa Plateau on your "Must Hike" list; it's the one place that looks much as it did 100 years ago.

CHAPTER 7

RIVERSIDE COUNTY

HIKE ON.

TELEGRAPH CANYON

HILLS-FOR-EVERYONE TRAIL

Along Ranch Road to McDermont Spring is 4 miles round trip with 400-foot gain; to Carbon Canyon Regional Park is 7.5 miles one way with 800-foot loss

Hills-for-Everyone Trail was named for the conservation group that was instrumental in establishing Chino Hills State Park. The trail follows a creek to the head of Telegraph Canyon. The creek is lined with oak, sycamore and the somewhat rare California walnut.

DIRECTIONS: Chino Hills State Park can be a bit tricky to find. The park is located west of Highway 71 between the Riverside Freeway (91) and the Pomona Freeway (60). From Highway 71, exit on Soquel Canyon Parkway and travel 1 mile to a signed left turn at Elinvar Road, which bends sharply left. Look immediately right for a signed dirt road—Bane Canyon Road (subject to closure and frequently undergoing repairs). Enter the park on this road (which returns to pavement in 2 miles) and follow signs to the park office and ranger station.

The road forks just before the ranger station. To the right is the ranger station and visitor center. Bear left 0.5 mile on the dirt road to a vehicle barrier and trailhead parking. The signed trailhead is located a short distance past the vehicle barrier on the right of the road.

THE HIKE: Hills-for-Everyone Trail descends to a small creek and follows the creek up canyon. Shading the trail—and shielding the hiker from a view of the many electrical transmission lines that cross the park—are oaks, sycamores and walnuts. Of particular interest is the walnut; often the 15- to 30-foot tall tree has several dark brown trunks, which gives it a brushy appearance.

The trail, passes a small (seasonal) waterfall. The slopes above the creekbed are carpeted with lush grasses and miners lettuce. Look for evidence of the park's ranching heritage, including lengths of barbed wire

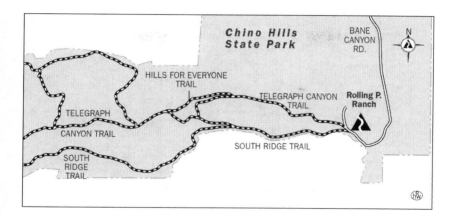

fence and old cattle troughs. For more than a century this land was used exclusively for cattle ranching.

Near its end, the trail ascends out of the creekbed to the head of Telegraph Canyon and intersects a dirt road. McDermont Spring is just down the road. Livestock ponds, constructed during the area's ranching days, still exist, and hold water year-round. McDermont Spring—along with Windmill and Panorama ponds—provides water for wildlife.

To Carbon Canyon Regional Park: Telegraph Canyon Trail (a dirt road closed to vehicular traffic) stays close to the canyon bottom and its creek. It's a gentle descent under the shade of oak and walnut trees. The walnuts are particularly numerous along the first mile of travel and the hiker not inclined to hike the length of Telegraph Canyon might consider exploring this stretch before returning to the trailhead.

The route passes an old windmill. Farther down the canyon, the walnuts thin out. A lemon grove, owned by the state park but leased to a farmer, is at a point where the dirt road intersects Carbon Canyon Road. Walk along the broad shoulder of the latter road 0.5 mile to Carbon Canyon Regional Park.

191

SAN JUAN HILL

SOUTH RIDGE TRAIL

To the top of San Juan Hill is 6 miles round trip with 1,200-foot elevation gain

When the land for Chino Hills State Park was purchased in the mid 1980s, there was much grumbling about the high cost—from the public, from politicians, and even from some conservationists, who figured purchasing a redwood grove or two was a better use of hard-to-come-by funds.

Nowadays the large park seems like a bargain. And nowhere is this more apparent than on the trail to the park's high point, San Juan Hill.

The first glimpse of the park's great value is obvious when hiking along South Ridge Trail and look at what you're leaving behind: suburbia pushing right up to the park's southern boundary. Without a park, every buildable slope would likely be smothered in subdivisions.

Farther up the trail, most traces of civilization vanish, and hikers enters a wonderfully pastoral landscape of rolling grassland and drifts of oak. Deer gambol through the high grasses, hawks circle overhead and a refreshing breeze (often) keeps the temperature down. It would be difficult to place a dollar value on this wonderful experience.

While that famed San Juan Hill in Cuba was a difficult charge for Theodore Roosevelt and his Rough Riders to make in an 1898 battle of the Spanish-American War, you should have a rather mellow time conquering the San Juan Hill perched on the border of Orange and San Bernardino counties. The trail to 1,781-foot San Juan Hill is a well-graded fire road.

DIRECTIONS: From the Orange Freeway (57) in Brea, exit on Imperial Highway (90) and head southeast 4.5 miles to Yorba Linda

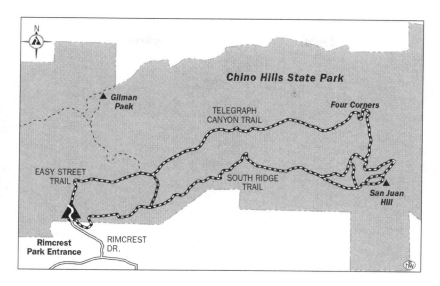

Boulevard. Turn left (east) and drive 1.3 miles to Fairmont Boulevard. Turn left (east) and drive 1.5 miles to Rim Crest Drive. Turn left and proceed 0.3 mile to the signed trailhead on the right. Park alongside Rim Crest Drive. Heed the curbside parking signs because public parking is permitted only on some lengths of Rim Crest Drive; some parking is for residents (by permit) only.

THE HIKE: Walk 40 yards up the fire lane to the park information bulletin board and the signed beginning of South Ridge Trail. Begin your journey eastward with an ascent that soon removes you from virtually all of the sights and sounds of civilization.

The moderate climb leads over hills covered with wild oats, rye, mustard and wild radish. Trees are few and far between atop these hills, which means both little shade and unobstructed views of the surrounding countryside. Only the high-voltage powerlines bisecting the hills detract from the near-pastoral landscape.

Nearly 3 miles out, reach a junction with the signed path to San Juan Hill. Walk 50 yards up a fire road toward a powerline tower, then join the narrow, unsigned footpath on the right leading 0.1 mile to the summit of San Juan Hill.

Crowning the hilltop is a concrete, hexagon-shaped column that reads: San Juan 1896. Enjoy the billowing grass and the usually breezy summit, as well as commanding vistas of the Chino Hills.

193

MT. RUBIDOUX

MT. RUBIDOUX TRAIL

3-mile loop with 500-foot elevation gain

The isolated, 1,337-foot high granite hill towering above the Riverside's western edge has long been a landmark to travelers and residents alike. The mountain was named for a 19th-century owner, wealthy ranchero Louis Robidoux.

Frank Miller, owner of the Mission Inn, purchased the mountain in 1906 with the intention of using it as an attraction to sell residential lots at its base. Developers constructed the road up Rubidoux as a "trail of shrines," an ascent past monuments of famous men to a long white cross. By some accounts, America's first Easter sunrise service took place atop Rubidoux in 1909.

Today's pilgrim views an eclectic assortment of monuments and memorials, including Peace Tower and Friendship Bridge. Local hikers access the mountain (closed to vehicles since 1992) from several trailheads, but the best route for first-time Rubidoux ramblers is by way of the Ninth Street gate. Hint: a sunset hike can be awesome.

DIRECTIONS: From the Pomona Freeway (60) in Riverside, exit on Market Street and proceed east into downtown. Turn west (right) on Mission Inn Avenue and drive 7 blocks to Redwood Drive. Turn left and head 2 blocks to Ninth Street, turn right and continue 2 more blocks to the distinct trailhead (gated Mt. Rubidoux Drive) on the left. Park on adjacent residential streets.

From the Riverside Freeway (91) in Riverside, exit on University Avenue and head west through downtown to Redwood Drive. Turn left, travel 1 block, turn right on Ninth Street, and proceed two more blocks to this hike's start on the left.

THE HIKE:

Pass through the
entry gate and walk
along a landscaped
lane past pepper
trees, eucalyptus and
huge beavertail cac-
tus. After 0.3 mile of
southbound travel,
the road makes a
tight turn north and
nearly intersects the
downward leg of
Mt. Rubidoux Road,
which makes a simi-
lar hairpin turn from
north to south. Note
this junction because

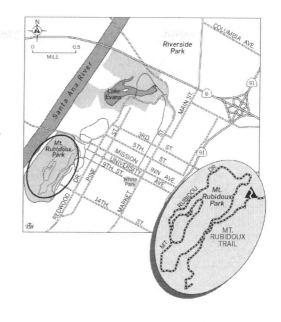

on the return journey you'll need to cross from one leg of the road to
the other to close the loop.

The road ascends rather bare slopes, dotted with brittlebush,
mustard and century plant. Lupine and California poppies brighten
the way in spring. After passing a memorial to Henry E. Huntington, "man of affairs, large in his bounty, yet wise," the road bends
west, then south. City views are exchanged for more rural ones,
including the Santa Ana River that gave Riverside its name. The
main Mt. Rubidoux road junctions a circular summit road, which
you'll join to see the sights—the Peace Tower, Friendship Bridge and
plenty of plaques.

From Father Junipero Serra Cross or from one of the peak's
other fine vista points, partake of the 360-degree panorama of great
mountains and metro-Riverside. Return to the main Mt. Rubidoux
Road for a short (0.75 mile) descent that loops south, east, then
back north. Just as this downward leg bends sharply south, leave the
road and step over to the other road leg that you used to ascend the
mountain. Retrace your steps a final 0.3 mile back to Ninth Street.

LAKE PERRIS

TERRI PEAK TRAIL

From Campfire Center to Terri Peak is 3.5 miles round trip with 800-foot elevation gain; to Indian Museum, return via lakeshore, is 6 miles round trip

More than a million visitors a year flock to Lake Perris State Recreation Area to beat the Inland Empire heat and enjoy the many recreational offerings: camping, boating, fishing, bicycling, boating, water skiing, swimming and horseback riding.

The park's 300 picnic sites are (thank goodness!) shaded by ramadas and have great views of the lake. Sites located near the swim areas at Moreno Beach and Perris Beach are the most popular.

While the park is oriented to water recreation, there is a network of trails for those visitors who wish to explore Perris by pathways. A nine-mile bike trail loops around the lake, as does a horse trail, which also ventures into the undeveloped part of the recreation area.

Springtime colors the hills around the lake with a host of wildflowers, including goldfields, California poppy, fiddleneck, baby blue eyes and blue dicks. Hikers can take the trail to Terri Peak and enjoy, on smog-free days, a fantastic view: the fast-growing Moreno Valley, as well as all of Lake Perris, Alessandro Island, and hundreds of boaters, anglers and swimmers.

Rock-climbers are drawn to Big Rock, a popular climbing spot. The giant granite rock, about 180 feet high, offers a number of routes for beginning and intermediate climbers.

The park's Regional Indian Museum includes exhibits interpreting the Cahuilla, Chemehuevi, Serrano and other desert tribes and how they adapted to life in the Mojave Desert region.

DIRECTIONS:
Located 11 miles
south of Riverside,
Lake Perris State
Recreation can be
reached by way
of Highway 60 or
I-215. From the
Pomona Freeway
(60), a few miles east
of its intersection
with I-215, exit on
Moreno Beach Drive
and proceed 4 miles
to the park. Imme-
diately after the day
use fee at the entry
kiosk, turn right on

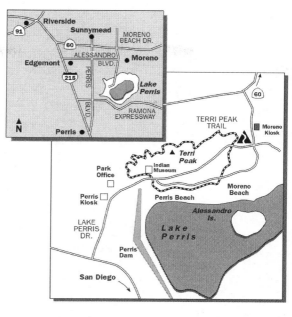

Alta Calle. Look sharply right for the amphitheater sign and park in
the lot nearby.

THE HIKE: The trail ascends gradually west and occasionally intersects a horse trail. The path is tentative and climbs boulder-strewn slopes up into a coastal scrub community.

Reaching a small flat meadow, the path turns southwest and
ascends more earnestly to Teri Peak. Enjoy clear-day view of the San
Bernardino Mountains to the northeast and the Santa Ana Mountains to the southwest. View all of Lake Perris, Alessandro Island, as
well as hundreds of boaters, anglers and swimmers.

Descend Terri Peak Trail, which bends sharply east and deposits
you at the Indian Museum's parking lot. From the museum, follow
the asphalt road to Alta Calle, cross this main park road and continue down to Perris Beach.

Improvise a route along the lakeshore using sidewalk and bike
trail until you spot the main campground entrance on your left.
Enter the campground, pass the kiosk, then pick up the intermittent
footpath that winds through the campground. This path and some
improvisation will bring you back to Alta Calle and the trailhead.

Santa Rosa Plateau Reserve
Coyote, Trans Preserve, Vernal Pool Trails

From Hidden Valley Trailhead to Vernal Pools is 6 miles round trip

Hike an early California landscape of oak woodlands, rolling grasslands and vernal pools and observe the remarkable biodiversity flourishing on Santa Rosa Plateau. Known for its rare Engelmann oaks, the plateau also hosts about half of all the species of plants and animals considered to be rare in the Inland Empire.

Good thing a sizeable portion of Old SoCal was preserved because off the plateau it's very much the 21st century; huge housing developments have pushed up Clinton Keith Road and left the 8,300-acre reserve something of an island on the land. The Nature Conservancy handles resources management of the reserve while Riverside County Regional Parks and Open Space District provides for visitors.

Trans Preserve and a supporting cast of trails offer a grand tour of the plateau. Hike for a few hours or an entire day on the reserve's 18 named trails.

This hike leads to the vernal pools atop Mesa de Colorado. Capped with basalt, the mesa is an ideal rainwater collector. Depressions in the rock collect water into seasonal ponds. One pool measures nearly 40 acres and is considered one of the largest in California.

The vernal pools offer habitat to the unusual fairy shrimp and rare plants that ring the waterline. In winter, the pools attract waterfowl, including grebes, Canada geese and green-winged teal. In spring, goldfields and other wildflowers surround them.

DIRECTIONS: In the Wildomar area, between Lake Elsinore and Murrietta, exit I-15 on Clinton Keith Road. Drive 5 miles

southwest to the Santa
Rosa Plateau Ecological
Reserve Visitor Center.
Continue another mile
as the road turns abrupt-
ly right (west) and con-
tinues as Tenaja Road.
Proceed another 0.5 mile
farther to Hidden Valley
Trailhead on the south
side of the road, parking
on both sides.

THE HIKE: Begin
on Coyote Trail, named
for one of the many
animals that roam the
reserve, though bird-
ers tend to watch for
white-tailed kites when
hiking along this path. A
half-mile's travel leads to

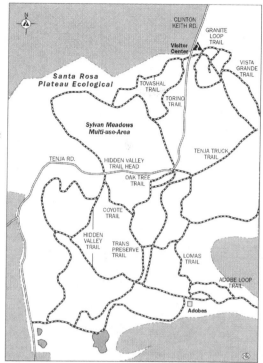

a junction; go right (south) on Trans Preserve Trail.

Hike across the reserve, over rolling hills and with views of
woodlands and native grasslands. Junctions for paths leading east
and west may tempt you, but stick with Trans Preserve Trail to the
top of Mesa de Colorado and a junction with Vernal Pool Trail.

Hike east and check out the vernal pools, then descend from the
mesa to the historic adobes, located a bit more than 3 miles from the
trailhead. After inspecting the oldest structures in Riverside County,
head north on Lomas Trail.

Bear right on Monument Road, and follow it only briefly,
because Lomas Trail soon resumes and you'll follow it northbound.
Cross Tenaja Truck Trail to reach Oak Tree Trail. Take the left fork
of this looping nature trail and hike in close company with the rare
Englemann oaks to Trans Preserve Trail, which you follow southwest
to the Coyote Trail. Retrace your steps 0.5 mile on Coyote Trail to
the trailhead.

Rim of the World Highway, leading
from San Bernardino up to Lake
Arrowhead and Big Bear Lake, offers a
grand scenic tour of the San Bernardino
Mountains and access to terrific trails.
Many quiet places in the mountains, under
the protection of the 700,000-acre San
Bernardino National Forest, beckon the
hiker to behold waterfalls, stunning fields of
wildflowers and golden eagles soaring above
lofty crags.

The "wildest" area in the Southland is
the San Gorgonio Wilderness, a magnificent
high country of alpine meadows, sparkling
lakes and mighty Mt. San Gorgonio (Old
Grayback, 11,502 feet), highest peak in
Southern California.

CHAPTER 8

SAN BERNARDINO MOUNTAINS

HIKE ON.

Champion Lodgepole Pine & Siberia Creek

Lodgepole Pine, Siberia Creek Trails

To Champion Lodgepole Pine is 1 mile round trip with 100-foot loss; to Siberia Creek Trail Camp is 12 miles round trip with 2,500-foot loss

California nurtures some superlative trees. The tallest tree on Earth is a coast redwood, the oldest tree a bristlecone pine. And in the San Bernardino Mountains gows the world champion lodgepole pine.

It's a pleasant stroll, suitable for the whole family, to the world champion. More ambitious hikers will enjoy tramping down Siberia Creek Trail to the appropriately named rock formation "The Gunsight," and on to Siberia Creek Trail Camp for a picnic.

Siberia Creek, born atop the high mountains near Big Bear Lake, is a delightful watercourse. It flows southwest through a deep coniferous forest and lush meadowlands, then cascades down a steep rocky gorge and adds it waters to Bear Creek.

Siberia Creek Trail passes the Champion Lodgepole, largest known lodgepole pine in the world. It then travels alongside Siberia Creek through a wet tableland, detours around a ridge while Siberia Creek crashes down a precipitous gorge, then rejoins the creek at Siberia Creek Trail Camp.

This is an "upside-down" hike; the tough part is the trek uphill back to the trailhead. Pace yourself accordingly.

DIRECTIONS: From Highway 18 at the west end of Big Bear Lake Village, turn south on Tulip Lane. A half mile from the highway, turn right on Mill Creek, which after 0.75 mile continues as Forest Service Road 2N10. Proceed 4 more miles and make a right on Forest Road 2N11. Drive 1 more mile to parking and the signed trailhead.

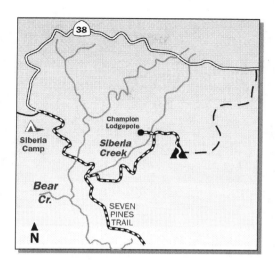

THE HIKE: The trail follows a fern-lined little brook. Notice some tall cornstalk-like plants—corn lilies—and a generous number of red flowers—Indian paintbrush. A half-mile's travel brings you to a signed junction. Go right 75 yards to the Champion Lodgepole, which towers above the east end of an emerald green meadow.

Lodgepole pines are usually found at higher elevations, but here at 7,500 feet, nurtured by the rich, well-watered soil, they not only thrive, but achieve mammoth proportions. The World Champion, 110 feet high, 75 inches in diameter (the species usually measures 12 to 24 inches), and is estimated to be more than 400 years old.

Lodgepoles are easily identified by their yellow-green paired needles; while hiking in Southern California, these pines are probably the only ones you'll come across that have two needles per bundle.

Return to the main trail and continue through open forest, skirting the meadowland. Cross and re-cross Siberia Creek. After the second crossing, the meadowland ends and the creek crashes down the gorge. The trail avoids the gorge and swings down and around the steep slopes of Lookout Mountain. About 1 mile from the Champion Lodgepole, an interesting rock formation called "The Gunsight" appears; squint through it at the metropolis below.

From The Gunsight, descend the slopes of Lookout Mountain. Switchbacks lead to junction with Bear right (north) on the Seven Pines Trail and proceed 0.75 mile to Siberia Creek Trail Camp. For the day hiker, this oak- and alder-shaded camp makes a nice picnic spot or rest stop.

FAWNSKIN

GROUT BAY, GRAYS PEAK TRAILS

From Grout Bay Picnic Area to Grays Peak is 6 miles round trip with 1,000-foot elevation gain

Even today, Grout Bay doesn't sound like a place to play. The name suggests mortar, not lakeshore, and offers no clue to the considerable attractions offered by the bay and the woodsy hiking trail that offers vistas of Big Bear Lake.

Back in 1919, Los Angeles businessmen William Cline and Clinton Miller ran into serious consumer resistance when they tried to lure vacationers to their upscale summer resort on the north shore of Big Bear Lake. Marketing a community called Grout was difficult to say the least; Grout had to go.

The developers changed the name to Fawnskin, appropriating the name from a nearby meadow. Fawnskin's origin is one guaranteed to upset an animal rights activist. Back in 1891, hunters shot many deer fawns, stretched their hides on trees, and promptly disappeared. As the story goes, subsequent travelers observed the fawn skins and began referring to the meadow and surrounding area as Fawnskin.

During the 1920s, Fawnskin expanded to include the Swiss chalet-style Fawn Lodge, a general store, post office, fairly pricey homes along the lakeshore and in the surrounding woods, as well as the Theatre of the Stars, a stage for musicals and dramas.

A bit west of Fawnskin proper stood Gray's Lodge, a pier, store and rental cabins owned by Alex Gray. Gray's name now graces a boat landing and a 7,880-foot peak.

As for the name Grout, it didn't entirely slip between the cracks: Grout Bay and Grout Bay Trail remain on the map, perhaps a reminder that a name isn't everything.

Grout Bay Trail begins in the piney woods above the lake and climbs to the summit of Grays Peak. The trail begins at the outskirts of the drowsy hamlet of Fawnskin, where a couple of eateries are located.

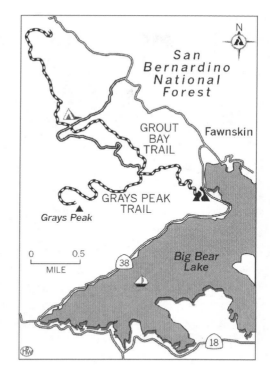

DIRECTIONS: From the far west end of Big Bear Lake at the junction of Highway 18 (Big Bear Boulevard) and Highway 38 (North Shore Drive), take the latter highway northeast 2.5 miles to the outer fringe of Fawnskin. Turn west into the trail parking lot of the Grout Bay Picnic Area.

THE HIKE: The well-graded, signed path begins a moderate ascent over wooded slopes and soon offers views of Fawnskin, Grout Bay and Windy Point. Vistas soon close up as the trail traverses more heavily timbered terrain.

A bit less than a mile out, Grout Bay Trail meets and joins dirt Forest Service Road 2N68E. Assisted by a couple of "Trail" signs, follow the road west about 0.4 mile. (Grout Bay Trail resumes as a footpath and heads north toward Fawnskin Valley.)

This hike leaves the road and follows the signed trail west toward Grays Peak. Long, finely engineered switchbacks aid the ascent past conifers, jumbo boulders and impressive specimens of manzanita.

The trail ends just short of the peak at a rock outcropping, which provides a superb overlook of the lake, valley and surrounding San Bernardino Mountains, as well as fine picnic spot.

Grand View Point

Pine Knot Trail

From Aspen Glen Picnic Area to Grand View Point is 6.5 miles round trip with 1,200-foot elevation gain

Rim of the World Highway offers the traveler a fine view of Big Bear Lake. A better view, a hiker's view, is available from Pine Knot Trail, which climbs the handsome, pine-studded slopes above the lake and offers far-reaching panoramas of the San Bernardino Mountains.

Big Bear Lake is a great place to escape the crowded metropolis, and Pine Knot Trail is a great way to escape sometimes-crowded Big Bear Lake.

The idea for Big Bear Lake came from Redlands citrus growers, who wanted to impound a dependable water source for their crops. Farmers and city founders formed Bear Valley Land and Water Co. and in 1884, at a cost of $75,000, built a stone-and-cement dam, thus forming Big Bear Lake. In 1910 a second, larger dam was built near the first one. This second dam is the one you see today.

Pine Knot Trail takes its name from the little community of cabins, stores and saloons that sprang up when Rim of the World Highway was completed. After World War II the town of Pine Knot changed its name to Big Bear Lake Village.

While Pine Knot Trail offers grand views of the lake, this hike's destination—Grand View Point—does not overlook the lake. The grand view is a breathtaking panorama of the San Gorgonio Wilderness and the deep canyon cut by the Santa Ana River.

DIRECTIONS: From California 18 in Big Bear Lake Village, turn southwest on Mill Creek Road and proceed about a half-mile to Aspen Glen Picnic Area on your left. The signed trail departs from the east end of the picnic area by Mill Creek Road.

THE HIKE: From Aspen Glen Picnic Area, Pine Knot Trail climbs a low, lupine-sprinkled ridge. The path follows a fence line for a short distance, then dips into and out of a willow-lined creek bed. You will get great over-the-shoulder views of the south shore of Big Bear Lake.

Ascending through Jeffrey pine and ponderosa pine forests, the trail meets and joins a fire road; after a short distance, it again becomes a footpath. Now your over-the-shoulder view is of the north shore of Big Bear Lake.

Pine Knot Trail passes near one of the runs of the Snow Forest Ski Area, then meanders through an enchanted area of castellated rocks. About 2 miles from the trailhead the trail intersects dirt Forest Service Road 2N17. Before you is a meadow, a rather amusing-looking landscape decorated with boulders, ponderosa pine, Indian paintbrush and skunk cabbage. Bear left on the dirt road for just 50 feet or so, then pick up the signed footpath again.

Passing black oak and willow, Pine Knot Trail skirts the moist meadow and soon arrives at Deer Group Camp. Benches and tables suggest a picnic or rest stop.

From the camp, continue on Pine Knot Trail, which crosses and then parallels another dirt Forest Service road. Ahead of you are tantalizing views of San Gorgonio Wilderness peaks—just a hint of things to come when you reach trail's end.

About a mile from Deer Group Camp, the trail intersects dirt Forest Service Road 2N11. Cross the road and follow the signed trail on a quarter-mile ascent to the top of a ridgeline.

From Grand View Point, enjoy the views of San Gorgonio Wilderness, a panorama of Southern California's highest peaks.

COUGAR CREST

COUGAR CREST TRAIL

From Highway 38 to Bertha Peak is 7 miles round trip with 1,100-foot elevation gain

Explore the North Shore of Big Bear Lake on a hike with many highlights: a forest of pine and cedar, an intriguing trail and a brief sampling famed Pacific Crest Trail, and grand views of the lake and

Cougar Crest Trail travels a sunny south slope so that it offers a longer "hiking season" than other paths near the lake; in fact sometimes you can hike here in spring when skiers are still swooshing down slopes above the south side of the lake.

On an early morning hike, you have a good chance of seeing wildlife along the trail—squirrels, raccoons, deer and coyote—and a late afternoon hike often provides a vantage point to watch colorful sunsets.

Cougar Crest, the forested ridge between Big Bear Lake and Holcomb Valley is a treat for hikers. From the ridge, as well as from Bertha Peak, enjoy great views of the lake, towering Mt. San Gorgonio and tranquil Holcomb Valley.

Holcomb Valley wasn't always so tranquil. In 1860, Billy Holcomb was out bear hunting and wandered over the ridge of hills that separates Bear Valley from the smaller, parallel valley to the north. He found gold. Prospectors swarmed into the valley from all over the West.

Be sure to check out nearby Big Bear Discovery Center, which offers recreation information for San Bernardino National Forest. Co-managed in partnership with the Southern California Mountains Foundation, the center offers exhibits and interpretive programs. You can begin this hike from the Discovery Center by following a 0.5

mile long paved pathway to the Cougar Crest Trailhead.

DIRECTIONS: From Highway 18 in the town of Big Bear Lake, turn north on Stanfield Cutoff, crossing to the north shore of the lake and a junction with Highway 38. Turn left, drive 1.4 mile to Big Bear Discovery Center, then 0.6 mile farther to the signed Cougar Crest trailhead and parking area off the north side of the highway.

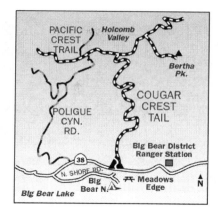

THE HIKE: From the signed trailhead, ascend Cougar Crest Trail through a pine and juniper woodland. After a mile, the trail ascends forested Cougar Crest via a series of well-constructed switchbacks. Enjoy over-the-shoulder views of Big Bear Lake and its dramatic backdrop—the high peaks of the San Gorgonio Wilderness.

From the top of the ridge, look south for grand vistas of all of Big Bear Lake, from Big Bear City to the dam, plus the ski slopes and resorts and mighty Mt. San Gorgonio. To the north is pretty Holcomb Valley. About 2.4 miles from the trailhead, Cougar Crest Trail intersects Pacific Crest Trail.

To reach Bertha Peak, bear right (east) on PCT and continue along the ridge crest for 0.2 mile to an intersection with an old dirt road. PCT continues straight at this junction, but you bear right on the dirt road and ascend 0.8 mile through pinyon pine and juniper woodland to the radio towers atop Bertha Peak. Best views are a bit below the peak.

SAN BERNADINO PEAK

SAN BERNADINO PEAK TRAIL

From Angelus Oaks Trailhead to Columbine Spring Camp is 9 miles round trip with 2,000-foot elevation gain; to Limber Pine Bench Camp is 12 miles round trip with 3,200-foot gain; to San Bernardino Peak is 16 miles round trip with 4.700-foot gain

Mt. San Bernardino, together with its twin peak, Mt. San Gorgonio, just 5 miles away and 900 feet higher, anchors the eastern end of the San Bernardino Mountains. Like Mt. San Gorgonio, Mt. San Bernardino (10,624 feet), is quite a SoCal landmark.

In 1852, Colonel Henry Washington and his Army survey party constructed a monument atop Mt. San Bernardino. The monument provided an east-west reference point from which all future surveys of Southern California would be taken.

This trail leads from deep pine forest to exposed manzanita slopes and visits the old survey monument. The higher slopes of Mt. San Bernardino are beautiful and rugged subalpine terrain. Trail camps along the way offer spring water and rest.

High elevation, coupled with a steep ascent, mean this trail is best left to experienced hikers in top form. Beyond Columbine Spring the trail becomes very steep.

Camp Angelus trailhead is less visited than others at the edge of San Gorgonio Wilderness, but does receive a lot of use, particularly during summer weekends.

DIRECTION: From Interstate 10 in Redlands, exit on Highway 38 and drive 20 miles to Angelus Oaks. Turn right at a sometimes signed junction for San Bernardino Peak Trail. Make an immediate left and drive past a fire station. Turn right on a dirt road (1W07). Staying right at two forks, drive 0.3 mile to a large dirt

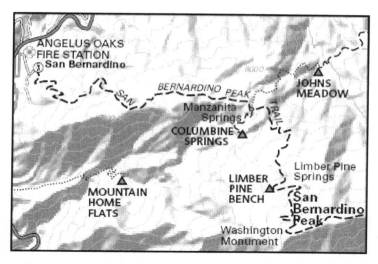

parking lot and signed San Bernardino Peak Trail. (Access to this trailhead has been known to change.)

THE HIKE: Ascend through mixed forest of pine, fir and oak, switchbacking up the beautifully wooded slope. Surmount a ridge, walk along its crest for a brief distance, and continue climbing. Reach a San Gorgonio Wilderness sign, 2 miles from the trailhead.

A little beyond the wilderness boundary, the grade lessens. Above 8,000 feet, the Jeffrey pine become widely spaced and the trail penetrates a manzanita-covered slope. Look for a side trail leading down to Manzanita Springs. (Don't drink the water.) The side trail continues on 0.25 mile to Columbine Springs Trail Camp (which usually has water later in the season than Manzanita.

A short distance beyond Manzanita Springs Trail Junction, the trail climbs more earnestly. The path ascends in fits and starts over slopes covered with manzanita and homely chinquapin; in 1.5 more miles, it reaches Limber Pine Springs Camp. (Actually, shade in the area is provided by lodgepole pines.) Another 0.25-mile up the trail is Limber Pine Springs, usually a dependable source of water.

The trail begins a long traverse south, switchbacking up to Camp Washington, a trail camp with plenty of view, but nothing to drink. One hundred yards from the trail is Colonel Washington's baseline monument, little more than a pile of stones. The trail climbs another 0.5 mile, where it intersects a brief side trail leading to the summit of Mt. San Bernardino.

MT. SAN GORGONIO
SOUTH FORK TRAIL

From South Fork to South Fork Meadows is 9 miles round trip with 1,500-foot elevation gain; to Dollar Lake is 13 miles round trip with 2,500-foot gain; to Mt. San Gorgonio Summit is 22 miles round trip with 4,600-foot gain

Most of us in the Southland have looked east and marveled at Mt. San Gorgonio, highest peak in Southern California. And some of us have decided to hike to the top of the 11,502-foot mountain—what can only be called a once-in-a-lifetime experience.

The reward? By far the best view of Southern California available to a hiker: a 360-degree panoramic view from the Mexican border to the southern Sierra, from the Pacific Ocean to the far reaches of the Mojave Desert.

Gorgonio got its name from an obscure fourth-century Christian martyr and its nickname "Grayback" because its bare, gravelly summit stretches laterally for some distance above the timberline, giving it the appearance of a long, gray back.

Subalpine vegetation includes carpets of buttercups, and that venerable survivor of inclement weather, the limber pine. Mountain lions, mule deer and bighorn sheep roam the high slopes, and golden eagles soar over the summit.

With a great trail, lovely meadows and small lakes, this hike is a wonderful tour through the heart of the San Gorgonio Wilderness and well worth doing even if the 21 miles round trip to the summit is out of your hiking range. Traveling as far as South Fork Meadow or Dollar Lake is no walk in the park and a heart-pounding, soul satisfying journey indeed.

Native American legend has it that San Gorgonio and San Jacinto peaks were brothers and sisters and among the first-born of

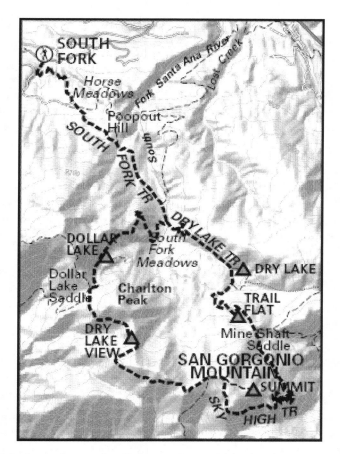

Earth Mother, who made all things. It would be hard to improve on Earth Mother's handiwork here. Mt. San Gorgonio's alpine vegetation includes carpets of buttercups, and that venerable survivor of inclement weather, the limber pine. Mountain lions, mule deer and bighorn sheep roam the high slopes, and golden eagles soar over the summit.

The San Gorgonio Wild Area was created by law in 1931, and San Gorgonio Wilderness in 1964. The wilderness has been expanded several times to include elevations as low as 2,300 feet, and now totals 94,702 acres.

DIRECTIONS: From Interstate 10 in Redlands, exit on California 38. Stop at the Mill Creek Ranger Station just beyond the hamlet of Mentone and pick up a wilderness permit. Follow the highway 19 miles past the ranger station to Jenks Lake Road. Turn right and proceed 2.5 miles to the South Fork trailhead and large parking lot.

THE HIKE: From the signed trailhead, the path ascends moderately through a mixed pine forest, passes wide Horse Meadow, and reaches the wilderness boundary, 2.4 miles out, at Poopout Hill. Hike east along forested slopes. After another mile, South Fork Creek appears on your left, and you parallel it toward South Fork Meadows, also known as Slushy Meadows in days gone by.

Dozens of tiny streams, which form the headwaters of the Santa Ana River, roam through the ferns and wispy waist-high grasses. Two former trail camps offer places to picnic; locate an idyllic picnic spot beneath the ponderosa pine and white fir.

The trail skirts the west edge of the meadow to a junctioin. Whitewater Trail, heads toward Dry Lake and the top of Gorgonio. Take the right fork, South Fork Trail.

After a mile of climbing, through ponderosa pine and then lodgepole pine, begin a long contour around the wall of the basin that holds Dollar Lake. The trail passes a manzanita-covered slope and reaches a junction 1.75 miles from South Fork Meadows. Go left.

In a few hundred yards you reach another junction and turn left again. Follow the easy 0.25-mile trail down the basin wall to the lake. Dollar Lake, so named because it gleams like a silver dollar, is one of the most popular backcountry spots in the San Gorgonio Wilderness and is another ideal place to picnic or laze away a day. Return to the main trail the way you came.

If you're headed for the summit, resume climbing for another mile to Dollar Lake Saddle (approx. 10,000 feet) and a three-way junction. One half mile beyond the junction, ypass another junction with the rocky side-trail that ascends Charlton Peak. In another 0.5 mile you pass Dry Lake View Camp, a waterless trail camp amidst great boulders. From here, you can look down into Dry Lake Basin, where you'll pass if you return from the peak via Sky High Trail. Soon you'll pass junctions with the Vivian Creek Trail and the Sky High Trail. Keep to your left at both junctions. Cross a last rise and climb to the summit of San Gorgonio.

No other Southern California mountain commands such an uninterrupted panoramic view. To the north are the deep green meadowlands of the upper valley of the Santa Ana River. To the west is the murky megalopolis. To the east is the Mojave. South is San Gorgonio Pass and just across from it, nearly level with your feet, is Mt. San Jacinto.

After enjoying this 360-degree view from the top of the world, return the way you came or via the Sky High Trail, which descends the east slope of San Gorgonio to Mine Shaft Saddle and Dry Lake and deposits you in South Fork Meadows where you intersect the trail back to South Fork.

From the summit, retrace your steps on the main trail to its intersection with the Sky High Trail. Begin your descent from the clouds on the latter trail, circling first east, then north around the mountain's great shoulders. As you descend there are good views of the Whitewater drainage, gorges bearing snowmelt from San Gorgonio and carrying waters to the desert sands below. The awesome Whitewater country was in 1984 added to the San Gorgonio Wilderness.

Three and a half miles from the summit you reach Mine Shaft Saddle on the divide between Dry Lake Basin and the Whitewater River. Continue your descent, and in two more miles you'll reach Dry Lake at 9,200 feet. Some years it is dry by midsummer, but in other years the lake is filled to the brim, its water lapping against the trail that surrounds the lake.

From the Dry Lake basin, you switchback down through pine and fir 1.75 miles to South Fork Meadows, where you intersect the trail back to South Fork trailhead.

VIVIAN CREEK

VIVIAN CREEK TRAIL

From Mill Creek Canyon to Vivian Creek Trail Camp is 3 miles round trip with 1,200-foot elevation gain; to Halfway Trail Camp is 6 miles round trip with 1,800-foot gain; to High Creek Trail Camp is 9.5 miles round trip with 3,400-foot gain; to Mt. San Gorgonio Peak is 17 miles round trip with 5,300-foot gain

A half-dozen major trails lead through the San Gorgonio Wilderness to the top of Mt. San Gorgonio, Southern California's highest peak. Oldest, and often regarded as the best, is Vivian Creek Trail. It's the shortest route to the top of San Gorgonio and one of the steepest.

Not long after the formation of San Bernardino Forest Preserve in 1893, pioneer foresters built Government Trail to the top of San Gorgonio. This path was later renamed Vivian Creek Trail because it winds along with its namesake watercourse before climbing the steep upper slopes of San Gorgonio.

Vivian Creek Trail begins in Mill Creek Canyon. Lower stretches of the canyon, traveled by Highway 38, display many boulders, evidence of great floods in years past. (Upper Mill Creek Canyon is where Big Falls falls. Tumbling from the shoulder of San Bernardino Peak, snowmelt-swollen Falls Creek rushes headlong over a cliff; check out Big Falls from the trailhead just down the road.

Leaving the head of Mill Creek Canyon, Vivian Creek Trail climbs into the valley cut by Vivian Creek, visits three inviting trail camps—Vivian Creek, Halfway and High Creek—and ascends rocky, lodgepole pine-dotted slopes to the top of Old Grayback.

DIRECTIONS: From Interstate 10 in Redlands, exit on Highway 38 and proceed 14 miles east to a junction with Valley of

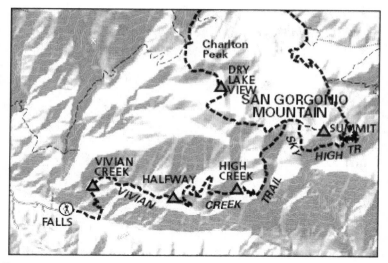

Falls Drive. (Halfway to this junction, on Highway 38, is Mill Creek Ranger Station; obtain a wilderness permit here.) Turn right and drive 4.5 miles to the signed trailhead and parking.

THE HIKE: The trail, an old dirt road, travels 0.75 mile through (closed) Falls Campground to another (the former) Vivian Creek trailhead. The trail, a dirt path from this point, crosses boulder-strewn Mill Creek wash, and begins a steep ascent over an exposed, oak-dotted slope. At 1.5-miles, reach Vivian Creek Trail Camp, where pine- and fir-shaded sites dot the creek banks.

Past the camp, Vivian Creek Trail follows its namesake, crossing from one side to the other and passing little lush meadows and stands of pine and cedar. Three miles out, reach Halfway Camp, about halfway between Vivian Creek and High Creek Camps Another 1.8 miles of steep climbing up forested slopes leads to High Creek Camp.

Above High Creek, located at 9,000-foot elevation, you leave behind the Ponderosa pine and cedar and encounter that hearty, high-altitude survivor, the lodgepole pine. Two miles high, you start getting some great views; at 11,000 feet, the trail ascends above the timberline.

When you reach a junction with the trail coming up from Dollar Lake you'll turn right (east). Soon you'll pass a junction with the Sky High Trail, cross a last rise and climb to the summit of San Gorgonio.

217

SANTA ANA RIVER

SANTA ANA RIVER TRAIL

From South Fork Campground to Heart Bar Campground is 9 miles round trip with 500-foot elevation gain

Southern California's largest river is study in contrasts.

Concrete-lined and channelized, the Santa Ana River that crosses Orange County is a thoroughly domesticated, watercourse, with a popular bike path that extends alongside it. In the San Bernardino Mountains, the Santa Ana runs wild and free with 33 miles of trail meandering along with it.

I suggest taking a hike at its headwaters high in the mountains, where the Santa Ana River waters a beautiful meadow and cuts through a deep canyon that separates the high peaks of the San Gorgonio Wilderness from the mountains of the Big Bear Lake area.

A fine length of Santa Ana River Trail parallels the river between South Fork Campground to Heart Bar Campground. The path stays in piney woods for most of its length. A few side trails allow passage to the river.

DIRECTIONS: From Interstate 10 in Redlands, take the Highway 38 exit and proceed north 32 miles to the turn-off for South Fork Campground. Look for the Santa Ana River trailhead and parking on the north side of the highway opposite the camp entrance.

If you want to make this a one-way hike arrange for transportation at Heart Bar Campground or at trail's end at Forest Road IN05.

THE HIKE: Santa Ana River Trail meanders by its namesake, then veers under the Santa Ana River Bridge. Notice the rugged construction of the bridge and the wide bed of the river, two indications of the Santa Ana's size and strength after a storm.

SART, reaches a second signed trailhead at the entrance to South Fork Campground heads briefly west, switchbacks up a slope and

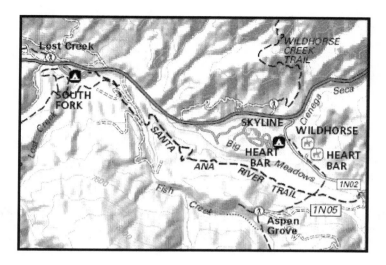

soon turns east—your direction for the rest of the hike.

Much of the climb occurs in the first mile. The trail travels through a mixed forest of ponderosa and Jeffrey pine, white fir and black oak. Ground squirrels are abundant, and deer are seen occasionally.

Above you, to the southwest, is the San Gorgonio Wilderness, dominated by its 11,502-foot signature peak, highest point in Southern California. To the north, above the forested canyon of the Santa Ana River, is Sugarloaf Mountain (9,952 feet), highest peak in the San Bernardinos outside the wilderness.

Continuing east, the trail offers great views of well-named Big Meadow. Watering the meadow are Heart Bar Creek, Coon Creek, Cienega Seca Creek and the headwaters of the Santa Ana. Big Meadow is especially pretty when a breeze sways the willows and tall grasses. During late spring and summer the meadow is splashed with colorful wildflowers.

The meadows where cattle (branded with heart with a bar beneath it) once grazed are now a valuable habitat for rabbits, foxes, skunks and raccoons.

About a mile from trail's end intersect a trail leading left down to Big Meadow and over to Heart Bar Campground. Take this path or continue straight at this junction to the end of this segment of SART at Forest Road 1N05.

ASPEN GROVE &
FISH CREEK MEADOW

ASPEN GROVE, FISH CREEK TRAILS

To Aspen Grove is 0.5 miles round trip; to Fish Creek Trail Camp is 8 miles round trip with 600-foot elevation gain

One of the prettiest sights of autumn is the fluttering of the aspen's golden-yellow leaves.

Botanists say the aspen is the most widely distributed tree on the North American continent, but the tree is a rarity in Southern California.

Happily, a handsome little grove of quaking aspens (*Populus tremuloides*) thrives in the San Bernardino Mountains. Aspen Grove, reached by a trail with the same name, is an ideal autumn excursion. After the first cold snap, the aspens display their fall finery, a display of color unrivaled in the Southland.

It's only a short saunter to the aspens but the trail continues up-creek, traveling through pine and fir forest and a lovely meadow to junction Fish Creek Trail; this path connects to several paths in the San Gorgonio Wilderness.

In addition to the aspens, get great views of San Gorgonio Wilderness peaks. To the west stands mighty Grinnell Mountain, named for famed zoologist Joseph Grinnell, who studied the animals of the San Bernardino Mountains. To the south is Ten Thousand Foot Ridge, headwaters for Fish Creek.

DIRECTIONS: From Interstate 10 in Redlands, exit on Highway 38 and proceed 32 miles east to the signed turnoff for Heart Bar Campground. (Along 38, stop at Mill Creek Ranger Station and obtain a wilderness permit or get one from Barton Flats Ranger Station located 6 miles west of Heart Bar Campground.) Turn south (right)

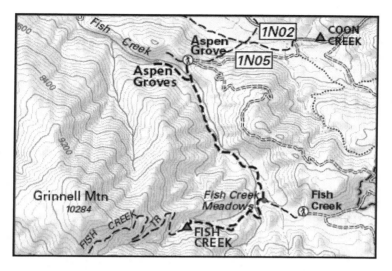

Forest Road 1N02, and drive 1.2 miles to a fork in the road. Stay right at the fork and follow Forest Road 1N05 on a 1.5-mile climb to a small parking area and signed Aspen Grove Trail.

THE HIKE: The trail descends toward Fish Creek and a sign marking the boundary of the San Gorgonio Wilderness. Cross the creek and view the aspens along Fish Creek. To see more aspens, join the path that leads right (northwest). Relax and enjoy a picnic among the whitewashed trunks and quaking leaves here.

After touring Aspen Grove, consider extending the hike by continuing with Aspen Grove Trail along the west side of Fish Creek. Make a mellow ascent amidst a forest of ponderosa pine, Jeffrey pine and Douglas fir. A mile out, reach little Monkey Flower Flat, seasonally sprinkled with monkeyflowers as well as lupine and columbine.

The path ascends briefly, descends to Fish Creek and crosses it, and leads another 0.8 mile along the east bank to Fish Creek Meadow and a junction, nearly 3 miles from the trailhead, with Fish Creek Trail. The left fork leads 0.6 mile back to a trailhead on Forest Road 1N05.

Take the right fork of the trail, which angles toward Upper Fish Creek. The path ascends above the creek, passes through a pine and fir forest and switchbacks up to Fish Creek Camp, 1.2 miles from the junction. This fir-shaded camp, with year-around water, is an ideal place to relax.

Many hikers compare this range with the High Sierra. The San Jacinto Mountains seem an island in the sky because of their incredibly rapid rise from the desert floor. No other place in California do alpine and desert vegetation thrive in such close proximity. Hikers get the feeling of hiking in Switzerland while gazing down on the Sahara.

The seasons are more distinct here than anywhere else in Southern California. One of those magical places that lure hikers back year after year, the range is a delight to hike whether you begin in charming Idyllwild or get a lift from the Palm Springs Aerial Tramway.

Chapter 9

San Jacinto Mountains

HIKE ON.

INTRO TO IDYLLWILD

ERNIE MAXWELL SCENIC TRAIL

5.2 miles round trip with 300-foot elevation gain

The late founder of the "Idyllwild Town Crier" and longtime Idlyllwild conservationist is honored by the Ernie Maxwell Scenic Trail, a woodsy path through the mountains on the outskirts of Idyllwild. Fairly flat and family-friendly, the trail leads from Humber Park to Saunders Meadow and delivers fine views along the way.

Maxwell explained that his trail came into being as a result of his horse's inability to get along with automobiles. After riding through the San Jacinto Wilderness, Maxwell and his fellow equestrians were forced to follow paved roads back through town to the stables.

Equine-auto conflicts were frequent. Maxwell thought: Why not build a trail from Humber Park, at the edge of the San Jacinto Wilderness, through the forest to the stables, thus avoiding the horse-spooking congestion of downtown Idyllwild?

Maxwell got cooperation from the U.S. Forest Service and from Riverside County inmates, who provided the labor. Ernie Maxwell Trail was completed in 1959.

Maxwell often wrote about what he wryly called "the urban-wildlands interface issue. That's the one that deals with more and more people moving into the hills."

Fortunately, Idyllwild and the mountains have had many conservation-minded friends like Ernie Maxwell.

The trail begins at Humber Park, the main jumping-off point to the San Jacinto Wilderness for hikers and rock climbers. You'll get frequent views of the dramatic pinnacles popular with SoCal climbers. The path meanders through a mixed forest of pine and fir and offers fine views of the granite face of Marion Ridge.

DIRECTIONS:
From Highway 243 in Idyllwild, turn east on North Circle Drive just below the ranger station and proceed 0.7 mile to Pinecrest Avenue. Go right and make an immediate right on South Circle Drive. Turn left on Fern Valley Road and go 1.8 miles to Humber Park. Signed Ernie Maxwell Trail is located across from the entrance to the park and parking is along Fern Valley Road. (BTW: bathrooms and Devil's Slide Trail can be found at a loop at the top of the road.)

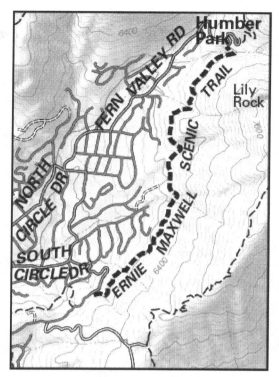

THE HIKE: Pause to admire the scene-stealing Tahquitz Rock then descend to a sparkling creek and cross it. About 0.2 mile out, pass an intersection with a climbers trail (to Tahquitz Rock of course) and continue on a slight descent (with a few dips and rises)

The trail contours gently around wooded slopes. Ponderosa, Jeffrey and Coulter pines, fir and incense cedar grace the mountainside and carpet the path with needles. Cross another bubbling creek about 1.5 miles out.

Saunders Meadow, more a pocket of residences than a big meadow, is named for Amasa Saunders, who in 1881 operated a huge sawmill not too far down slope in Strawberry Valley. Be thankful that not all trees around Idyllwild became grist for Saunders' mill.

Ernie Maxwell Scenic Trail ends somewhat abruptly and ingloriously at Tahquitz View Drive.

Idyllwild Nature Center

Yellow Pine Forest, Steep, Hillside Trails

0.5 mile round trip loop; 2.5 miles round trip loop

With its towering pines and incense cedar, great boulders and lively creeks, Idyllwild County Park offers a family-friendly introduction to the pleasures of the San Jacinto Mountains. Such pleasures are visited by a couple of miles of trail that tour the forest and climb to viewpoints for far-reaching vistas of the stony ramparts of the range.

The adventure begins at the Idyllwild Nature Center, located just a mile north of the town of Idyllwild. Exhibits present the natural and cultural history of the mountains.

The center hosts environmental education programs and guided hikes.

A half-dozen, short, family-friendly trails explore the area surrounding Idyllwild Nature Center. Enjoy a post-hike picnic at tables set beneath tall pines. There's also access by trail from the park's campground, a pleasant place to overnight with 88 forested sites.

Opt for a little loop with Yellow Pine Trail and Nature Trail or a little longer loop with Perimeter Trail. "The Loop" is a combo of the Steep and Hillside Trails. Most hikers prefer to hike up the Steep Trail first, continuing to the summit, and traveling back along Hillside Trail. However you go, this hike travels a slope punctuated by some impressive boulders as well as a mixed forest of oak, pine and cedar

DIRECTIONS: From the town of Idyllwild, drive a mile north on Highway 243 to the signed turnoff for Idyllwild County Park (entrance fee). Proceed to the last parking lot and walk up the path to the Idyllwild Nature Center, where Yellow Pine Forest Trail begins. The longer loop begins behind the nature center.

THE HIKE: Enjoy the awesome trees as you set out on Yellow Pine Forest Nature Trail, which departs from the nature center.

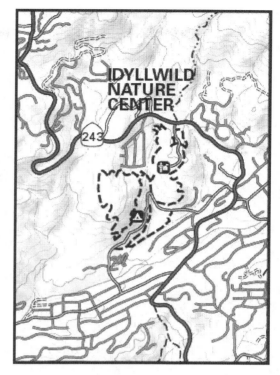

The trail passes impressive specimens of manzanita, and meanders past black oak and boulders. With its soft reddish bark and stately stature, the incense cedars en route seem to personify tranquility.

About halfway along, the nature trail travels near Lily Creek and arrives at an impressive bit of bedrock where the native Cahuilla ground seeds and acorns. The resultant grinding holes, morteros, are evidence of exactly where the Cahuilla went to work—a scenic spot indeed for such labor! Close the loop with Nature Trail.

The longer loop trail begins behind the visitor center with a 0.3 mile hike to a bridge crossing of Lily Creek. Walk another 0.1 mile to a junction with left-forking Hillside Trail and straight-ahead leading Steep (aka Summit) Trail. Go straight. When the path turns south leading to handsome boulders and grand mountain views, particularly of Tahquitz Peak.

Continue south, looping toward the park campground and to a junction with Hillside Trail and a connector trail leading to the campground. Join Hillside Trail and hike 0.6 mile to close the loop. Go right, re-cross the bridge over Lily Creek and retrace your steps back to the nature center.

Tahquitz Peak

South Ridge Trail

From South Ridge Road to Tahquitz Peak is 7 miles round trip with 2,000-foot elevation gain

Tahquitz Peak dominates the southern San Jacinto Mountains, lording over Strawberry Valley and Idyllwild on one side, and Tahquitz Valley on the other. Considered the second-most prominent peak in the range, Tahquitz (pronounced Taw-kits or Taw-kwish) has long been associated with rock-climbing.

Southland rock climbers have practiced their craft on the superb rock walls of Tahquitz since the 1930s. By some accounts, Tahquitz Rock, also known as Lily Rock, was the first major practice ground for the sport of technical rock climbing in North America.

A lookout tower, staffed by volunteers is perched on the summit. The view from the peak is inspiring: clear-day vistas of the San Jacintos, the desert and the distant Santa Rosas.

South Ridge Trail, true to its name, ascends the steep south ridge of Tahquitz Peak. The trail climbs through stands of fine and fir and offers great views of Strawberry Valley and the storybook hamlet of Idyllwild.

If you want a longer hike than the one to Tahquitz Peak, there are a number of ways to extend your trek. By arranging a car shuttle, you could descend Tahquitz Peak to Humber Park at the outskirts of Idyllwild. For a very long loop hike, you could even follow the Ernie Maxwell Trail from Humber Park down to the foot of South Ridge Road, then up the road to the South Ridge trailhead.

DIRECTIONS: Obtain a wilderness permit from the Forest Service Station in Idyllwild, then head along the south edge of town on Highway 243 and make a left turn on Saunders Meadow Road.

After 0.75 mile, turn left on Pine Avenue, drive 0.25 mile, then turn right on Tahquitz View Drive and proceed another 0.25 mile. Turn right on South Ridge Road and travel a mile to parking and signed South Ridge Trail.

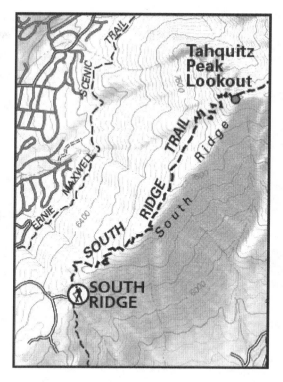

THE HIKE: From the trailhead at the top of South Ridge Road, the well-constructed path zigzags through a forest of Jeffrey pine and white fir. You'll get fine south views of Garner Valley and Lake Hemet, Thomas Mountain and Table Mountain. Far off to the west, on a clear day, you'll be able to pick out the Santa Ana and San Gabriel Mountains.

South Ridge Trail climbs to a boulder-strewn saddle, which marks the trail's halfway point. Here you'll find a rock window-on-the-world, a great place to rest or to frame a picture of your hiking mate.

From the saddle, the trail climbs in earnest past thickets of spiny chinquapin, and past scattered lodgepole pine. You'll sight the fire lookout tower atop Tahquitz Peak and many a switchback above you, but the last mile of trail goes by faster than you might expect with a slow, steady pace.

Enjoy the summit views, then either return the same way or continue farther into the backcountry and take another route through the San Jacinto Wilderness and back down to Humber Park and Idyllwild.

SUICIDE ROCK

DEER SPRINGS TRAIL

From Idyllwild to Suicide Rock is 6.6 miles round trip with 1,900-feet elevation gain

Suicide Rock is a sheer, granite outcropping that provides the romantic with a tale of star-crossed lovers, and rewards the hiker with splendid views of Strawberry Valley and a forest wonderland of pine and fir.

Native Cahuilla legend has it that the rock got its tragic name from an Indian princess and her lover who leaped to their deaths over the precipice rather than be separated, as their chief had commanded. That's right, Romeo and Juliet set on the slopes San Jacinto Peak.

Suicide Rock is very popular with rock climbers; more than 300 climbing routes have been described over the granite outcrop

Suicide Rock is a splendid place to observe the ever-changing four seasons (though you'd have a hard time climbing the rock in winter!). Seasons fade in and out with clarity and distinction in the San Jacintos. Fall colors tint the black oak and azalea, winter brings a white blanket, spring is heralded by a profusion of wildflowers, and the long, hot summers are tempered with thunder and lightning displays. Views like this bring hikers back again and again to sample the beauty of the San Jacinto Mountains.

Deer Springs Trail is one of four great hiking trails that ascend the west face of San Jacinto. Some hikers like this route because the ascent is more gradual and the trail less-traveled than other approaches to the peak; however, this is long way to go—19 miles round trip and a 5,200-foot gain from the trailhead.

DIRECTIONS: Deer Springs Trailhead is located across the highway from the Idyllwild Nature Center, one mile north of

Idyllwild on Highway 243. Park in the large dirt pullout. All paths from the pullout lead to Deer Springs Trail. Obtain the necessary wilderness permit from Mount San Jacinto State Park Ranger Station, located 0.5 mile south of the trailhead on Highway 243.

THE HIKE: Signed Deer Springs Trail picks its way through manzanita, and for short lengths of the journey there's an almost high desert-like feel to the hike. After 0.5 mile enter the

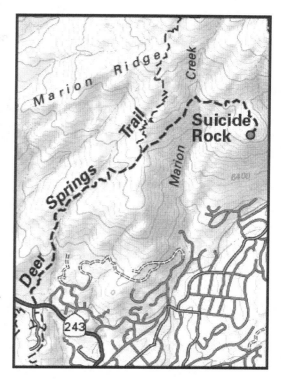

wilderness and at about the 0.75-mile-mark, gain a fine vista extending west to Hemet and an eye-popping view of Tahquitz Peak to the east.

Ascend past black oaks and tall pines, switchbacking up a ridge to incense cedar and to Suicide Junction, 2.3 miles from the trailhead. Depart Deer Springs Trail and bear east, contouring across Marion Ridge. Cross Marion Creek, whose performance is seasonal, and on wet years, inspiring. After what seems a very long mile of hiking from Suicide Junction, reach the back side of Suicide Rock.

From the white granite rock look down at tiny Idyllyllwild, across Strawberry Valley and over to Lily Rock and Tahquitz Peak. Kick back on one of the white granite rocks and enjoy the views. But be careful to watch your step near the edges of the rock and to watch where you sit (the rock attracts more than its fair share of rattlesnakes).

DEER SPRINGS &
LITTLE ROUND VALLEY

SEVEN PINES, MARION MOUNTAIN TRAILS

**From Dark Canyon to Deer Springs is 7.6 miles round trip with
2,600-foot elevation gain; to Little Round Valley Camp is 10.6
miles round trip with 3,600-foot elevation gain; to San Jacinto
Peak is 13.8 miles round trip with 4,500-foot gain**

Seven Pines Trail ascends the cascading North Fork of San Jacinto River to its headwaters at Deep Springs. Energetic hikers will join the Deer Springs Trail for an ascent of Mt. San Jacinto.

Heavily forested, with a fair share of switchbacks, Seven Pines Trail is a pretty enough path, but not a very popular one: seems like hikers much prefer other ways to go into the wilderness and to ascend San Jacinto Peak. I don't know the reason for that because the trail itself whether hiking a mile or so amidst the pines and handsome boulders or the whole length to Deer Springs—has a lot to offer.

OK, there might be one reason for its unpopularity. Remote as it is, the trail doesn't seem to get much maintenance. Every time I've hiked it there are deadfalls across the trail and the trail gets sketchy and hard to follow in places. I've given silent thanks for those who've placed ducks to help us hikers stay on track.

DIRECTIONS: Take Highway 243 about 20 miles from Banning or 6 miles from Idyllwild. Just east of Alandale Ranger Station, take paved Marion Mountain Road turnoff and drive 1 mile to Dark Canyon Campground. Follow the one-way loop camp road through the campground and rejoin (dirt) Marion Mountain Road (4S02) at the top of the loop. Follow this road 1.5 miles to the trailhead. (Note: Campground access road closed November to May.)

THE HIKE: Seven Pines Trail ascends the ridge between Dark Canyon and the canyon cut by the North Fork. You hike out of the San Bernardino National Forest into Mt. San Jacinto State Park. After a mile, the trails tops the ridge and descends eastward to the North Fork. In spring, when the river is swollen with snowmelt, the North Fork has quite a heady flow.

The trail climbs along a pine- and incense cedar-covered slope, re-crosses the river, and reaches a junction with Deer Springs Trail, which is also famed Pacific Crest Trail. (A right turn on the trail leads toward Strawberry Junction and Suicide Rock).

Follow Deer Springs Trail left (east) 0.25 mile to Deer Springs. The former camp boasts an all-year water supply and its pleasant locale makes for an ideal lunch or rest stop.

A short walk hike past Deer Springs leads to another junction. The leftward fork is Fuller Ridge Trail, which leads northwest 5 miles to Black Mountain Camp. Bear right at this junction and ascend a very steep mile (900-foot gain) to Little Round Valley Trail Camp.

Then it's more climbing through stands of lodgepole pine and in 1.3 miles arrive at a junction with San Jacinto Peak summit trail. Ascend this trail 0.3 mile, passing a stone shelter cabin, and reaching the top of the 10,084-foot peak.

MT. SAN JACINTO

MT. JACINTO TRAIL

From Mountain Station to Round Valley is 4 miles round trip with 600-foot elevation gain; to San Jacinto Peak is 11 miles round trip with 2,300-foot gain

Palm Springs Aerial Tramway makes it easy for hikers to enter Mt. San Jacinto State Wilderness. Starting in Chino Canyon near Palm Springs, a tram takes passengers from 2,643-foot Lower Tramway Terminal (Valley Station) to 8,516-foot Upper Tramway Terminal (Mountain Station) at the edge of the wilderness.

The gondola rapidly ascends from palms to pines over one of the most abrupt mountain faces in the world. When you disembark at Mountain Station, you'll have quite a head start up 10,834-foot Mt. San Jacinto.

This a classic hike, beginning in one of California's finest state parks and ending atop of one of the Southland's most prominent peaks with panoramic vistas you'll long remember. "No Southern California hiker worth his salt would miss climbing 'San Jack' at least once," write John W. Robinson and Bruce D. Risher, authors of *The San Jacintos*.

DIRECTIONS: From Interstate 10, exit on California 111 (the road to Palm Springs). Proceed 9 miles to Tramway Road, turn right, and follow the road 4 miles to its end at Mountain Station. Contact the Tramway office for information about prices and schedules.

THE HIKE: From Mountain Station, walk down the cement walkway through the Long Valley Picnic Area. Soon you will arrive at the state park ranger station. Obtain a wilderness permit here.

Continue west on the trail, following signs to Round Valley. The trail parallels Long Valley Creek through a mixed forest of pine and

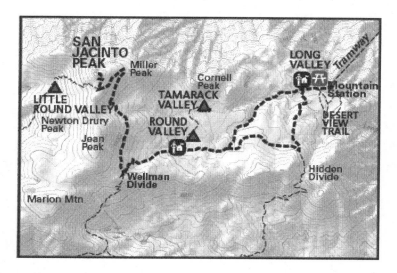

white fir, then climbs into lodgepole pine country. Lupine, monkey-flower, scarlet bugler are a few of the wildflowers that add seasonal splashes of color.

After passing a junction with a trail leading toward Willow Creek, another 0.3 of a mile of hiking leads to Round Valley. A trail camp and a backcountry ranger station are located in the valley, as are splendid places to picnic. (On the return trip, consider making a little loop with Willow Creek Trail; it adds some variety and almost no extra mileage to the hike.)

From Round Valley, a sign indicates you may reach the peak by either Tamarack Valley or Wellman Divide Junction. Take the trail toward Wellman Divide Junction. From the Divide, a trail leads down to Humber Park. At the divide, enjoy spectacular views of Tahquitz Peak and Red Tahquitz, as well as more distant Toro Peak and Santa Rosa Mountain. Continue toward the peak on vigorous switchbacks. The lodgepole pines grow sparse among the crumbly granite.

At another junction, 0.5 mile from the top, the trail continues to Little Round Valley but you take the summit trail to the peak. Soon reach a stone shelter hut, then boulder-hop to the top of the peak.

The view from the summit—San Gorgonio Pass, the shimmering Pacific, the Colorado Desert, distant Mexico—has struck some visitors speechless, while others found superlatives. John Muir called the view "the most sublime spectacle to be found anywhere on this earth!"

Marion Mountain

Marion Mountain, Pacific Crest Trails

From Fern Basin to San Jacinto Peak is 12 miles round trip with 4,400-foot elevation gain

It's the shortest, the steepest and, in the opinion of some hikers, the most scenic ascent of San Jacinto Peak. Marion Mountain Trail gains 2,400 feet in just 2.5 miles. The rest of the climb to the peak via Pacific Crest and Deer Springs trails is nearly as steep.

While reaching the summit of the great mountain is ample return on investment for most hikers, Marion Mountain Trail scatters additional rewards along the way. This is a hike for tree-lovers, a climb to remember through Conifer-Land.

Marion Mountain's lower elevations support stands of Jeffrey pine and even oaks. Higher up the mountain grow ranks of sugar pine and white fir and higher still, lofty lodgepole pine.

Marion Mountain Trail is a great conditioning hike for anyone planning a High Sierra adventure. The altitude and altitude gain of this hike approximates some Sierra sojourns.

DIRECTIONS: From Interstate 10 in Banning, exit on Highway 243 and ascend south some 19 winding miles. Just east of Alandale Ranger Station, take paved Marion Mountain Road (4S02) turnoff, fork left at a junction, and proceed a mile to a junction with Marion Mountain Campground Road. Bear right and drive 0.5 mile (passing the entrance to Fern Basin Campground) to a parking area and the trailhead located just below the campground. (Wilderness permit required.)

THE HIKE: Begin what is briefly (0.2 mile) a mellow ascent through piney woods. Soon pass a spur trail leading down to the campground and begin a vigorous ascent of the northwest flank of Marion Mountain.

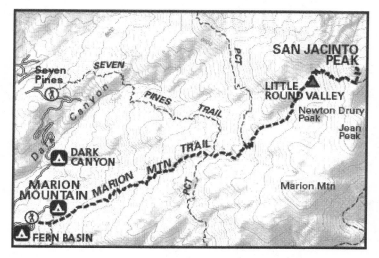

A bit more than 1.25 miles up the trail, reach a wilderness boundary sign. The trailside view briefly opens up to reveal Highway 243 snaking through the mountains far below and the murky flatlands of the Inland Empire to the north.

Almost immediately, it's back to the trees, interspersed with ferns and big boulders.

After 2.5 miles of ascent, you'll come to a junction. It's not quite the perfect four-way intersection pictured on trail maps, but it's well signed. You'll first encounter Pacific Crest Trail (Deer Springs Trail) coming in from the right (south). Turn left and walk 50 feet to a second junction. Seven Pines Trail descends to the north, but you continue your climb east on signed PCT.

After a 0.3-mile ascent on the very well engineered and maintained PCT, pass gurgling Deer Springs. The modest springs-spawned creek forms part of the headwaters of the North Fork of the San Jacinto River.

The ascent continues another 0.25 mile up the other side of the creek canyon and junctions Fuller Ridge Trail. Keep right, and keep switchbacking for another mile to Little Round Valley, where a small trail camp is located.

The trail curves east, still climbing, still switchbacking for another 1.3 miles and 800-foot elevation gain to San Jacinto Peak's summit ridge. A final 0.3-mile ascent via the summit trail leads past a stone mountaineers hut to the peak.

FULLER RIDGE

PACIFIC CREST TRAIL (FULLER RIDGE TRAIL)

From Fuller Ridge to San Jacinto Peak is 15 miles round trip with 3,200-foot elevation gain

True, you get a 7,700-foot head start, but that doesn't make the ascent from Fuller Ridge the easiest hike to the top of Mt. San Jacinto.

Do the math and the hike seems a moderate enough exercise: a climb that averages under 500 feet per mile.

Do the hike and the math seems fuzzy and downright irrelevant. Fuller Ridge is a much more difficult ascent than its numbers suggest. Other paths to San Jacinto Peak lead through cool forest and, while by no means a walk in the park, offer a woodsy solace to the hiker. The trail following Fuller Ridge is a challenging ("tortuous" some hikers say) series of tight switchbacks zigzagging amongst stone ramparts and wind-thrashed fir.

The attraction of ascending the mighty mountain by way of Fuller Ridge is more obvious to veteran hikers than novices. What you get is a trek on a grand, seldom-used stretch of Pacific Crest Trail, fabulous views of mountain ranges, the desert and the San Andreas Rift Zone, as well as the satisfaction of seeing the quizzical looks of hikers when you tell them you conquered San Jacinto Peak by way of Fuller Ridge. "You came from where?" is the likely response from those taking shorter and easier routes.

Fuller Ridge is a good conditioning hike for that upcoming trek to Nepal; however, the 4-mile round trip hike to the Fuller ridgeline and far-reaching views is a fine, short day hike.

DIRECTIONS: From Interstate 10 in Banning, exit on Highway 243 and ascend southeast 15 winding miles to Black Mountain

Road (usually closed November-May). From Idyllwild, drive 8.5 miles north to Black Mountain Road. Proceed 6 miles north to Black Mountain Campground and another 1.5 miles to a brief, right-forking spur that leads to parking and the trailhead.

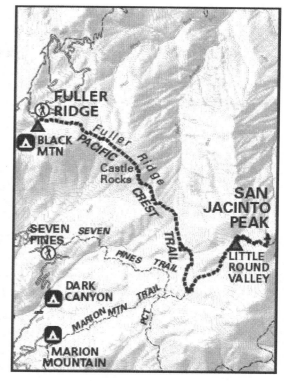

THE HIKE: The path ascends a mile (in a mellow manner at first) through open forest to a saddle. Another mile of ascent, past aptly named Castle Rocks, leads to Fuller Ridge.

The path twists atop the ridgeline, dodging great boulders and contorted white fir. Savor eye-popping vistas of Mt. San Gorgonio and other tall peaks of the San Bernardino Mountains. Also get impressive views of Coachella Valley.

After a bit more than a mile of squirming atop the ridgeline, PCT abandons it for the southern slopes of Mt. San Jacinto. PCT switchbacks and contours across the broad shoulders of the mountain past the headwaters of the north fork of the San Jacinto River and reaches a junction with Deer Spring Trail, 5 miles from the start.

Join this path, turn northeast and keep switchbacking for another mile to Little Round Valley, where a small trail camp is located.

The trail curves east, still climbing, still switchbacking for another 1.3 miles with a 800-foot elevation gain to San Jacinto Peak's summit ridge. A final 0.3-mile ascent via the summit trail leads past a stone mountaineers hut to the peak.

Along with wonderful beach walks, San Diego offers some enjoyable hikes in the hills and canyons around the city.

The Palomar Mountains, extending 25 miles along the northern boundary of San Diego County offer a few fine day hikes near Julian. Hike amidst blue lupine on sunny slopes, tiger lilies in the shade and azalea in damp canyons. And hike the oak valleys, pine forests and spring-watered grasslands of Palomar Mountain.

Plentiful rain and a location between coast and desert make the Cuyamaca Mountains a unique ecosystem. The range offers four-season hiking at its best—particularly in autumn with its colorful foliage. More than 100 miles of hiking trails pass through Cuyamaca Rancho State Park, which protects a good portion of the mountains.

Chapter 10

San Diego and Beyond

HIKE ON.

COWLES MOUNTAIN

COWLES MOUNTAIN TRAIL

To summit is 3 miles round trip with 930-foot elevation gain

Cowles Mountain, highest summit within San Diego City limits, offers grand views of downtown and far beyond. In a city known for its considerable coastal attractions, Cowles is a close as it gets to being San Diego's iconic summit.

By mountain standards Cowles is not very high (1,591 feet), but as any hiker ascending L.A.'s Mt. Hollywood (1,625 feet) will tell you, it's not the elevation but the experience and vistas that makes hiking to the top of a city landmark so compelling.

The classic south approach, leads to the summit by way of a nearly shadeless series of switchbacks. Low brush cloaks the mountainside and the hiker is treated to mostly uninterrupted views from the footpath. If you want double the distance and fun, consider continuing from Cowles to Pyles Peak.

Expect company, lots of it, on the mountain named for 19th-century rancher-businessman George Cowles. More than 500 hikers climb Cowles on a busy day. Cowles (pronounced "Coals") Mountain is the most popular trail in the greater San Diego area. Trail users include families with kids, scores of SDSU students, and hikers and joggers of all ages, shapes and sizes.

Cowles Mountain is a must-do-at-least-once hike for any proud San Diegan, and a great trail to take your (reasonably fit) out-of-town visitors. For hikers on holiday, who can tear themselves away from the attractions of the coast and want to do one inland hike, Cowles is a top choice. The summit is a romantic place to watch the sunset; just be sure you have a headlamp for the descent in the dark back to the trailhead.

DIRECTIONS:

From Interstate 15 in San Diego, exit on Friars Road East and head east (Friars continues as Mission Gorge Road). After 5 miles, past the main turnoff to Mission Trails Regional Park, reach Golf Crest Drive. Turn right and drive 1 mile to the trail on the left side of Golf Crest where it meets Navajo Road. The staging area is shaded (but the trail is not) and has a native plant garden, helpful with the ID of the flora

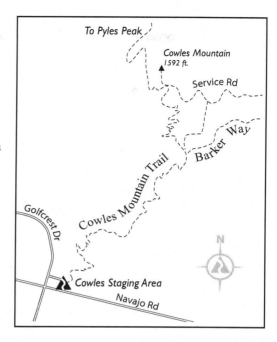

that you may see along the trail. The modest-sized lot is often full, though plentiful curbside parking is nearby.

THE HIKE: Up you go, usually with lots of company. The trail can seem even busier than it is because everyone is traveling at a different pace, so you are constantly passing or getting passed by fellow travelers. (BTW, don't cut switchbacks; loose granite soil and high traffic make this trail subject to erosion.)

A bit more than halfway, the trail reaches the top of the mountain's south shoulder and a junction with a Barker Way Trail that crosses the east side of the mountain and meets a service road on the north ridge. Above the shoulder, switchbacks lead to the summit and spectacular views of downtown, Point Loma, San Diego Bay, across the border into Baja, Cuyamaca Peak and many more San Diego County peaks.

Oak Canyon

Oak Canyon Trail

**From Old Mission Dam to Oak Canyon is 3.4 miles round trip
with 200-foot elevation gain**

Oak Canyon Trail offers a look at the Old Mission Dam built in
the early 1800s, leads past intriguing rock formations, and delivers
the promises in its name—an oak-lined canyon. It's one of the best
hikes in the park.

Every season has its charms. Winter rains swell the creek cours-
ing through Oak Canyon and the resultant pools, cascades and a
small waterfall are a delight to the eye. In early- and mid-Spring the
creek is still sprightly and wildflowers bloom in the canyon and in
the adjacent Grasslands Area of the park. In summer and fall, the
plants and grasses turns shades of brown and gold and the creek is
usually dry revealing slickrock boulders with a casual resemblance to
one of the Utah's slot canyons.

Oak Canyon is definitely one of San Diego's hidden gems. At
times Mission Dam is a tourist jam, but it's easy to get away from
the crowds and even find a measure of peace and tranquility with a
hike into Oak Canyon.

This hike has at least two great add-ons. Ascend South Fortuna
Mountain with an extra 2.4 miles round trip (and a robust elevation
gain!). Or take the Grassland Loop Trail (1.2 miles) as part of an
alternative return route.

DIRECTIONS: From I-8 in San Diego,805, take the Mission
Gorge Road exit. Turn north on Mission Gorge Road and drive 4.2
miles to the signed Mission Trails Regional Park entrance. Turn left
on Father Junipero Serra Trail, and drive 1.7 miles on the one-way
road to the Old Mission Dam. The small parking lot is often full so

expect to park along-
side the road.

THE HIKE: Walk
past the Old Mission
Dam and surprisingly
extensive ruins of the
first major irrigation
project on the West
Coast. Join signed
Oak Canyon Trail and
head across the steel
footbridge spanning
the San Diego River.
Head up-river on the
path and, in 0.2 mile,
look right for a wood
stairway ascending
a hillock to an im-
pressive vista of Old
Mission Dam.

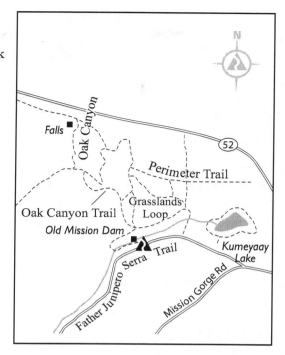

Continue along with Oak Canyon Creek, staying left at junctions and noting the wide Grasslands Loop Trail (a possible return
route). Meet signed Fortuna Saddle Trail (that leads 0.6 mile to
the saddle between South Fortuna and North Fortuna peaks; from
the saddle, it's another 0.6 mile to the top of South Fortuna Peak.)
Join right forking and signed Oak Canyon Trail North. This path
weaves its way around rocks and crisscrosses the creek. You can
almost imagine you're in the wilderness—except for the towering
Highway 52 overpass looming ahead.

Trail's end is a junction with North Fortuna/Perimeter Trail. For
an optional return, go right on this trail and take a hilly 0.7-mile
hike to meet the Grasslands Loop Trail. Join this path to trek across
a portion of the grasslands. Reconnect with Oak Canyon Trail and
retrace your steps to the trailhead.

South Fortuna Mountain

South Fortuna Mountain Trail

To summit is 4.6 miles round trip with 1000-foot elevation gain

This is a great cardio workout and conditioning hike with grand vistas from the top of the mountain.

South Fortuna Mountain and environs offered an altogether different kind of "workout" for U.S. Marines during World War II when this locale was part of Camp Elliott and used as a training ground. The Marines who trained here fought on the island of Iwo Jima and, when they captured the isle's high point Mt. Suribachi (528 feet) from the Japanese, were immortalized in that iconic photograph, "Raising the Flag on Iwo Jima."

South Fortuna Mountain (1,094 feet) is a member in good standing of a group of peaks of about the same height extending from North Fortuna Mountain in the north to Cowles Mountain in the south. To reach the summit, there are a few ways to go—all of them steep and strenuous. The killer climb requires ascent of the long South Fortuna Staircase, sometimes referred to as the "Stairway to Heaven."

A century ago, South Fortuna and North Fortuna, separated by a low saddle, were referred to as one twin-peaked mountain known as "Long Mountain." Add another mile to this hike and get to the top of nearby North Fortuna peak but be warned: South Fortuna, the smaller of the two peaks, has better views.

DIRECTIONS: From I-15 northbound, just north of I-8, exit on Friars Road/Mission Gorge Road and follow Mission Gorge Road 4 mile to Jackson Drive. Turn left into the San Diego River Crossing Trailhead parking area. The trailhead is at Jackson Drive and Mission Gorge Road.

THE HIKE:

Head northwest on the wide pathway (Visitor Center Loop Trail). As the story goes, what is now a hiking trail was the beginnings of a road route intended to connect Jackson Drive north to Highway 52.

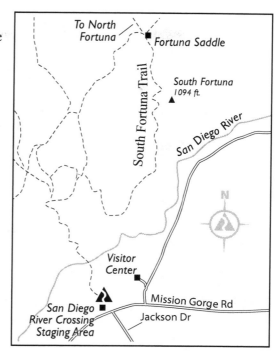

About 0.3 mile out, reach the San Diego River and part company with the VC Trail at a signed junction. Walk across a concrete berm to the trail on the other side of the river. (Use caution; may be impassable at times of high water.)

Begin a very steep 0.5 mile ascent and reach a junction. Head east (staying right at every trail junction), descend a bit and enter Suycott Wash at about the 1.2-mile mark. Stay right at every trail junction. Follow the trail and additional signs to meet Suycott Wash Trail, and go right once more to join South Fortuna Trail.

Cross a footbridge, hike through an oak woodland, and head out toward the exposed south-facing slopes of South Fortuna Mountain. The trail gets ever steeper, levels for a short distance, then reaches the stairs. Whew!

Is the staircase really just 0.3 mile long? Could South Fortuna Mountain really be more than 2,000 feet high? Did trail-builders forget an invention called the "switchback" that could have been used here?

Reward for reaching the top of the staircase are views of downtown San Diego and a parade of peaks: nearby North Fortuna Mountain, Kwaay Paay Peak, Pyles Peak and Cowles Mountain. Finish the hike by following the now mercifully mellow trail 0.4 mile to the summit.

Palomar Mountain

Observatory National Recreation Trail

From Observatory Campground to Palomar Observatory is 4 miles round trip from 800-foot elevation gain

Astronomer George Hale will be remembered both for his scientific discoveries and his vision of constructing great observatories. His first vision materialized as the Yerkes Observatory with its 40-inch telescope, his second as Mt. Wilson Observatory with its 60- and 100-inch telescopes, and finally Palomar Observatory with its 200-inch telescope.

The Great Glass at Palomar is the most powerful telescope in America and has greatly increased our knowledge of the heavens. Most visitors traveling to Palomar drive their cars all the way to the top, visit the Observatory and drive back down. Too bad! They miss a nice hike. Observatory Trail roughly parallels the road, but is hidden by dense forest from the sights and sounds of traffic.

Palomar Mountain lacks the distinct cone shape of a stereotypical mountaintop. It soars abruptly up from the San Luis River Valley to the south, but flattens out on top. Atop and just below the long crest, are oak valleys, pine forests, spring-watered grasslands and lush canyons.

Palomar Mountain provides a bird's-eye view of much of Southern California. Miles and miles of mountains roll toward the north, dominated in the distance by peaks of the San Bernardino Mountains. Southward, Mt. Cuyamaca is visible, and even farther south, the mountains of Baja California. On the western horizon, orange sunset rays floodlight the Pacific.

Observatory National Recreation Trail is a delightful introduction to the geography of the Palomar Mountains. It leads from

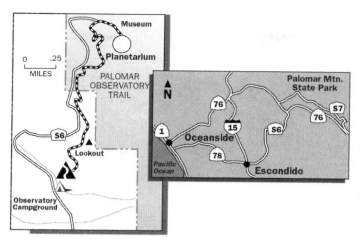

Observatory Campground to the peak, where you can learn about the geography of the heavens.

DIRECTIONS: From Interstate Highway 15 near Fallbrook, exit on Highway 76 and drive 21 miles east. Proceed to Rincon Springs. For a couple of miles, S6 joins with Highway 76. Turn north on S6, forking to the left at South Grade Road and proceeding 9 miles to Observatory Campground and up to the Observatory. Follow the campground loop until you spot the signed trailhead and parking near the amphitheater.

You could just as well hike the Observatory Trail from top to bottom and have a friend with a vehicle meet you at the bottom. To reach the upper trailhead, continue up the road to the Observatory parking area. The upper trailhead is just outside the gates of the Observatory grounds.

THE HIKE: The signed trail begins at the edge of the campground. Begin climbing over wooded slopes and soon get a grand view of Mendenhall Valley. Continue ascending over slopes watered by the headwaters of the San Luis Rey River.

The last part of the trail climbs more abruptly up manzanita-covered slopes. Soon you see the silvery dome of the 200-inch Hale telescope. This obelisk of symmetry and precision dwarfs nearby trees. Ever-changing patterns of sunlight and shade play upon the top of the dome.

Visit the Observatory gallery to see the great telescope. Check out the nearby museum and exhibits that explain some of the mysteries unraveled by the big telescope.

Palomar Mountain State Park

Scott's Cabin Trail

From Silver Crest Picnic Area to Scott's Cabin; Cedar Grove Campground and Boucher Lookout is a 3.5-mile loop with 800-foot elevation gain

Palomar Mountain is a state park for all seasons. Fall offers dramatic color changes, and blustery winter winds ensure far-reaching views from the peaks. In spring, the dogwood blooms, and during summer, when temperatures soar, the park offers a cool, green retreat.

A mixed forest of cedar, silver fir, spruce and black oak invites leisurely exploration. Tall trees and mountain meadows make the park especially attractive to the SoCal hiker in search of a Sierra Nevada-like atmosphere.

Native peoples lived in this lovely area of the Palomars for many hundreds of years.

This day hike is a grande randonnée of the park, a four-trail sampler that leads to a lookout atop 5,438-foot Boucher Hill.

DIRECTIONS: From Interstate 5 in Oceanside, drive northeast on State Highway 76 about 30 miles. Take County Road S6 north; at S7, head northwest to the park entrance. There is a day use fee. Park in the lot at Silver Crest Picnic Area just inside the park.

THE HIKE: A trail sign points the way to Scott's Cabin, 0.5-mile away. Noisome Steller's jays make their presence known along this stretch of trail. Scott's Cabin, built by a homesteader in the 1880s, is found on your left. The crumpled remains aren't much to view.

Descend steeply through a white fir forest and junction Cedar-Doane Trail, which heads right (east). This steep trail, formerly known as the Slide Trail because of its abruptness, takes the hiker

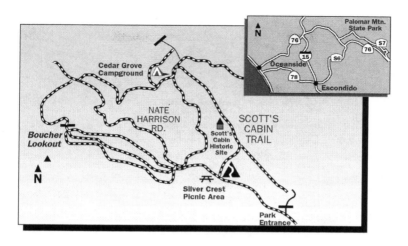

down oak-covered slopes to Doane Pond. The pond is stocked with trout, and fishing is permitted. A pondside picnic area welcomes the hiker.

Continue past the Cedar-Doane Trail junction a short distance to Cedar Grove Campground. Follow trail signs and turn left on the campground road, and then right into the group campground. Look leftward for the signed Adams Trail, which cuts through a bracken fern-covered meadow. Once across the meadow, encounter a small ravine where dogwood blooms during April and May. The trail winds uphill past big cone spruce and reaches Nate Harrison Road, named in honor of Nathan Harrison, a Southern slave who followed his master to the California gold rush—and freedom—in 1849. Harrison had a successful hay-making and hog-raising operation here, despite numerous run-ins with bears and mountain lions.

Across the road, your path becomes Boucher Trail, which ascends a north-facing slope through white fir, then through bracken ferns and black oaks, to the summit of Boucher Hill. Atop the hill is a fire lookout and communication facilities. From the summit, get views of the surrounding lowlands, including Pauma Valley to the west.

Return to the parking area via Oak Ridge Trail, which descends one mile between the two sides of the loop road that encircles Boucher Hill. The trail descends an open ridgeline to a junction of five roads, where it's a mere hop, skip and a jump back to the Silver Crest Picnic Area.

STONEWALL PEAK
STONEWALL PEAK TRAIL

From Paso Picacho Campground to summit is 4 miles round trip with 900- foot elevation gain; Return via California Riding and Hiking Trail, Cold Stream Trail is 5.5 miles round trip.

Rounded Mount Cuyamaca (6,512 feet) is the highest peak in the range, but Stonewall Peak is more prominent. "Old Stony" is about 1,000 feet lower, but its huge walls of granite and crown of stone make it stand out among neighboring peaks.

(In 2003, Cedar Fire devastated the state park, burning black oak and pine forests, grassland and riparian corridors. It was the worst wildfire loss in state park history. However, nature's healing powers are truly miraculous. The park (except for its stands of pine) is recovering in extraordinary fashion.)

Popular Stonewall Peak Trail leads to the top of the peak (5,730 feet) and offers grand views of the old Stonewall Mine Site, Cuy-amaca Valley and desert slopes to the east. An optional route lets you descend to Paso Pichacho Campground via the California Riding and Hiking Trail and the Cold Stream Trail.

DIRECTIONS: From San Diego, drive east on Interstate 8. Exit on Highway 79 north. The highway enters Cuyamaca Rancho State Park and climbs to a saddle between Cuyamaca and Stonewall peaks. Park near the entrance of Paso Picacho Campground. The trail to Stonewall Peak begins just across the highway from the campground.

THE HIKE: From Paso Picacho Campground, the trail ascends moderately, then steeply through oak and boulder country. The black oaks display vivid colors in fall.

The trail switchbacks up the west side of the mountain. From the blackened forest, views from the north unfold. Cuyamaca Reservoir is the most obvious geo-graphical feature.

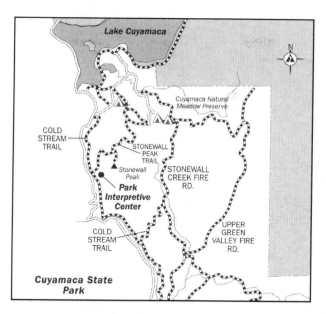

Vegetation grows more sparse and granite outcroppings domi-
nate the high slopes as the trail nears the top of Old Stony. A hundred feet from the summit, a guardrail with steps hacked into the
granite helps you reach the top. Far-reaching vistas east and west
are not possible because a number of close-in mountains block your
view. You can, however, orient yourself to Cuyamaca geography from
atop Stonewall Peak. Major Cuyamaca peaks, from north to south,
are North Peak, Middle Peak and Cuyamaca Peak.

It's exciting to be atop Stonewall Peak when a storm is brewing over
the Cuyamacas, but beware that the peak has been known to catch a
strike or two. Black clouds hurtle at high speed toward the peak.

Return the way you came or via the California Riding and
Hiking Trail by backtracking 100 yards on the Stonewall Peak Trail
to a junction. From here, bear right (north). The trail descends
steeply at first, then levels off near Little Stonewall Peak (5,250 feet).
It then descends moderately to the California Riding and Hiking
Trail, which traverses the west side of the park. Travel for 1 mile on
the CR&H Trail, which is actually part of the Stonewall Peak Trail.
It forks to the right and crosses Highway 79. Don't take the fork,
but continue a half-mile down the Cold Stream Trail, paralleling the
highway, back to Paso Picacho Campground.

CUYAMACA PEAK

CUYAMACA PEAK TRAIL

Paso Picacho Campground to Summit is 7 miles round trip with 1,600-foot elevation gain

Of the more than 100 miles of trails in Cuyamaca Rancho State Park, the route offering the most spectacular views is surely the Cuyamaca Peak Trail, which climbs through a forest of oak, as well as charred pine and fir to the summit. From the 6,512-foot peak, the hiker has an open view from the Pacific to the Salton Sea.

Over the years, many day hikers expressed their surprise to me about discovering such a densely forested mountain in Southern California. Encircling Mount Cuyamaca are silver fir and cedar, plus Coulter, sugar, ponderosa and Jeffrey pine. Or were. Many oaks survived the 2003 Cedar Fire, but the conifers were devastated in the conflagration.

Even before the 2003 fire, the road to Cuyamaca Peak passed through an area that was scorched by severe forest fires in 1950 and 1970. Quite a few tall trees were lost in those blazes, too.

The name Cuyamaca is believed to have been derived from the Native American word *ekui-amak*, variously meaning "rain from above," "rain from behind," and "place beyond rain."

The trail, Cuyamaca Peak Fire Road, is a paved one-lane road (closed to public vehicle traffic) that winds slowly to the summit. While this guide and its author generally avoid pavement like the plague, an exception has been made for this road; it offers a most enjoyable hike and a memorable view. One view is of a park, of a mountain range, making an amazing recovery from the effects of wildfire.

DIRECTIONS: You may begin this hike from two places, neither of which has good parking. The Cuyamaca Peak Fire Road

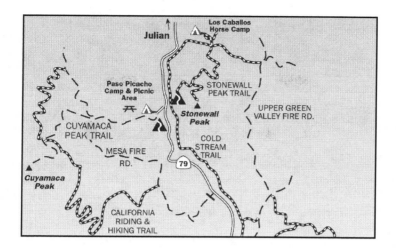

intersects Highway 79 just south of the park interpretive center. Look for a legal place to park along Highway 79. Or you can pick up the trail at the southernmost campsites in Paso Picacho Campground. There's a state park day use fee.

THE HIKE: The ascent, shaded by oaks, is moderate at first. Look over your shoulder for a fine view of Stonewall Peak. After passing the junction with the California Riding and Hiking Trail, the route grows steeper. Pine and fir predominate high on the mountain's shoulders.

Just about at the halfway point, the road levels out for a short distance and you'll spot Deer Spring on the left (south) side of the road. Near the top, better and better views of Cuyamaca Reservoir and the desert are yours.

The road veers suddenly south, passes junctions with Conejos Trail and Burnt Pine Fire Road, and arrives at the summit.

The peak, located nearly in the exact center of San Diego County, provides quite a panorama, including the Santa Rosa and Laguna mountains. You can look across the desert into Mexico and westward over to Point Loma, the Silver Strand and the wide Pacific. Atop Mount Palomar, the white observatory can be seen sparkling in the distance.

Return the same way, or perhaps improvise a return route back to Paso Picacho Campground via the California Riding and Hiking Trail and the Azalea Glen Trail.

The air and water temperatures are Mediterranean, the place names Spanish, and the hiking, once you escape the mass-use beaches, is excellent. The SoCal offers not only those white sand beaches depicted on postcards, but a wide variety of shoreline features—the palms of La Jolla and Santa Monica, the cliffs and bluffs of Torrey Pines, San Clemente, Palos Verdes and Malibu.

Each of the Southland's five coastal counties—San Diego, Orange, Los Angeles, Ventura and Santa Barbara—has its own character. And each individual beach seems to have its own personality: best surfing, clearest water, grandest panoramic view or most birdlife.

CHAPTER 11

SOUTHERN CALIFORNIA COAST

HIKE ON.

CABRILLO NATIONAL MONUMENT

BAYSIDE TRAIL

From Old Point Loma Lighthouse to Monument boundary is 2 miles round trip

Cabrillo National Monument, located on the tip of Point Loma, marks the point where Portuguese navigator Juan Rodriguez Cabrillo became the first European to set foot on California soil. He landed near Ballast Point in 1542 and claimed San Diego Bay for Spain.

Cabrillo liked this "closed and very good port" and said so in his report to the King of Spain. Turns out the explorer landed on what is now the most southwesterly spot in the contiguous United States.

As for Cabrillo himself, little is known. Historians do not know for certain where he was born or what he looked like. Cabrillo National Monument itself is historic. Created it 1913, it's one of the oldest national parklands and predates the founding of the National Park Service in 1916.

One highlight of a visit to the national monument is the Old Point Loma Lighthouse. This lighthouse, built by the federal government, first shined its beacon over bay and ocean in 1855. Unfortunately the lighthouse was built at 422 feet above sea level; fog and low clouds often obscured the light. The station was abandoned in 1891 and a new one was built on lower ground at the tip of Point Loma.

The older lighthouse has been wonderfully restored to the way it looked when Captain Israel and his family lived there in the 1880s. Park staff leads walks and give talks to explain the lighthouse's colorful history.

The 1891 lighthouse is still in service today, operated by the U.S. Coast Guard. Check out the "New" Point Loma Lighthouse from Whale Overlook, located 100 yards south of Old Point Loma Lighthouse.

Rangers lead walks (at low tides) to the rich tide pools located on the western side of Point Loma. Check on the tides and walk schedule at the park visitor center, where you can learn more about lighthouses and marvel how Cabrillo made his way here with 16th century navigational instruments.

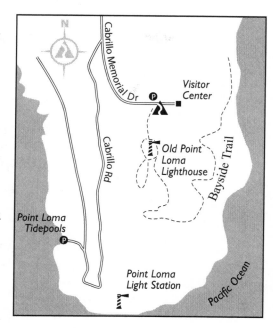

Bayside Trail begins at the old lighthouse and winds past yucca and prickly pear, sage and buckwheat. The Monument protects one of the last patches of native flora in southernmost California, a hint at how San Diego Bay may have looked when Cabrillo's two small ships anchored here.

DIRECTIONS: Exit Interstate 5 on Rosecrans Street (Highway 209 south) and follow the signs to Cabrillo National Monument.

THE HIKE: From the visitor center parking lot, walk across the road and up the walkway toward Old Point Loma Lighthouse. The first part of Bayside Trail winding down from the old lighthouse is a paved road. At a barricade, bear left on a gravel road, once a military patrol road. During World War II, the Navy hid bunkers and searchlights along these coastal bluffs.

Bayside Trail provides fine views of the San Diego Harbor shipping lanes. Sometimes when ships pass, park rangers broadcast descriptions of the vessels.

Also along the trail is one of Southern California's most popular panoramic views: miles of seashore, 6,000-foot mountains to the east and Mexico to the south.

The trail dead-ends at the park boundary. Return the way you came.

Sunset Cliffs Natural Park

Sunset Cliffs Trail

From Sunset Cliffs Blvd to Sunset Cliffs Park is 3.6 miles round trip

Sunset Cliffs, on the ocean side of Point Loma, are projections of sculpted sandstone, that frame small pocket beaches. Sunset fans marvel at the brilliant light reflecting off golden cliffs, which extend south from Ocean Beach.

Sunset Cliffs Natural Park attracts plenty of regulars and repeat sunset-viewers, friendly folks happy to help first-timers locate the tide pools, hidden grottos, and the best photo ops. Quantity and quality of sunset photos posted on social media is amazing.

(A less obvious reason for the cliffs considerable popularity is that the other nearby sunset-viewing venue, Cabrillo National Monument, usually closes before sunset.)

A long and narrow block of sandstone uplifted some 400 feet above sea level by fault action from long ago, Point Loma forms a kind of natural breakwater between the ocean and the bay behind it. Cliff erosion is severe here and elaborate bulwarks designed to dissipate the relentless energy of the waves have been constructed to keep the shoreline road from being undermined.

Sketchy trails lead along the edge of the Sunset Cliffs, providing a bird's-eye view of the surfing action below and grand vistas of the coastline. The park includes hillsides above the coast and below the campus of Point Loma Nazarene University.

Access the beach by hiking down paths of varying quality through fissures and narrow openings in the cliffs. Or relax on the occasional bench, strategically placed for your sunset-gazing pleasure. Watch for gulls, great blue herons, and a multitude of seabirds. And for daredevil young adults who, heedless of the many cliff-edge warning signs, jump, indeed somersault, into the water.

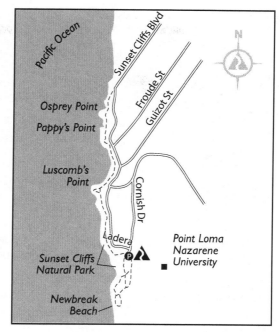

After you enjoy this wonderful walk, partake of post sunset hike refreshment just north in Ocean Beach, which offers a generous assortment of bars, coffee houses and cafés.

DIRECTIONS:
From its junction with I-5 (San Diego Freeway) in San Diego, follow I-8 (Ocean Beach Freeway) 2 miles west to its end. Turn left on Sunset Cliffs Boulevard and drive 2.5 miles to Ladera Street and parking in a dirt lot two blocks up from shore at Ladera and Corning Streets.

THE HIKE: Before joining the coastal trail, enjoy the northern section of the park, which is perched above Newbreak Beach and below the university. Wander the paths amidst eucalyptus trees. Their blue and white foliage, peeling bark and wild fragrance get your hike off to a good start.

Next, from near the point where Sunset Cliffs Drive ends at Ladera, head north on the blufftop paths. Luscomb's Point is an intriguing assemblage of beaches, caves and arches. Continue along severely eroded cliffs past Ross Rock to "The Arch," a sandstone formation that arcs over the water at Pappy's Point. A cove here is the scene of illegal cliff-diving.

Gaze out at rocks well-populated by birds as you make your way to Osprey Point and trail's end near an oceanfront parking lot.

Mission Bay

Mission Bay Trail

From Kendall Frost Marsh to Sail Bay and Belmont Park is 2 to 6 miles round trip

Sail Bay, Fiesta Bay, Vacation Island and Paradise Island.

Is this place named for fun or what?

Fun comes in many forms around Mission Bay: swimming, sailing, water-skiing and cycling.

And the walking is pretty good, too. Observe scores of resident and migratory waterfowl as well as SoCal beach culture to the max from beaches and walkways along Mission Bay's west side.

In the early 1960s, the city of San Diego transformed what was a seriously degraded marshland into a world-class resort area by constructing waterfront hotels, marinas and Mission Bay City Park, said to be the largest aquatic park in the world. About 25 percent of the 4,235-acre park, including famed Sea World, is used for commercial enterprises. The balance, including more than 27 miles of shoreline of which 19 are sandy beaches, is for public use.

My favorite Mission Bay walk begins at the Kendall-Frost Mission Bay Marsh Preserve, an environment of cordgrass and pickleweed that hints at how the whole bay may have appeared a hundred years ago. From the preserve, beach trails and the Bayside Walk lead into ever-more developed terrain, but definitely fun in its own way.

DIRECTIONS: From Interstate 5 in San Diego, exit on Clairemont Drive. The Visitor Information Center is just west of the freeway. Follow East Mission Bay Drive, then Mission Bay Drive north to Grand Avenue, bearing left (west). Turn left onto Lamont Street and drive to the bay shore at Crown Point Drive. Park in the large lot. Your bay walk adventure begins at the far (east) end of the Crown Point Drive parking lot.

THE HIKE: From the east end of the lot by Kendall-Frost Marsh Reserve, head southwest along the shell-strewn sand beach, passing water-ski take-off and landing areas. The beach, Crown Point Shores, is known for its annual sand castle building contest.

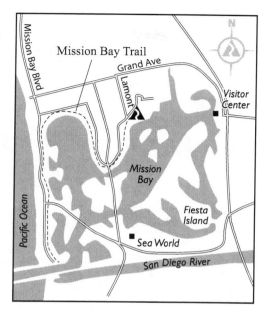

Your beach path passes below the Ingraham Street overpass leading to Vacation Island, and rounds Crown Point. On the far side of the point, check out the low eroded cliffs and the old (200,000 years by some estimates) sand dollars poking out of them.

Continue up the beach, known as Riviera Shores here and follow horseshoe-shaped Sail Bay. Bay Walk begins at Riviera Shores and offers a paved, parallel alternative to beach walking. As you walk south, pass two distinct points—Santa Clara and El Carmel—with a fine sandy beach located between them.

At Mission Bay Drive, reach Belmont Park, a historic oceanfront amusement park that opened in 1925. Rides and attractions that remain from the park's earliest days include Giant Dipper, a wooden rollercoaster, and The Plunge, an indoor swimming pool.

A good place to relax is atop the grassy hillside of Bonita Cove Park. To extend your walk, continue a mile along Bayside Walk to the entrance channel to Mission Bay. For a change of pace, walk the first 2 miles of your return trip along Mission Beach.

TORREY PINES STATE RESERVE

PARRY GROVE, GUY FLEMING, DEL MAR BEACH TRAILS

From 0.4 to 1 mile nature trails; to Del Mar Beach is 6 miles round trip

Atop the bluffs of Torrey Pines State Reserve lies a microcosm of old California, a garden of shrubs and succulents.

Most visitors come to view the 3,000 or so *Pinus torreyana*, which grow only here and on Santa Rosa Island, but the reserve also offers the walker a striking variety of native plants. Be sure to check out the interpretive displays at the park museum and the native plant garden near the head of the Parry Grove Trail. Plant and bird lists, as well as wildflower maps (February through June) are available for a small fee.

Parry Grove Trail was named in honor of Dr. C.C. Parry, a botanist assigned to the boundary commission that surveyed the Mexican-American border in 1850. Parry investigated a tree called the Soledad (Spanish for "solitude") pine and sent samples to his teacher and friend, Dr. John Torrey of Columbia. Parry requested that, if it proved to be a new species, it be named for Torrey. The Soledad pine became Pinus torreyana, or Torrey pine, in honor of the famous botanist and taxonomist.

The 0.4-mile-loop trail leads past toyon, yucca, and many other coastal shrubs. Alas, a long drought followed by an infestation of the Five Spined Engraver beetle devastated Parry Grove.

Broken Hill Trail visits a drier, chaparral-dominated landscape, full of sage, ceanothus and manzanita. From Broken Hill Overlook, view of Torrey pines clinging to life in an environment that resembles a desert badlands.

Guy Fleming Trail is a 0.6-mile-loop that travels through stands of Torrey pine and leads to South Overlook, where you might glimpse a migrating California gray whale.

For a fine adventure, take Beach Trail to Torrey Pines State Beach and hike up-coast to Del Mar.

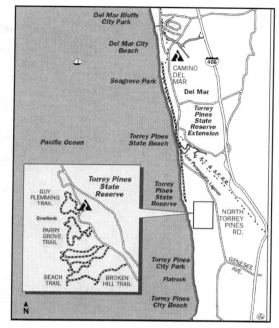

DIRECTIONS: From Interstate 5, exit on Carmel Valley Road and head west to North Torrey Pines Road (also known as old Highway 101). Carmel Valley Road dead-ends at a T; turn left (south) on North Torrey Pines Road. The main entrance to the reserve is at the base of the bluffs, where the park road climbs to a parking area near the reserve visitor center. You can also leave your car along the highway next to Torrey Pines State Beach and walk up the reserve road.

THE HIKE: Beach Trail leads to Yucca Point and Razor Point and offers precipitous views of the beach below. The trail descends the bluffs to Flat Rock, a fine tidepool area.

Hike up-coast along Torrey Pines State Beach a mile to South Beach and the Reserve entrance. Another 0.5 mile of travel takes you to Los Penasquitos Lagoon, a saltwater marsh patrolled by native and migratory waterfowl, and to a picnic area across the S21 highway bridge on the north side of the marsh.

Continue along the beach between the pounding breakers and high cliffs to downtown Del Mar, the train station or as far as time and tides permit.

SAN CLEMENTE STATE BEACH

TRESTLES TRAIL

From State Beach to San Mateo Point is 3 miles round trip

"Our beach shall always be free from hurdy-gurdies and defile-ment. We believe beauty to be an asset as well as gold and silver, or cabbage and potatoes."

This was the pledge of Norwegian immigrant Ole Hanson, who began the town of San Clemente in 1925. It was quite a promise from a real estate developer, quite a promise in those days of shame-less boosterism a half-century before the California Coastal Com-mission was established.

Thanks in part to Hanson's vision, some of the peaceful ambi-ance of San Clemente, which he regarded as "a painting 5 miles long and a mile wide" has been preserved.

A great shore to walk, San Clemente State Beach is mercifully walled off from the din of the San Diego Freeway and the rest of the modern world by a handsome line of tan-colored bluffs. Only the occasional train passing over tracks located near the shore interrupt the cry of the gull and the roar of the breakers.

At the north end of the beach, wind- and water-sculpted marine terraces resemble Bryce Canyon in miniature. The trestles located at the south end of the beach at San Mateo Point give Trestles Beach its name. Trestles is one of the finest surfing areas on the west coast. When the surf is up, the waves peel rapidly across San Mateo Point (the boundary line between Orange and San Diego counties), creat-ing a great ride. From Trestles, you can continue several miles south to San Onofre State Beach.

You can begin this hike from the state beach day-use area. Look for two signed trails that lead to the beach. Or begin from Calafia

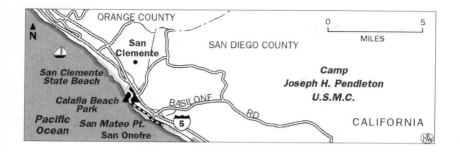

Beach Park, cross the railroad tracks and make your way down an embankment to the beach.

DIRECTIONS: Southbound on the San Diego Freeway (5) in San Clemente, exit on Avenida Calafia and head west very briefly to the entrance of San Clemente State Beach (day use fee) or 0.5 mile to Calafia Beach Park (metered parking). Northbound on I-5, exit at Cristianitos Road, turn left, go over the freeway onto Ave. Del Presidente and drive north to the parks.

THE HIKE: Head south on San Clemente State Beach, frequented by plenty of shorebirds, surfers, body surfers, and swimmers.

At distinct San Mateo Point, find San Mateo Creek. Rushes, saltgrass and cattails line the creek mouth, where sandpipers, herons and egrets gather.

You can usually safely ford the creek mouth (except after winter storms) and continue south several more miles toward San Onofre State Beach.

For an alternate return route: Walk under the train trestles and ascend the park service road up the bluffs, to join San Clemente Coastal Bike Trail. Walk through a residential area to an entrance to San Clemente State Beach Campground, improvise a route through the camp to the park's entry station. Join the nature trail on a descent through a prickly pear- and lemonade berry-filled draw to Calafia Beach Park.

Crystal Cove Beach and Bluffs

Bluff Trail

From Reef Point to Pelican Point is 4 miles round trip (with shorter and longer options)

Between the Pacific Coast Highway and the wide blue Pacific, and between Laguna Beach and Newport Beach, lie the beautiful blufftops of Crystal Cove State Park.

A paved, multi-use path extends along most of the 3.2-mile length of the bluffs.

Eight connector trails—dirt and paved ones as well as a boardwalk—invite the hiker to leave the main route (Bluff Trail) and explore tide pools, rocky coves and sand strands.

Be sure to detour from Bluff Trail through Los Trancos Canyon to the Crystal Cove Historic District and view the funky 1930s to 1950s-era wood-frame beach houses.

In 1979, California State Parks acquired the Crystal Cove area as parkland, and the little houses as well. Several cottages have been renovated, frozen in time with vintage furnishings and historical details. Since mid-2006 they've been in high demand as vacation getaways. The Beachcomber Café is also located here.

At low tide, the beach is passable; you can hike the bluffs oneway and the beach the other. This beach attracts its share of surfers, swimmers and sun-bathers but still gives the feeling of being away from it all.

DIRECTIONS: Crystal Cove State Park's Reef Point entrance is located off Pacific Coast Highway, three miles north of Laguna Canyon Road in Laguna Beach and 3.5 miles south of MacArthur Boulevard in Newport Beach.

THE HIKE: Walk up-coast on the Bluff Trail. Note the stairway that descends to popular Scotchman's Cove. The Reef Point area is a

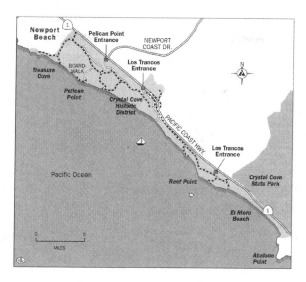

native plant-lover's paradise. Saltbush, toyon, buck- wheat, California sagebrush, mulefat, coast prickly pear, deer weed, lemonadeberry, coyote bush… Of course, plenty of non-natives cling to the bluff tops, too, including scads of ice plant, Australian salt bush and mustard.

Bluff Trail travels (too) close to PCH and delivers you to the counter of the Shake Shack, located on the bluffs above Crystal Cove. This roadside refreshment stand has been a landmark to locals and coastal travelers since 1945; now it's Ruby's Shake Shack offering great shakes like the Monkey Flip and the same menu as the restaurant chain. Parking is scarce…ah, it's great to be a hiker.

A bit beyond the Shake Shack, look for the service road that descends to Crystal Cove Historic District. Walk past the cottages and across Crystal Cove, a very pretty place; however, it's not a cove or coastal indentation of any kind here. Certainly it's no more crystal-line- appearing than any other Southland beach.

Back on Bluff Trail, the hiker is soon tempted with more trails leading down to Crystal Cove and a boardwalk descending to Pelican Point. Continue to the edge of the blufftops at the park boundary and curve coastward to join View Point Path. Enjoy vistas from above Little Treasure Cove and Treasure Cove.

Return to Reef Point the way you came or via the beach. (To extend your walk from Reef Point, descend the bluffs on a steep path leading to Scotchman's Cove. Head down-coast along El Moro Beach.)

269

HUNTINGTON AND BOLSA CHICA

HUNTINGTON BEACH TRAIL

From Huntington State Beach to Bolsa Chica State Beach is 6 miles round trip; to Bolsa Chica north boundary is 7.5 miles one way

Huntington and Bolsa Chica are the perfect locations for a beach party. They're wide and long, and dotted with numerous fire pits for summertime fun long after the sun has set. The state beaches (with Huntington City Beach sandwiched in the middle) extend some 9 miles along northern Orange County's coast, from the Santa Ana River to just-short of the San Gabriel River.

In many ways, Huntington/Bolsa Chica has always been a kind of blue-collar beach. Until Bolsa Chica beach came under state control in 1961, nobody did much to keep the beach clean—hence its once-popular name of Tin Can Beach. Despite a couple of boutiqued blocks where Main Street meets the shore, and upscale subdivisions more in keeping with OC inland 'burbs, Huntington Beach still has rough edges, including bad-boy surfers and shoulder-to-shoulder oil wells.

Before Huntington Beach received its present name, the long shoreline was a popular camping spot. Millions of small clams were washed up on its sands and old timers called it Shell Beach. In 1901 a town was laid out with the name of Pacific City, in hopes it would rival Atlantic City. In 1902, Henry E. Huntington, owner of the Pacific Electric Railroad, bought a controlling interest and renamed the city after himself. Today, though, it's known by the officially trademarked name, "Surf City USA.™"

This hike takes you north along wide sandy Huntington State Beach to Bolsa Chica State Beach and adjacent Bolsa Chica

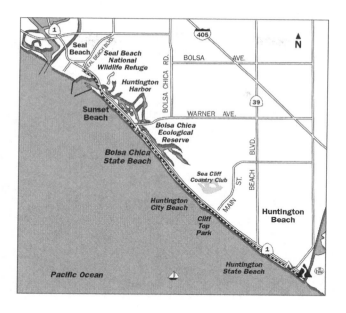

Ecological Reserve. You can also make this a one-way jaunt by taking advantage of OCTD Bus #1 which makes several stops along Pacific Coast Highway.

This is an ideal beach trail to bike and hike. A bike path extends the length of Bolsa Chica Beach to the Santa Ana River south of Huntington Beach. You can leave your bike at Bolsa Chica State Beach and hike up to it from Huntington Beach.

DIRECTIONS: From the San Diego Freeway (405) in Huntington Beach, exit on Beach Boulevard and travel 5.5 miles south to the boulevard's end at Huntington State Beach.

THE HIKE: Walk north along the northernmost mile of the three-mile- long sandy state beach. The state beach blends into Huntington City Beach just before the pier. The beach is best known as the site of international surfing competition. The 1,800-foot Huntington Pier was built in 1914.

Beyond the pier is Bolsa Chica State Beach, The southern end has steep cliffs rising between Pacific Coast Highway and the beach. Huntington Beach Mesa or "The Cliffs" is popular with surfers and oil well drillers.

The northern three miles of the beach packs in all the facilities: showers, food concessions, picnic areas and more.

271

Long Beach
Long Beach Trail

From Aquarium of the Pacific to Long Beach City Beach is 3 miles round trip; to Belmont Pier is 6 miles round trip; to Alamitos Bay is 10 miles round trip

You won't be bored on this beach hike! The Aquarium of the Pacific and nearby waterfront attractions, plus long and sandy Long Beach add up to plenty of natural and cultural sights-to-see.

The aquarium is a must-see, a collection of more than 11,000 creatures in tanks and exhibits that introduce visitors to the special life and seascapes of the Pacific, as well as the particular conservation challenges this ocean.

The first length of this shoreline saunter delivers various views of the Queen Mary, at one time the largest passenger liner ever built. Once past Shoreline Village and the city marina, you'll hit the beach and walk along water's edge.

You can take a very long walk along Long Beach; the strand is very long—and wide. Long Beach City Beach extends nearly 5 miles from the city's downtown marina to Alamitos Bay. The beach, 100 yards wide in places, offers some of the most gentle ocean swimming in Southern California.

Near the aquarium, a walkway leads around Rainbow Harbor to a point with a model lighthouse and interpretive panels that tell of the Pike, the naval shipyard and other tales from Long Beach's long and colorful history. Great views, too!

Those preferring a one-way walk along Long Beach, can arrange return transport by making use of the AquaBus Water Taxi or AquaLink for a ride on the waterways.

DIRECTIONS: Head south on the Long Beach Freeway (710) to its end and follow the Downtown Long Beach/Aquarium signs.

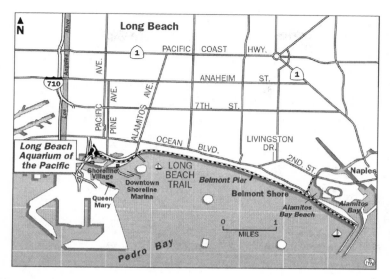

The signs lead you onto Shoreline Drive and to the Aquarium's multi-level, 1,500-vehicle parking structure on the right.

THE HIKE: From the aquarium, join the beige- and brown-brick path along Rainbow Harbor. You'll pass an display about the Transpacific (Long Beach to Honolulu) yacht race. The promenade leads by the pedestrian overpass that links the convention center to the waterfront and passes Shoreline Village, a waterside shopping center.

Continue 0.5 mile or so down-coast along the inland side of the marina to a second breakwater, beach volleyball courts and the beginning of Long Beach City beach.

Walk along the wide sandy beach. In summer, pass brigades of beach-goers; in winter, the walk is a more tranquil one, often in the company of curlews, godwits, sandpipers and other shorebirds.

Cross into the trendy Belmont Shores and reach the 1,620-foot long Belmont Pier. From the pier, walk a mile to the foot of Bay Shore Avenue. For a fun side trip, follow the avenue a mile around the horseshoe of Alamitos Bay to Appian Way Bridge and Naples, a residential community of three islands separated by canals.

To complete the Long Beach walk, head out onto Alamitos Peninsula, which extends from 54th Place to the entrance channel of Alamitos Bay. Stick with the sandy and rocky beach or join Bay Shore Walk, a public walkway that extends along the bay from 55th to 65th Place.

PALOS VERDES PENINSULA

PALOS VERDES PENINSULA TRAIL

From Malaga Cove to *Dominator* is 4 miles round trip

Palos Verdes Peninsula, famed for its rocky cliffs rising from 50 to 300 feet above the ocean and for its 13 wave-cut terraces is quite a contrast to the stereotypical Southland shoreline of sandy beaches.

Offshore, divers explore the rocky bottoms for abalone and shellfish. Onshore, hikers enjoy wave-scalloped bluffs, rocky shores and splendid tidepools.

Many sojourners are drawn to PV's shores by a shipwreck. On March 13, 1961, the *Dominator*, an old radar-less WWII ship, bound from Vancouver for Algiers with a cargo of wheat, ran aground on a reef 100 yards offshore from Rocky Point while searching for the San Pedro Harbor entrance in the fog.

After more than a half century not much is left of the wave-battered ship's exoskeleton. What remains is a tractor-like hoisting device with gears and large hook as well as two sections of rusted orange hull.

Reach the shipwreck by hiking (at low tide) 2 miles along the rocky Palo Verdes shoreline. Trek over a surface resembling broken bowling balls under tall cliffs, and visit abundant tide pools before arriving at the wreckage, strewn over a couple hundred yards of coastline.

DIRECTIONS: Take Pacific Coast Highway to Palos Verdes Boulevard. Bear right on Palos Verdes Drive. Near Malaga Cove Plaza, turn right at the first stop sign (Via Corta). Make a right on Via Arroyo, then another right into the parking lot behind the Malaga Cove School. The trailhead is on the ocean side of the parking area where a wide path descends the bluffs above the Flat Rock Point tide pools. A footpath leaves from Paseo Del Mar, 0.1 mile past Via Horcada, where the street curves east to join Palos Verdes Drive West.

THE HIKE:

Descend the wide path to the beach. At several places along this walk note where the coastal terraces are cut by steep-walled canyons. The first of these canyon incisions can be observed at Malaga Cove, where Malaga Canyon slices through the north slopes of Palos Verdes Hills, then cuts west to empty at the cove.

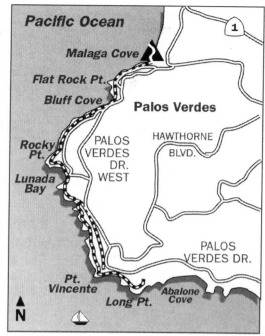

The coastline curves in a southwesterly direction and Flat Rock Point comes into view. Jade-colored waters swirl around the anvil-shaped point, creating great conditions for the rich tide pools here. Above the point, the cliffs soar to 300 feet.

Rounding Flat Rock Point, pick your way among the rocks, seaweed and the flotsam and jetsam of civilization to Bluff Cove, where sparkling combers explode against the rocks and douse the unwary with their tangy spray. Enjoy views of Santa Monica Bay, the Santa Monica Mountains in gray silhouette and on the far horizon, the Channel Islands.

A mile beyond Bluff Cove, Rocky (also called Palos Verdes) Point juts out like a ship's prow. Hike to the rusted remains of the Greek freighter *Dominator*, a victim of the treacherous reef surrounding PV Peninsula.

You can continue your trek (3 more miles) on rocky shore around Rocky Point to horseshoe-shaped Lunada Bay, and around Resort Point to Point Vincente.

SANTA MONICA BAY

CALIFORNIA COASTAL TRAIL

From Torrance to Santa Monica Pier is 20 miles one way

Fringed by palm trees, with the Santa Monica Mountains as dramatic backdrop, the wide sandy beaches along Santa Monica Bay draw visitors from around the world.

Locals tend to get a bit blasé about this beauty in their backyard, and often fail to take advantage of what is, in my opinion, one of the world's great beach walks.

Favorite bay walks enjoyed by tourists include Venice Beach and the Venice Boardwalk, the Santa Monica Pier and Palisades Park in Santa Monica. These are pleasant enough excursions, but I would suggest something more ambitious: a walk around the entire bay.

Such a hike will surely be a very long day—or a weekend—to remember. You'll get a real feel for the bay, not only as a collection of beaches and seashore sights, but as a living, dynamic ecosystem whose health and well-being depends heavily on government and citizen action.

Geographically, Santa Monica Bay is a mellow intrusion by the Pacific Ocean into the western edge of the Los Angeles lowlands. The bay's magnificent curving beaches are cooled by a prevailing ocean breeze, which protects the coast from the temperature extremes—and smog—that are characteristic of the interior.

Alas, all views along Santa Monica Bay are not picture-perfect; huge smokestacks from power plants tower over some South Bay beaches, while jets departing LAX fly low and loud over others. And the bay has its share of well-documented environmental problems, too. Sewers and storm drains empty into the bay. Organizations such as Heal the Bay have undertaken the Herculean task of educating the

public and public offi-
cials that the bay is not
merely a series of sand
strands, but a complex
ecosystem.

Pick a brisk fall
or winter weekend to
walk the bay and you'll
be surprised at how
much shoreline solitude
you'll enjoy. It's possible
to walk the bay from
Torrance to the Santa
Monica Pier in a very
long day, but the 20-
mile beach hike is more
comfortably completed
in two days.

If bay-walking
agrees with you, con-
sider walking the rest
of the bay—another 20
miles from the Santa
Monica Pier to Pt.
Dume.

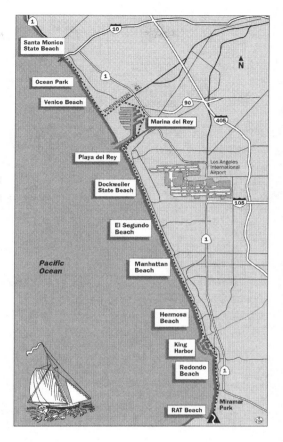

Arrange a car shuttle or use the bus system to return to your
day's start point. Better yet, leave a bicycle at the end of your walk
and cycle back to the trailhead along the South Bay Bicycle Trail.
Super-jocks will relish the challenge of what I call the Triathlon Trail:
Walk the 20 miles from Torrance County Beach to the Santa Monica
Pier, cycle the South Bay Bicycle Trail, then take a long refreshing
swim.

Malibu Beach

Malibu Beach Trail

1 mile round trip around Malibu Lagoon, to Malibu Pier; 4 to 6 miles round trip up-coast

When Southern California natives say "Malibu Beach," this popular surfing spot is what they mean. Immortalized in 1960s-era beach-blanket movies and Beach Boys songs, it is today a great place to hang. The state beach—formerly known as Surfrider—is a mixture of sand and stone. More than 200 bird species have been observed at Malibu Lagoon.

For Frederick Hastings Rindge, owner of 22 miles of Southern California coast, life in the Malibu of a century ago was divine. "The enobling stillness makes the mind ascend to heaven," he wrote in his memoir, *Happy Days in Southern California*, published in 1898.

Long before Malibu meant good surfing, a movie star colony and some of the most expensive real estate on earth, "The Malibu" was a shorthand name for Topanga-Malibu-Sequit, an early 19th-century rancho. This rancho extended from Topanga Canyon to the southeast to Ventura County on the northwest, from the tideline to the crest of the Santa Monica Mountains.

Malibu Lagoon hosts many different kinds of waterfowl, both resident and migratory. The beach is rock cobble on the ocean side of the lagoon. To the land- ward side of the lagoon stretches the alluvial fill flatland deposited by Malibu Creek. The city of Malibu is situated here.

This beach hike is best done at low tide. And please respect the privacy of the beachside homeowners.

DIRECTIONS: Malibu Lagoon State Beach is located at Pacific Coast Highway and Cross Creek Road in Malibu.

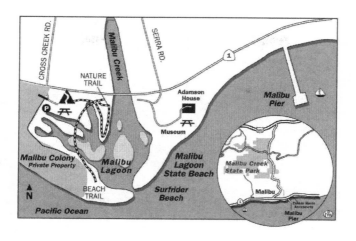

THE HIKE: First follow the nature trails around the lagoon. Next, head down-coast to the historic 700-foot Malibu Pier, built in 1903. It's a favorite of anglers and tourists.

Farther down-coast is Zonker Harris Accessway, long the focus of debate between the California Coastal Commission, determined to provide access to the coast, and some Malibu residents who would prefer the public stay out. The original sign read "Zonker Harris Memorial Beach," honoring a character from the Doonesbury comic strip whose primary goal once was to acquire the perfect tan.

Up-coast, you'll pass Malibu Point; here the strong southwest swell refracts against a rock reef and creates the waves that makes Malibu so popular with surfers. Next you walk the narrow and sandy beach lined by the exclusive Malibu Colony residences, home to many a movie star. Toward the west end of The Colony, the beach narrows considerably and houses are built on stilts, with the waves sometimes pounding beneath them.

As you walk along Malibu Beach, rejoice that you do not see State Highway 60, the Malibu Freeway. In the 1960s a plan was hatched to build a causeway along Malibu Beach, supported on pilings offshore. A breakwater would have converted the open shore into a bay shore. The wonderful pounding surf would have been reduced to that of a lake.

The beach is wider and more public at Corral State Beach, located at the mouths of Corral and Solstice Canyons.

Point Dume

Zuma-Dume Trail

From Zuma Beach to Point Dume is 1 mile round trip; to Paradise Cove is 3 miles round trip

Point Dume State Beach packs an astonishing number of natural features into 63-acres located at the northern end of Santa Monica Bay: rich tide pools, dunes, a terrific vista point for whale-watching, an intact and diverse coastal scrub community, and, this being Malibu, a beach that's starred in many motion pictures.

More than half the beach is designated Point Dume State Preserve in recognition of its ecological significance and the need to afford it a high level of protection. Protected it is, but accessible as well: 2 miles of trail crisscross the point.

During whale-watching season (December through March), visitors ascending to the lookout atop Point Dume have a good chance of spotting a migrating California gray whale. The creatures swim rather close to the point, as do dolphins, harbor seals and sea lions.

A rocky triangle projecting into the Pacific, Point Dume includes dense black Zuma volcanics and the much softer white sedimentary beds of the sea cliffs. The volcanics have resisted the crashing sea far better than the sedimentary rock and have protected the land behind from further erosion, thus forming the triangle shape of the point.

Hike to the point from Zuma Beach, one of the finest white sand strands in California, lies on the open coast beyond Santa Monica Bay and thus receives heavy breakers crashing in from the north. From sunrise to sunset, board and body surfers try to catch a big one.

DIRECTIONS: From Pacific Coast Highway, about 18 miles up-coast from Santa Monica and just down-coast from Zuma Beach

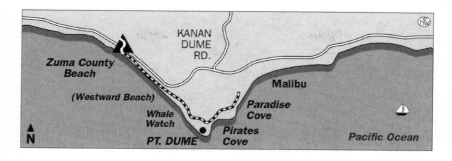

County Park, turn oceanward on Westward Beach Road. There's limited parking along the road (free); or drive to its end at a convenient and (fee) parking lot.

THE HIKE: Head down-coast along sandy Zuma (aka Westward) Beach and look for a distinct path leading up the point. The trail ascends amidst sea fig and sage, coreopsis and prickly pear cactus to a lookout point.

From atop Point Dume, view Pirate's Cove, 200 yards of beach located on the west side of the point and tucked away between two rocky outcroppings. In decades past, this beach was the scene of much dispute between nude beach advocates, residents and the county sheriff.

Memorable scenes in the old Planet of the Apes flicks (remember the Statue of Liberty buried in the sand?) were filmed at Pirate's Cove and at Westward Beach. Many TV and movie productions make use of the beaches around the point.

Retrace your steps a short distance and continue on the trail over the point. Take the stairway down to the beach located east of the point.

It it's low tide, check out the extensive tide pools and abundant marine life: urchins, anemones, crabs and sea stars in several colors.

A mile of beach-walking leads to secluded Paradise Cove, the scene of much television and motion picture filming. The Sand Castle restaurant and a private pier are located at the cove.

McGrath State Beach

McGrath Beach Trail

From State Beach to McGrath Lake is 4 miles round trip; to Oxnard Shores is 8 miles round trip; to Channel Islands Harbor is 12 miles round trip

McGrath State Beach in Ventura County gets a lot of use. About 130,000 visitors a year come to camp, surf, fish, hike and bird-watch.

The 2-mile long beach has faced difficult challenges in recent years: first, funding (the park's antiquated plumbing needed replacement and there was no money available to fix it). Then after a cooperative effort by government and private citizens secured funding, the park had to cope with flooding. After a very dry year, the Santa Clara River lacked the flow necessary to knock out the sand berms that annually build up at its mouth. Consequently the river overflowed its low banks and flooded the park, which was closed

On this hike, walk the edge of 3 watery environments: Santa Clara Estuary Natural Preserve, McGrath Lake, and along the Pacific shore. The variety of habitat attracts more than 200 species of birds, including black-shouldered kites, northern harriers, owls and herons. A great park for bird-watching!

Begin on a nature trail through the Santa Clara River Estuary and travel miles of sandy beach to Channel Islands Harbor. (Check on status of McGrath State Beach; if it's closed, consider beginning this hike at Oxnard Shores.)

DIRECTIONS: From Highway 101 southbound, take the Seaward Avenue off-ramp to Harbor Boulevard, turn south, and travel 4 miles to the park. From Highway 101 northbound, exit on Victoria Avenue, turn left at the light to Olivas Park Drive, and right to Harbor Boulevard. Turn left on Harbor and proceed 0.7 mile to the park. The signed nature trail leaves from the day use parking lot.

THE HIKE: Follow the nature trail through the estuary. The riverbank is a mass of lush vegetation: willow, silverweed and yerba mansa. (If the beach is not accessible via the estuary and a trail that leads atop an old levee, head for higher and drier ground and just tramp over the low dunes to the shoreline.)

However you get to the beach, head down-coast. Pass sunbathers and surf fishermen and, about 2 miles out, head inland a short distance, to observe McGrath Lake, tucked behind dunes.

Continue south, along more sandy beach and dunes. Pass a huge old Edison power plant and arrive at Oxnard Shores, a development famous for getting clobbered by heavy surf at high tide. The beach is flat, and at one time was eroding at the phenomenal rate of 10 feet a year.

Past Oxnard Shores, a mile of beach walking brings you to historic Hollywood Beach. "The Sheik," starring that great silent movie idol Rudolph Valentino, was filmed on the desert-like sands here. Real estate promoters of the time attempted to capitalize on Oxnard Beach's instant fame and laid out subdivisions called Hollywood-by-the-Sea and Silver Strand, suggesting to customers that the area was really a movie colony; the development never attracted stars or their fans. This walk ends another mile down-coast at the entrance to Channel Islands Harbor.

CARPINTERIA BEACH

CARPINTERIA BEACH TRAIL

From Carpinteria State Beach to Harbor Seal Preserve is 2.5 miles round trip; to Carpinteria Bluffs is 4.5 miles round trip

Carpinteria is one of the state park system's more popular beachfront campgrounds. A broad beach, gentle waves, fishing and clamming are among the reasons for this popularity. A tiny visitors center (open weekends only) offers displays of marine life and Chumash history.

Carpinteria residents boast they have "The World's Safest Beach" because, although the surf can be large, it breaks far out, and there's no undertow. As early as 1920, visitors reported "the Hawaiian diversion of surfboard riding."

Surfers, hikers and bird-watchers have long enjoyed the bluffs, which rise about 100 feet above the beach and offer great views of Anacapa, Santa Cruz and Santa Rosa islands. The Carpinteria Bluffs extend from the state park boundary down-coast for more than a mile and were preserved by local conservationists after a two-decade-long battle with developers.

The Carpinteria Beach hike heads down-coast along the state beach to City Bluffs Park, an oil-company owned pier and a small pocket beach with a Harbor Seal Preserve. From December through May this beach is seals-only; at these times watch the boisterous colony, sometimes numbering as many as 150 seals from a blufftop observation area.

After seal-watching, sojourn over the Carpinteria bluffs or continue down the beach to Rincon Point on the Santa Barbara-Ventura county line

The Carpinteria Tar Pits once bubbled up near Carpinteria Beach. Around 1915, crews mined the tar, which was used to pave

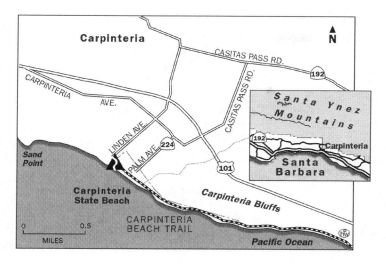

the coast highway in Santa Barbara County. Long ago, the tar pits trapped mastodons, saber-toothed tigers and other prehistoric animals. Unfortunately, the pits, which may have yielded amazing fossils like those of the La Brea Tar Pits in Los Angeles, became a municipal dump.

On August 17, 1769, the Captain Portola's Spanish explorers observed the native Chumash building a canoe and dubbed the location *La Carpinteria,* the Spanish name for carpenter shop. The Chumash used the asphaltum to caulk their canoes and seal their cookware.

DIRECTIONS: From Highway 101 in Carpinteria, exit on Linden Avenue and head south (oceanward) 0.6 mile through town to the avenue's end at the beach. Park along Linden Avenue (free, but time restricted) or in the Carpinteria State Beach parking lot (fee).

THE HIKE: Head down-coast. After a half-mile's travel over the wide sand strand you'll reach beach-bisecting Carpinteria Creek. During the summer, a sand bar creates a lagoon at the mouth of the creek. Continue over the sand bar or, if Carpinteria Creek is high, retreat inland through the campground and use the bridge over the creek.

Picnic at City Bluffs Park or keep walking a short distance farther along the bluffs past the oil company parking lot and oil pier to an excellent vista point above the Harbor Seal Preserve.

From the seal preserve, you can walk another mile across the Carpinteria Bluffs. Time and tides permitting, you can continue still farther down-coast along the beach to Rincon Beach.

Santa Barbara

East Beach Trail

From Stearns Wharf to Cabrillo Pavilion is 2.5 miles round trip

It's the postcard view of Santa Barbara: sandy beach, Chase Palm Park, white walls and red roofs, the Riviera and the Santa Ynez Mountains.

East Beach is the classic Southern California beach—long, sandy and rarely crowded. It's the place to play—beach volleyball, boogie boarding, sand sculpture contests—and the place to relax, with ample square footage of sand for the discriminating sunbather.

By the 1870s, wealthy health-seekers were flocking to Santa Barbara. And East Beach is where they flocked. Horse-drawn streetcars (electrified in 1896) traveled the length of East Beach, bringing bathers from the bathhouses to the beach.

The quintessential Santa Barbara citizen of her era, Pearl Chase, crusaded to preserve the coastline. Chase and her brother Harold were honored when the city renamed Palm Park, created in 1931, Chase Palm Park.

Explore East Beach via the sidewalk along Cabrillo Boulevard (the best option on Sundays when a weekly art sale takes place), along the beach itself, or with a stroll through Chase Palm Park. I suggest beginning with a walk in the park and returning via the beach.

Begin (or complete) your exploration with a walk (0.5 mile or so round trip) atop Stearns Wharf. Fun, fish and great sunset views are some of the highlights for the pedestrian on the longest wharf between Los Angeles and San Francisco. It's not uncommon to overhear a half-dozen languages on the wharf; the most-visited Santa Barbara destination, it attracts visitors from around the world.

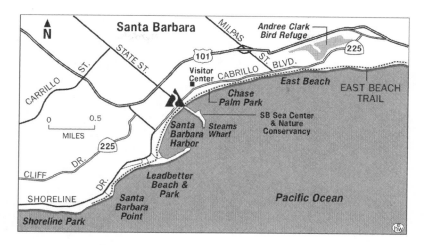

DIRECTIONS: Begin at the foot of Stearns Wharf at the intersection of State Street and Cabrillo Boulevard. Park curbside on Cabrillo Boulevard (note the time restrictions) or in one of the fee lots on the beach side of Cabrillo.

THE HIKE: Your path among palms soon takes you over the mouth of Mission Creek. At the foot of Santa Barbara Street, you'll find a plaque commemorating Pearl and Harold Chase for their civic and conservation efforts. You can't miss Skater's Point, a skateboard park constructed in 2000. Look across Cabrillo Boulevard at the tiny visitor information center. Built in 1911, the sandstone structure formerly housed a fish market and restaurant.

Chase Palm Park is a bit more than a mile long. Guests at the fine hotels cross Cabrillo Boulevard to the park, popular with locals for jogging and playing soccer. When you reach the east end of the park, cross a parking lot to Cabrillo Pavilion, where you can break for refreshments, see an art show or rent a boogie board.

Beyond Cabrillo Pavilion is another half-mile of East Beach with a turfed picnic area and very popular beach volleyballs courts. Those in the mood for beach-walking should head down to the shore; it's a bit more than a mile down-coast (passable at low tide) to the famed Biltmore Hotel and its narrow beach.

Enjoy the easy saunter along East Beach back to Stearns Wharf. It's fun to walk under the pilings of the wharf to West Beach and beyond.

ANACAPA ISLAND

ANACAPA ISLAND LOOP TRAIL

2 miles round trip

Anacapa, 12 miles southwest of Port Hueneme, is the most accessible Channel Island. It offers the hiker a sampling of the charms of the larger islands to the west. Below the tall wind-and-wave-cut cliffs, sea lions bark at the crashing breakers. Gulls, owls, and pelicans call the cliffs home.

Anacapa is really three islets chained together with reefs that rise above the surface during low tide. West Anacapa is the largest segment, featuring great caves where the Chumash Indians are said to have collected water dripping from the ceiling. The middle isle hosts a wind-battered eucalyptus grove.

The east isle, where the national park has a visitor center, is the light of the Channel Islands; a Coast Guard lighthouse and foghorn warn ships of the dangerous channel. It's a romantic approach to East Anacapa as you sail past Arch Rock.

What you find on top depends on the time of year. In February and March, you may enjoy the sight of 30-ton gray whales passing south on their way to calving and mating waters off Baja California. In early spring, the giant coreopsis, one of the island's featured attractions, is something to behold. It is called the tree sunflower, an awkward thick-trunked perennial that grows as tall as 10 feet.

Anacapa is small (a mile long and a quarter of a mile wide), but perfect-sized for the usual visit (2 to 3 hours). By the time you tour the lighthouse and visitor center, hike the self-guided trail and have lunch, it's time to board the boat for home.

Be sure to check out the national park's visitor center in Ventura Harbor for a sneak preview of the splendid park out there in the

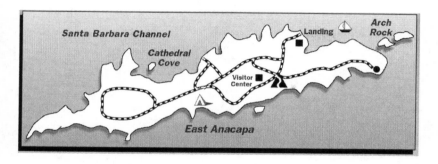

Pacific, 12 to 60 miles away, a series of blue-tinged mountains float-ing on the horizon. The visitor center not only has island history and ecology exhibits, but provides up to the minute boat transportation information.

The boat ride to Anacapa helps get a hiker oriented to the Chan-nel Islands, which parallel the Southern California coast—but a coast that is extending in a more or less east-west direction. In 1980, five of the eight Channel Islands—Anacapa, San Miguel, Santa Barbara, Santa Cruz and Santa Rosa—became America's fortieth national park. The waters surrounding the national park islands are protected as the Channel Islands National Marine Sanctuary.

DIRECTIONS: For the most up-to-date information about boat departures to Anacapa and to the other islands, contact Chan-nel Islands National Park at (805) 658-5730 or the park concession-aire, Island Packers (IslandPackers.com) in Ventura Harbor at (805) 642-1393.

THE HIKE: The nature trail leaves from the visitor center, where you can learn about island life, past and present.

Along the trail, a campground and several inspiring cliff-edge nooks invite you to picnic. The trail loops in a figure-8 through the coreopsis and returns to the visitor center.

Santa Cruz Island

Cavern Point, Potato Harbor, Smugglers Cove Trails

From Scorpion Anchorage to Cavern Point is 1.2 miles round trip with 300-foot elevation gain; to Potato Harbor is 4.5 miles round trip with 300-foot elevation gain; to Smugglers Cove is 7 miles round trip with 500-foot elevation gain

When viewed from Ventura or Santa Barbara shores, Santa Cruz Island doesn't look that big. However, hike a trail up to one of the commanding east isle promontories and the island appears massive: row upon row of mountains alternating with deep canyons, as well as a seemingly endless series of stark bluffs extending to the horizon.

The first time I took in this view I figured I was looking at a neighboring island but no, it was all Santa Cruz, all 96 square miles and 62,000 acres of it. For you city-slickers, the isle measures about four times the size of Manhattan.

Santa Cruz definitely offers hikers plenty of room to roam, as well as a far-reaching trail system composed mainly of old ranch roads. The only limitation on the hiker is time: day-trippers are allowed about 5 hours on the island before it's necessary to boat back to the mainland.

A short walk from the Scorpion Anchorage leads to picnic tables, restrooms and a historic two-story ranch house, now a visitor center.

DIRECTIONS: With a newer, higher-speed boat, the national park's primary concessionaire, Island Packers (805-642-1393), now transports hikers from Ventura Harbor to Scorpion Anchorage on Santa Cruz Island in a little over an hour.

THE HIKES: With limited time on the isle, hikers have a choice of 3 trails, which can be combined to fashion hikes of various lengths. The Trailmaster's favorites:

CAVERN POINT (From Scorpion Anchorage to Cavern Point is 1.2 miles round trip with 300-foot elevation gain) The short, but steep, climb on Cavern Point Trail leads the hiker to a stunning viewpoint. Look for seals and sea lions bobbing in the waters around the point, as well as cormorants, pigeon guillemots and black oyster-catchers swooping along the rugged volcanic cliffs.

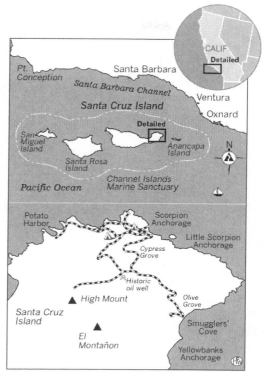

POTATO HARBOR (From Scorpion Anchorage to Potato Harbor is 4.5 miles round trip with 300-foot elevation gain) The jaunt to Potato Harbor begins on a right-forking road just beyond the upper end of the campground. After a heart-stirring half-mile climb, the road levels and heads west.

This hike parallels the mainland coast so it's fun to look back at the cities and civilization you left behind—a unique perspective indeed. Two miles out a spur trail leads oceanward to an overlook of the distinctly tater-shaped cove backed by rugged cliffs.

SMUGGLERS COVE (From Scorpion Anchorage to Smugglers Cove is 7 miles round trip with 500-foot elevation gain) The signed dirt road to Smugglers Cove climbs east then west as it passes a cypress grove. At the two-mile mark, a spur trail leads to San Pedro Point, a worthy destination for the time-short hiker.

The road descends to an airstrip, then down to the beach. Note the century-old eucalyptus and olive trees in the vicinity of Smugglers Cove.

CATALINA ISLAND
AVALON CANYON ROAD, HERMIT GULCH TRAIL, DIVIDE ROAD, MEMORIAL ROAD

From Avalon to Hermit Gulch Campground is 3 miles round trip with 200-foot elevation gain; loop via Hermit Gulch Trail and Botanical Garden is 6.5 miles round trip with 1,000-foot gain

This hike is a great intro to the natural and cultural attractions of Catalina Island. First, check out the Botanical Garden, a show-case for plants native to Catalina. At the head of Avalon Canyon stands the imposing Wrigley Memorial, a huge monument honoring chewing gum magnate William Wrigley, who purchased most of the island in 1919.

Don't miss The Nature Center, located just down Avalon Canyon Road from Hermit Gulch Campground. The center, operated by the Catalina Island Conservancy, offers nature and history exhibits and is the place to go for the latest trail information and (free) hiking permits.

I really like the grand tour of Avalon Canyon: ascending Hermit Gulch Trail to the head of the canyon for grand views, descending to the Botanical Garden, and sampling Catalina's rugged and bold terrain.

DIRECTIONS: Several boat companies offer ferry service to Catalina Island, with departures from San Diego, Newport Beach, Long Beach and San Pedro. The modern fleet makes the 22-mile crossing to Catalina in a bit more than an hour from Long Beach.

If you want to skip the walk along island byways to the trailhead, the Avalon Trolley (modest fee) departs from the waterfront and downtown (3rd Street) locations and makes stops at Hermit Gulch Campground (where Hermit Gulch Trail begins) and Botanical Garden.

THE HIKE: Head uphill along Catalina Street past shops and residences, jog briefly right on Tremont Street, and join Avalon

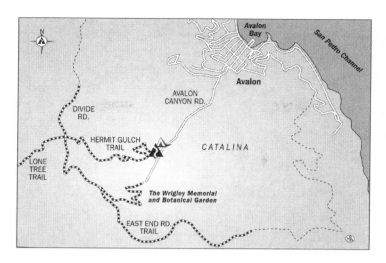

Canyon Road. Walk past the country club and golf course to the Wrigley-created, Bird Park, which once held thousands of unusual birds in the "largest bird cage in the world." On the other side of the road, baseball fans will stop for a view of a baseball field and pay homage to the one-time spring training camp of Wrigley's beloved Chicago Cubs.

At Hermit Gulch Campground, located a few hundred yards below road's end and the Botanical Garden, join signed Hermit Gulch Trail and begin a vigorous ascent. Climb 1.7 miles along the waterless canyon to the top of a divide and an intersection with aptly named Divide Road. From the 1,000-foot high divide, read the poetry on a plaque, and partake of commanding views of the isle and mainland.

Bear left on Divide Road. Walk along the divide, which bristles with prickly pear cactus. After about 0.75 mile of walking atop the divide, join Memorial Road.

The descent on Memorial Road offers excellent views of Avalon Harbor. You may flush a covey or two of Catalina quail from the brush as you follow the fire road down to the back gate of Botanical Garden. Enter the garden and soon come face-to-face with the Wrigley Memorial, where Wrigley was once entombed. Climb the many stairs to the 232-foot-wide, 130-foot-high monument, and enjoy great vistas of Avalon Harbor.

Walk amongst the fascinating flora to the garden entrance and return to Avalon by foot or by trolley.

Situated south of the Tehachapi Mountains and northwest of the San Gabriel Mountains, the Antelope Valley makes up the western frontier of the Mojave Desert. The West Mojave presents great sandscapes, many flat areas and isolated ridges and buttes.

The valley's natural attractions include a reserve for the state's official flower—the California poppy. Only in the Antelope Valley does the showy flower blanket whole hillsides in such brilliant orange sheets. Other parks preserve a Joshua tree woodland (Saddleback Butte State Park) and display the remarkable earthquake-fractured geology of this desert (Devil's Punchbowl County Park).

CHAPTER 12

ANTELOPE VALLEY

HIKE ON.

Vasquez Rocks

Geology, Pacific Crest Trails

From 1 to 3 miles round trip

You've probably seen Vaquez Rocks in the movies–old Westerns, sci-fi flicks and many more . And you've probably seen Vasquez Rocks while motoring along the Antelope Valley Freeway; the famed formations are a short distance from California 14.

Best place to see the Southland's most famous geological silhouette is Vasquez Rocks Natural Area Park. Hiking trails circle the rocks, which are not only enjoyable to view, but fun to climb.

From a distance, the rocks look insurmountable; actually, the sandstone outcrops stand only 100 to 150 feet high and are rather easy to climb.

The rocks are tilted and worn sandstone, the result of years of earthquake action and erosion by elements. Before being hung for his crimes, notorious highwayman Tiburcio Vasquéz, who hid from the law here during the 1850s and 1860s left his name on the rocks.

The trail system at Vasquez Rock is a bit informal. Because of the open nature of the terrain, hikers can – and do – tend to wander where their rock fancy takes them. A favorite route of mine, a clockwise tour of three miles or so, is described below; however, part of the fun of Vasquez Rocks is going your own way.

DIRECTIONS: From the Antelope Valley Freeway (14), a few miles northeast of the outskirts of Canyon Country, exit on Agua Dulce Road and head north 1.5 miles. Agua Dulce Canyon Road swings west and you join Escondido Canyon Road, proceeding 0.25 mile to the Vasquez Rocks Natural Area Park entrance. Park just inside the entrance at a small parking area or continue to the main lot near the largest of the rock formations.

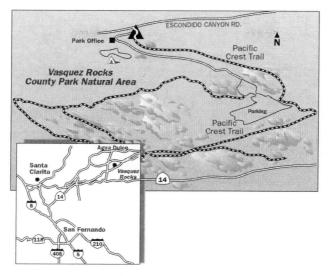

THE HIKE: Begin at the signed trailhead for Geology Trail just across the park road from the parking lot. Soon after beginning your trail-side study of strata, intersect Pacific Crest Trail and you'll head right.

The mile-long stretch of PCT through the park is part of a segment that connects the San Gabriel Mountains to the south with the Sierra Pelona area of Angeles National Forest to the north. The path parallels the park road.

PCT joins a dirt road at the edge of the picnic area and continues west atop the north wall of Escondido Canyon. Few park visitors, it seems, hike here, though the rock formations are stunning and a seasonal creek flows through the canyon. Only the annoying hum of the nearby Antelope Valley Freeway disturbs the natural beauty.

You can cross the creek with the PCT, double back along the other side of Escondido Canyon, and continue your exploration of the little-known southern part of the park. To continue to the main rock formations, stay west with the dirt road, pass a junction with the park's horse trail, and continue a short distance farther and join a foot trail.

The Vasquez Rocks area is a transition zone between mountain and desert environments. Yucca, buckwheat, sage and California juniper are among the plants you'll pass en route. The footpath drops northwestward then heads east to visit the most dramatic of the Vasquez Rocks.

DEVIL'S PUNCHBOWL NATURAL AREA

BURKHART, PUNCHBOWL TRAILS

From Visitor Center to Devil's Chair is miles round trip with 200-foot elevation gain; from South Fork Campground to Devil's Chair is 6 miles round trip with 500-foot gain

Southern California has many faults, and the mightiest of these is the San Andreas. Nowhere is the presence of this fault more obvious than in Devil's Punchbowl County Park. The dun-colored rocks have been tilted every which way and weathered by wind and rain. They are a bizarre sight to behold.

Punchbowl Trail takes you into the Devil's domain, a satanically landscaped rock garden on the desert side of the San Gabriel Mountains. The trip offers views of the Punchbowl Fault and the San Jacinto Fault—part of what seismologists call the San Andreas Rift Zone.

Winter is a fine time to visit the Punchbowl. Winds scour the desert clean and from the Devil's Chair, you can get superb views of this land, as well as the seemingly infinite sandscape of the Mojave.

Note that the six-mile-long Punchbowl Trail may be hiked from two directions or as a one-way with a car shuttle.

If you're looking for a much shorter hike check out the one-third mile-long nature trail, Pinyon Pathway, which introduces visitors to park geology and plant life, and a one-mile loop trail that offers grand views of the Punchbowl.

DIRECTIONS: From Highway 138 on the east edge of Pearblossom, exit on County Road N6 (Longview Road) and proceed south 7.5 miles to the entrance of Devil's Punchbowl Natural Area County Park.

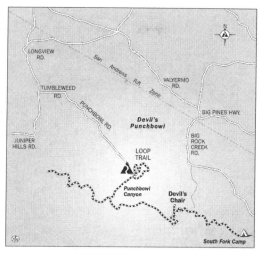

To South Fork Campground: From Pearblossom Highway (Highway 138) in Pearblossom, turn south onto Longview Road, then briefly left on Fort Tejon Road and right on Valyermo Road. Continue three miles to Big Rock Creek Road. Two-and-a-half miles past this junction, turn right on a signed dirt road to South Fork Campground and proceed 1 mile to the special day use/ hiker's parking lot below the campground.

THE HIKE: At the south side of the parking lot, join signed Burkhart Trail, tracing the Punchbowl's northwest rim. A half-mile out, the path merges with a retiring road and reaches a trail junction amidst Coulter pine in another 0.25 mile.

Join Punchbowl Trail, contouring around the heads of steep canyons that plunge into the Punchbowl. Descend steep switchbacks to a trail junction. A 0.1 mile, a connector trail leads across a narrow ridge (with some strategically placed protective fencing) to the Devil's Chair.

Take in the awesome panorama of the Punchbowl and its jumbled sedimentary strata. The somersaulted sandstone formation resembles pulled taffy. If you look west to the canyon wall, you can see the vertical crush zone of the fault, marked by white rocks.

From South Fork Campground: Join Punchbowl Trail and stay on it past the junction with South Fork Trail. Cross Big Rock Creek and begin a climb through manzanita and heat-stunted pinyon pine to a saddle where there's a view of the park and its faults. Descend from the saddle, down chaparral-covered slopes and over to Holcomb Canyon. Along the way, notice the strange dovetailing of three plant communities: yucca-covered hills, oak woodland, and juniper and piney woods.

From Holcomb Creek, the trail ascends steeply up another ridge through a pinyon pine forest to the Devil's Chair.

Antelope Valley California Poppy Reserve

Antelope Loop Trail

From Visitors Center to Antelope Butte Vista Point is 2.5 miles round trip with 300-foot elevation gain

The California poppy blooms on many a grassy slope in the Southland, but only in the Antelope Valley does the showy flower blanket whole hillsides in such brilliant orange sheets. Surely the finest concentration of California's state flower (during a good wildflower year) is preserved at the Antelope Valley California Poppy Reserve in the Mojave Desert west of Lancaster.

The poppy is the star of the flower show, which includes a supporting cast of fiddlenecks, cream cups, tidy tips and goldfields. March through Memorial Day is the time to saunter through this wondrous display of desert wildflowers.

The poppy has always been recognized as something special. Early Spanish Californians called it *Dormidera*, "the drowsy one," because the petals curl up at night. They fashioned a hair tonic/restorer by frying the blossoms in olive oil and adding perfume.

At the reserve, pick up a map at the Jane S. Pineiro Interpretive Center, named for the painter who was instrumental in setting aside an area where California's state flower could be preserved for future generations to admire. Some of Pineiro's watercolors are on display in the center, which also has wildflower interpretive displays and a slide show. Built into the side of a hill, the center boast an award-winning solar design, windmill power and "natural" air conditioning.

Antelope Loop Trail—and all trails in the reserve—are easy walking and suitable for the whole family. Seven miles of gentle trails

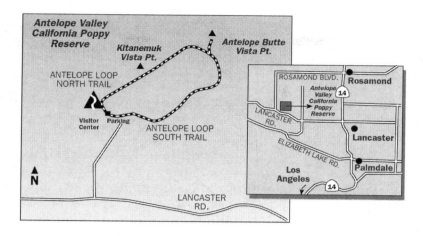

crisscross the 1,760-acre reserve; many hikers take every trail in the park without getting too tired.

DIRECTIONS: From the Antelope Valley Freeway (California 14) in Lancaster, exit on Avenue I and drive west 15 miles. Avenue I becomes Lancaster Road a few miles before the Poppy Reserve. The reserve (day use fee) is open 9 A.M. to 4 P.M. daily.

Spring wildflower displays are always unpredictable. To check on what's blooming where go online or call the park at (661) 942-0662 before making the trip.

THE HIKE: Begin on the signed Antelope Loop Trail to the left of the visitor center. The trail passes through an orange sea of poppies and fiddlenecks, then climbs briefly to Kitanemuk Vista Point, 0.75 mile from the visitor center. Atop Vista Point are those flowery symbols of faithfulness and friendship, forget-me-nots, and an unforgettable view of the Mojave Desert and the snow-covered Tehachapis.

After enjoying the view, continue on to Antelope Butte Vista Point, where another lookout offers fine desert panoramas. From here, join the south loop of the Antelope Loop Trail and return to the visitor center.

After you've circled the "upper west side" of the Poppy Reserve, you may wish to extend your hike by joining the Poppy Loop Trail and exploring the "lower east side."

SADDLEBACK BUTTE

SADDLEBACK BUTTE TRAIL

From Campground to Saddleback Peak is 4 miles round trip with 1,000-foot elevation gain; Season

Rarely visited Saddleback Butte State Park, located on the eastern fringe of Antelope Valley, is high-desert country, a land of creosote bush and Joshua trees. The park takes the name of its most prominent feature – 3,651-foot Saddleback Butte, a granite mountaintop that stands head and shoulders above Antelope Valley.

Richard Dowen Nature Trail is a good introduction to the Joshua tree and other plant life found in this corner of the desert. The trail to the boulder-strewn summit of Saddleback Peak takes a straight-line course, with most of the elevation gain occurring in the last half-mile. From atop the peak, enjoy far-reaching desert views.

The Spartan country around the butte once supported thousands of pronghorn antelope--hence the name Antelope Valley--and the numerous Native American tribes who hunted them. The antelope are all gone now, victims to hunting and encroaching civilization. By interrupting the antelope's migration, Southern Pacific railroad tracks also doomed the animals; the antelope could easily cross the tracks, but instinct prevented them from doing this, and they soon perished from exposure to harsh winters and the shrinkage of their habitat.

Today's park visitor may glimpse several other animals native to Antelope Valley, including coyote, jackrabbits, lizards and the Antelope ground squirrel. Some fortunate hikers may even witness the unhurried progress of a desert tortoise.

DIRECTIONS: From Highway 14 (Antelope Valley Freeway) in Lancaster, take the 20th Street exit. Head north on 20th and turn

east (right) on Avenue J. Drive 18 miles to Saddleback Butte State Park. Follow the dirt park road to the campground, where the trail begins. Park (day use fee) near the trail sign.

THE HIKE: The signed trail heads straight for the saddle. The soft, sandy track, marked with yellow posts leads through impressive Joshua tree woodland.

With the exception of pathfinder John C. Fremont, who called them "the most repulsive tree in the vegetable kingdom," most California travelers have found Joshua tress to be quite picturesque. Mormon pioneers thought that the tree's outstretched limbs resembled the prophet Joshua pointing to the promised land.

After 1.5 miles, the trail switchbacks steeply up the rocky slope of the butte. An invigorating climb brings you to the saddle of Saddleback Butte. To reach the peak, follow the steep leftward trail to the summit.

From the top, look south to the San Gabriel Mountains and Mount Baldy, dominating the eastern end of the range. At the base of the mountains, keen eyes will discern the California Aqueduct, which carries water to the Southland from the Sacramento Delta. To the east is the vast Mojave Desert, to the north is Edwards Air Force Base. To the west are the cities of Lancaster and Palmdale and farther west, the rugged Tehachapi Mountains.

For some visitors, the Joshua trees are not only the essence but the whole of the Joshua Tree National Park experience. Here in its namesake park, it reaches the southernmost limit of its range. The park, however, is more than a tableau of twisted yucca and beckons the hiker with a diversity of desert environments: sand dunes, palm oases, cactus gardens and jumbles of jumbo granite.

In JT, hikers get to roam two different deserts—the Mojave with its Joshua trees and mountains and the flatter, hotter Colorado with its cholla, ocotillo, smoketree and native California fan palms.

Chapter 13

Joshua Tree National Park

HIKE ON.

RYAN MOUNTAIN

RYAN MOUNTAIN TRAIL

To Ryan Mountain is 3 miles round trip with 800-foot elevation gain

The path to Ryan Mountain is a superb example of the trail builder's art. Stone steps have been crafted (from the abundant supply of rocks found nearby!) and well integrated into steeper sections of the route to Ryan's roundish summit.

Ryan Mountain is named for the Ryan brothers, Thomas and Jep, who had a homestead at the base of the mountain. The views from atop Ryan Mountain, located near the center of the park, are impressive to say the least. From the 5,457-foot summit, enjoy far-reaching vistas of vast Joshua tree forests, the Wonderland of Rocks and many more of the highlights that make this national park so special.

At the west end of the trailhead parking lot, note the brief and well-worn trail leading to Indian Cave. Bedrock mortars found in the cave suggest its use as a work site by its aboriginal inhabitants. It's typical of the kind of shelter sought by the nomadic Cahuilla and Serrano Indian clans that traveled this desert land.

DIRECTIONS: From Park Boulevard, 2 miles east of its junction with Keys View Road, look for the signed turnoff for Ryan Mountain on the south side of the road. Park in the large lot.

THE HIKE: Hike south through what seems like a natural granite gateway. In 0.2 mile, reach a side trail that passes through a lunar landscape of rocks and Joshua trees and leads to Sheep Group Camp (also an alternate trailhead for this hike).

Continuing past the junction, Ryan Mountain Trail ascends moderately-to-steeply toward the peak. En route, pass some very old rocks, which make up the core off this mountain and the nearby Little San Bernardino range. For eons, these rocks have, since their

creation, been metamor-
phosed by heat and pres-
sure into completely new
types, primarily gneiss
and schist.

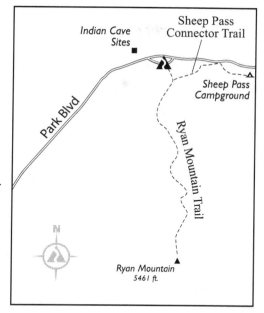

Indian Cave Sites

Sheep Pass Connector Trail

Sheep Pass Campground

Park Blvd

Ryan Mountain Trail

N

Ryan Mountain
5461 ft.

You don't have to
reach the top to get some
views. Look out from the
west slope of the moun-
tain at the Little San
Bernardino Mountains off
to the west. A half-mile
out, it's the granite formations on the face of Ryan
Mountain that capture
the hiker's attention.

The path works its
way up to the ridgeline
at the 1-mile mark. While we hikers appreciate JT's hikes up washes
and along old mining roads, it's great to take a hike on well-designed
and built trail like the one on Ryan Mountain.

Look out at Ryan Mountain's false summits to the north and
east as you ascend the last 0.5 mile (with a stiff 400-foot elevation
gain) to the true summit, marked by a pile of rocks.

The view from atop Ryan Mountain is one of the finest in the
park. Right down below to the west is Ryan Campground and Ryan
Ranch. Take in panoramic views of Lost Horse, Queen, Hidden and
Pleasant valleys as well as clear-day vistas of the San Jacinto Moun-
tains and San Bernardino Mountains, including SoCal high point
Mount San Gorgonio.

LOST HORSE MINE

LOST HORSE MINE TRAIL

To Lost Horse Mine is 4 miles round trip with 400-foot elevation gain; loop is 6.2 miles

Lost Horse Mine was the most successful gold mining operation in this part of the Mojave. More than 9,000 ounces of gold were processed from ore dug here in the late 1890s. The mine's 10-stamp mill still stands, along with a couple of large cyanide settling tanks and a huge winch used on the main shaft. The trail to the mine offers a close-up look back into a colorful era and some fine views into the heart of the national park.

Many are the legends that swirl like the desert winds around the Lost Horse Mine. As the story goes, Johnny Lang in 1893 was camping in Pleasant Valley when his horse got loose. He tracked it out to the ranch belonging to Jim McHaney, who told Lang his horse was "no longer lost" and threatened Lang's health and future.

Lang wandered over to the camp of fellow prospector Dutch Diebold, who told him that he, too, had been threatened by McHaney and his cowboys. A pity too, because he, Diebold had discovered a promising gold prospect, but had been unable to mark his claim's boundaries. After sneaking in to inspect the claim, Johnny Lang and his father, George, purchased all rights from Diebold for $1,000.

At first it looked like a bad investment, because the Langs were prevented by McHaney's thugs from reaching their claim. Partners came and went, and by 1895, Johnny Lang owned the mine with the Ryan brothers, Thomas and Jep.

Peak production years for the mine were 1896 through 1899. Gold ingots were hidden in a freight wagon and transported to Indio. The ruse fooled any would-be highwaymen.

But thievery of another sort plagued the Lost Horse Mine. The theft was of amalgam, lumps of quicksilver from which gold could later be separated. Seems in this matter of amalgam, the mill's day shift, supervised by Jep Ryan, far out-produced the night shift, supervised by Lang. One of Ryan's men espied Lang stealing part of the amalgam. When Ryan gave Lang a choice—sell his share of the mine for $12,000 or go to the penitentiary—Lang sold out.

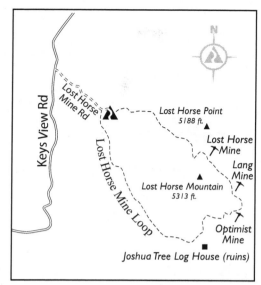

DIRECTIONS: From Park Boulevard, 2.5 miles south of Keys View Road, turn left on signed dirt road for Lost Horse Mine and travel 1 mile southeast to road's end, parking, and the signed trailhead.

THE HIKE: The trail, the old mine road, climbs above the left side of a wash. Pinyon pine and the nolina (often mistaken for a yucca) dot the wash. Nolina leaves are more flexible than those of yucca, and its flowers smaller.

A bit short of 2 miles, Lost Horse Mine comes into view. Note the stone foundations opposite the mill site. A little village for mine workers was built here in the late 1890s. Scramble up to the top of the hill (Lost Horse Point, elevation 5,188 feet) above the mine for a panoramic view of Queen Valley, Pleasant Valley and the desert beyond. Return the same way or complete the loop (4.2 miles).

BARKER DAM AND WONDERLAND OF ROCKS

BARKER DAM NATURE TRAIL

Loop through Wonderland of Rocks to Barker Dam is 1.4 miles

One of the many wonders of Joshua Tree National Park is the Wonderland of Rocks, 12 square miles of massive jumbled granite. This curious maze of stone hides groves of Joshua trees, trackless washes and several small pools of water.

Easiest, and certainly the safest way to explore the Wonderland is to follow the Barker Dam Nature Trail, which interprets the botanical highlights of the area and visits petroglyphs.

This hike's main destination is the small lake created by Barker Dam. A century ago, cowboys took advantage of the water catchment of this natural basin and brought their cattle to this corner of the Wonderland of Rocks. Barker and Shay Cattle Co. constructed the dam, which was later raised to its present height by Bill Keys and his family in the 1950s.

By park service regulation, the area is open only from 8 a.m. to 6 p.m.; this restriction is designed to allow the shy bighorn sheep a chance to reach water without human interference.

DIRECTIONS: From Park Boulevard, 1.5 miles north of the intersection with Keys View Road, turn north on the signed road to Wonderland of Rocks and drive 1.5 miles to the large parking area.

THE HIKE: From the north end of the parking area, join the signed trail that immediately penetrates the Wonderland of Rocks. You'll pass a special kind of oak, the turbinella, which has adjusted to the harsh conditions of desert life.

Interpretive signs point out the unique botany of this desert land. The path squeezes through a narrow rock passageway and leads to the edge of Barker Dam Lake. Bird-watching is excellent here because many migratory species not normally associated with the desert are attracted to the lake. Morning and late afternoon hours are particularly tranquil times to contemplate the ever-changing reflections of the Wonderland of Rocks on the water.

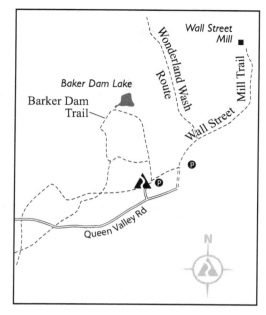

The trail is a bit indistinct near Barker Dam, but resumes again in fine form near a strange-looking circular water trough, a holdover from the area's cattle ranching days. A toilet-like float mechanism controlled the flow of water to the thirsty livestock.

The path turns southerly and soon passes a huge boulder known as Piano Rock. When this land was in private ownership, a piano was hauled atop this rock and played for the amusement of visitors and locals.

Beyond Piano Rock the trail enters a rock-rimmed valley. A brief leftward detour at a junction brings you to the Petroglyphs. In less-enlightened times, the native rock art was painted over by a film crew in order to make it more visible to the camera's eye.

Back on the main trail, you'll parallel some cliffs, perhaps get a glimpse of some Indian bedrock mortars, and loop back to the parking area.

BLACK ROCK CANYON

BLACK ROCK CANYON TRAIL

From Black Rock Campground to Warren Peak is 5.5 miles round trip with 1,000-foot elevation gain

A hike through Black Rock Canyon has just about everything a desert hike should have: plenty of cactus, pinyon pine-dotted peaks, a sandy wash, dramatic rock formations, a hidden spring, grand vistas. Tucked away in the northwest corner of the park, the area also hosts forests of the shaggy Joshuas.

More than 200 species of birds, including speedy roadrunners, have been observed in and around Black Rock Canyon. Hikers frequently spot mule deer and rabbits—desert cottontails and black-tailed jackrabbits.

Black Rock Canyon rarely makes the "must see" list of JT's natural attractions, even though it is one of the easiest places to reach. The canyon is close to Yucca Valley's commercial strip and residential neighborhoods and yet matches the allure of much more remote regions of the national park.

Black Rock Canyon Trail follows a classic desert wash, and then ascends to Warren Peak at the wild west end of the Little San Bernardino Mountains. Desert and mountain views from the peak are stunning.

DIRECTIONS: From Highway 62 in Yucca Valley, turn south on Joshua Lane and drive 4.6 miles to a T-intersection. Turn right then bend left on Black Rock Canyon Road, which leads a mile to Black Rock Campground. Park near the visitor center and walk up to the trailhead by campsite #30.

THE HIKE: From the upper end of the campground, the trail leads 0.2 mile to a water tank, goes left a very short distance on a park service road, then immediately angles right, continuing east.

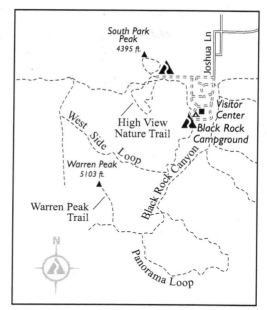

About 0.6 mile from the trailhead, the path drops into the dry, sandy creekbed of Black Rock Canyon. Bear right and head up the wide canyon mouth, passing Joshua trees, desert willow and cholla. Signs reading "WP" for Warren Peak keep the hiker on track.

Wash-walking leads to the remains of some so-called "tanks," or rock basins built by early ranchers to hold water for cattle. Farther up the wash is Black Rock Spring, sometimes dry, sometimes a trickle. Beyond the spring, the canyon narrows. Wend your way around beavertail cactus, pinyon pine and juniper.

Stay right at a junction (with the Panorama Loop Trail heading left), and a second right in 0.4 mile where the loop trail rejoins the trail to Warren Peak. Continue 0.3 mile to a Y junction; the spur trail to the left leads to Warren View. Stay right and climb to a dramatic ridge crest of the Little San Bernardino Mountains, then angle right (west) along the crest. The rough trail ascends steeply 0.4 mile (with a 400-foot gain) past contorted wind-blown juniper and pinyon pine to the top of Warren Peak.

What a grand clear-day view! Look north to the Mojave Desert, west to the San Bernardino Mountains; to the southwest behold mighty Mt. San Jacinto, Palm Springs and the Coachella Valley.

FORTY-NINE PALMS

FORTY-NINE PALMS TRAIL

To Forty-nine Palms Oasis is 3 miles round trip with 350-foot elevation gain

Forty-nine Palms Oasis has retained a wonderful air of remoteness. An old trail climbs a steep ridge and offers the hiker expansive views of the Sheephole and Bullion mountain ranges.

On the exposed ridge, barrel cacti, creosote, yucca, and brittlebush brave the heat. As the trail winds up and over a rocky crest, the restful green of the oasis comes into view.

At the oasis, nature's personality abruptly changes and the dry, sun-baked ridges give way to dripping springs, pools, and the blessed shade of palms and cottonwoods.

Unlike those oases strung out for miles along a stream, Forty-nine Palms Oasis is a close-knit palm family centered on a generous supply of surface water. Seeps and springs fill numerous basins set among the rocks at different levels. Mesquite and willow thrive alongside the palms. Singing house finches and croaking frogs provide a musical interlude.

Perched on a steep canyon wall, Forty-nine Palms Oasis overlooks the town of Twentynine Palms, but its untouched beauty makes it seem a lot farther removed from civilization.

DIRECTIONS: From Highway 62 about 5.5 miles west of Twentynine Palms and 11 miles east of the town of Joshua Tree, turn south on Fortynine Palms Canyon Road and follow it 2 miles to its end at a National Park Service parking area and the trailhead.

THE HIKE: The trail rises through a Spartan rockscape dotted with cacti and jojoba. After a brisk climb, catch your breath atop a ridgetop and enjoy the view of Twentynine Palms and the surrounding desert.

Colorful patches of lichen adhere to the rocks. Lichen, which conducts the business of life as a limited partnership of algae and fungi, is very sensitive to air pollution; the health of this tiny plant is considered by some botanists to be related to air quality. Contemplate the abstract impressionist patterns of the lichen, inhale great draughts of fresh air, then follow the trail as it descends from the ridgetop.

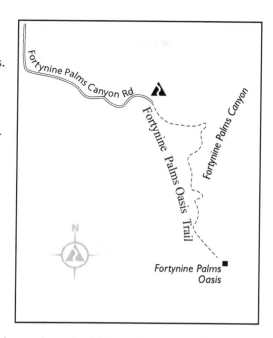

The trail leads down slopes dotted with barrel cactus and mesquite. Soon the oasis comes into view. Lucky hikers may get a fleeting glimpse of bighorn sheep drinking from oasis pools or gamboling over nearby steep slopes.

As the path leads to the palms, notice many fire-blackened tree trunks. The grove has burned several times before—and after—its inclusion in the national park.

Forty-nine Palms Oasis celebrates life. Native California fan palm cluster near handsome boulder-lined pools. Fuzzy cattails, ferns and grasses sway in the breeze. An oasis like this one gives the hiker a chance to view the desert in terms that are the exact opposite of its stereotypical dry hostility. If the desert is the land God forgot, then the Creator must have had a sudden afterthought and decided to sprinkle this parched land with oases, reminders of His lush handiwork.

LOST PALMS OASIS

LOST PALMS OASIS TRAIL

**From Cottonwood Springs to Lost Palms Oasis is 7.4 miles
round trip with 300-foot elevation gain**

With the help of significant underground springs, more than
100 California fan palms thrive at Lost Palms Oasis. A classic trail
connects Cottonwood Oasis and Lost Palms Oasis and leads to the
largest group of palms in Joshua Tree National Park.

The trail begins at largely man-made Cottonwood Spring Oasis,
once a popular overnight stop for freight-haulers and prospectors
during the mining years of 1870 to 1910. (See Cottonwood Spring
Oasis hike description.)

While summertime is a brutal time for hikers to visit Lost Palms
Oasis, it's a good time to spot wildlife, dependent on the waters and
plants of the oasis for survival. Bighorn sheep frequent Lost Palms
Oasis, which is day-use only for humans in order to protect the creatures' access to water.

Unlike other trails to palm oases that are straight shots up
canyons to reach palm groves, Lost Palms Oasis Trail passes through
a cactus garden, crosses a number of desert washes and travels up
and down ridges. The path is well way-marked with signs and with
arrows at turns, junctions and wash-crossings.

By the time you reach this hidden gem of an oasis you'll really
feel like you're having an adventure. The memorable journey matches the destination—families of palms in a deep canyon whose steep
igneous walls sparkle in the desert sun.

DIRECTIONS: From Highway 62 in Twentynine Palms, travel
9 miles south on Utah Trail to the Pinto Y junction, bear left, and
travel 32 miles to Cottonwood Visitor Center. Turn left and drive

1.2 miles to the Cotton-
wood Spring parking lot
and trailhead.

From Interstate 10,
some 25 miles east of
Indio, exit on Cotton-
wood Canyon Road
and head north 8 miles
to Cottonwood Spring
Visitor Center. Turn
right and drive 1.2 miles
to the Cottonwood
Spring parking lot and
trailhead.

THE HIKE: From
Cottonwood Spring,
home to a wide variety

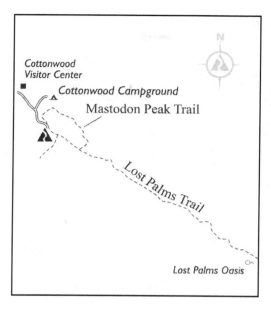

of birds and a large number of bees, the trail marches over sandy
hills, past heaps of huge rocks and along sandy draws and washes.
A number of Park Service signs point the way at possibly confusing
junctions.

Finally, about three miles from the trailhead, you rise above the
washes and climb to an ocotillo-dotted ridge for grand desert vistas,
including the Salton Sea. Dip into a minor canyon and then ascend
to a rocky outcropping overlooking the canyon harboring Lost Palms
Oasis at the 3.5-mile mark. From the overlook, descend the steep
path around boulders to the palms.

Little surface water is present at Lost Palms Oasis, but enough is
underground for the palms to remain healthy. Lost Palms remained
relatively untouched throughout the mining years, though some
of its water was pumped to settlements eight miles to the south at
Chiriaco Summit. Adjacent to Lost Palms Canyon is a handsome
upper canyon called Dike Springs. A challenging, rocky, use trail
leads to another palm family known as the Victory Palms.

Early 20th-century health-seekers and nature lovers recognized Palm Springs for what is was: a true oasis, a palm-dotted retreat where ancient springs gushed forth. Here was nature, simple and unadorned. While Palm Springs and satellite communities have achieved international resort status, a wild side remains and ample opportunities to experience the desert of old.

Especially compelling to the hiker are the Indian Canyons—Palm, Murray, Andreas and Tahquitz. The Living Desert Preserve, Big Morongo Canyon and the Coachella Valley Preserve are quiet places for the hiker to commune with the desert nature writer Joseph Smeaton Chase called "nature in her simplest expression."

CHAPTER 14

PALM SPRINGS

HIKE ON.

Big Morongo Canyon

Marsh, Yucca Ridge, Canyon Trails

2-mile loops via nature trails; through Morongo Canyon is 9.8 miles round trip with 1,800-foot elevation gain

The relative abundance of water is the key to Big Morongo's long human history and botanical uniqueness. Springs bubble up in the reserve and one of the California desert's very few year-around creeks flows through the canyon. Dense thickets of cottonwood and willow, as well as numerous water-loving shrubs line Big Morongo Creek.

Big Morongo is an oaisis, crucial water supply for wildlife from coyotes to chuckawallas to California tree frogs. The canyon is known for its variety of birds (more than 240 species counted), numerous because the canyon is at the intersection of two deserts, and because the oasis is such an attractive stopover for migrating birds.

Several short trails lead through the canyon, managed by the BLM with the assistance of the Friends of Big Morongo Canyon Preserve. First-time visitors will enjoy combining a couple of the nature trails into 2- or 3-mile loops; for a longer jaunt, head out for a mile or two along Canyon Trail.

DIRECTIONS: From Interstate 10, 15 miles east of Banning and a bit past the Highway 111 turnoff to Palm Springs, exit on Highway 62. Drive 10 miles north to the signed turnoff on your right for Big Morongo Canyon Preserve. Turn east and, after 0.1 mile, look for the entry road leading to a parking area.

THE HIKE: Wide and full-access Marsh Trail (0.6 mile) leads along and across cottonwood- and willow-lined Morongo Creek. The boardwalk and viewing decks help the hiker check out the marsh area, said to support the second-highest density of breeding birds (1,400 pairs per square kilometer) in the U.S.

If Marsh Trail is for the birds, then Yucca Ridge Trail (0.7 mile) is for the views: Big Morongo Canyon and the high peaks of the San Bernardino and San Jacinto ranges. The path ascends slopes clad with creosote bush, assorted cacti and Mojave yucca.

Desert Willow Trail (0.7 mile) Hike alongside mesquite thickets into (what can be a mighty warm)desert wash dotted with yerba santa and desert willow. Relax and cool-off on benches strategically placed in shady locales.

Mesquite Trail (0.5 mile), complete with bridges and board-walks, is another path that leads along the moist environs of Big Morongo Creek. Contemplate the lush scene nearby and the much drier desertscape in the distance from a large octagon-shaped deck.

Hike the west branch of West Canyon Trail (0.8 mile) to the top of a ridge for a grand view of Big Morongo Canyon, and descend to the canyon floor to junction Canyon Trail.

Canyon Trail (9.8 miles round trip from the parking lot) makes a mellow descent through Big Morongo Canyon from one desert to another—from a higher, cooler Mojave Desert environment to a lower and hotter Colorado Desert one. The path sticks with the canyon and willow-bordered creek. Admire the steep canyon walls and near trail's end enjoy a stirring view of snow-capped Mt. San Jacinto, which lies straight ahead.

Palm Springs

Museum, Lykken Trails

From Palm Springs Art Museum to Overlook is 2 miles round trip with 800-foot elevation gain; return via Ramon Drive is 4 miles round trip

Museum and Lykken Trails offer a good overview of the resort. This hike begins at Palm Springs Art Museum (formerly the Palm Springs Desert Museum). Founded in 1938, the institution specializes in regional art, the performing arts and natural history for the city and surrounding Coachella Valley. Natural science exhibits recreate the unique ecology of Palm Springs and the Colorado Desert.

What makes Palm Springs and the Coachella Valley so compelling to the hiker is the majestic mountains backdrop. The mountains beckon the sojourner afoot with world renowned scenic beauty, unique cultural and historical sites, exceptional biodiversity, and a wide-ranging collection of parklands. You get a taste of that from this short hike, an excellent introduction to Palm Springs.

The Palm Springs area offers hiking for all levels of ability and degrees of enthusiasm. Former Palm Springs Mayor Frank Bogert contributed much to the Palm Springs trail system, as well as to trails statewide. Check out what the BLM calls the Bogert Trail complex, an assemblage of Garstin, Berns, and Shannon Trails.

This is a great in-town hike and excellent aerobic workout. Museum Trail is one of the steepest trails around.

This trail delivers terrific vistas. Yes, you see the modern resort sprawling across the valley (how many golf courses can you count?). And you also get a glimpse of the lovely setting and understand why in the early years of the 20th century Palm Springs was called a "Desert Eden," "Our Araby," and "A Garden in the Sun."

Museum Trail ascends the western base of Mt. San Jacinto and junctions with Lykken Trail, which winds through the Palm Springs hills north to Tramway Road and south to Ramon Road. Lykken Trail honors Carl Lykken, Palms Springs pioneer and the town's first postmaster. Lykken, who arrived in 1913, owned a general merchandise store, and later a department/hardware store.

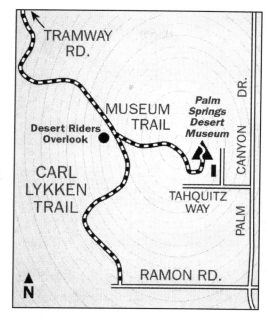

DIRECTIONS: From Highway 111 (Palm Canyon Drive) in the middle of downtown Palm Springs, turn west on Tahquitz Drive, then a right on Museum Drive. Park in Palm Springs Art Museum's north lot.

THE HIKE: The trail ascends the rocky slope above the museum. Soon you'll intersect a private road, jog left, and resume trail walking up the mountainside.

As you rapidly gain elevation (phew, this is a steep trail!), the view widens from the Desert Fashion Plaza to the outskirts of Palm Springs to the wide-open spaces of the Coachella Valley. A mile's ascent brings you to a picnic area, originally built by the Desert Riders, local equestrians whose membership included the colorful Frank Bogert and Carl Lykken.

Bear left (south) on North Lykken Trail, which travels the hills above town before descending to Ramon Road near the mouth of Tahquitz Canyon. Return to the trailhead via the streets of Palm Springs.

THE LIVING DESERT

NATURE TRAILS

1-mile loop; loop via Eisenhower Trail and Eisenhower Mountain is 5 miles round trip with 500-foot elevation gain

A superb introduction to desert plant life and wildlife, The Living Desert is a combination zoo, botanic garden and hiking area. The 1,200-acre, nonprofit facility is dedicated to conservation, education and research. Gardens represent major desert regions including California's Mojave, Arizona's Sonoran and Mexico's Chihuahuan, plus Madagascar and East Africa.

Wildlife-watchers will enjoy observing coyotes in their burrows, bighorn sheep atop a mountain peak, as well as many more creatures—Arabian oryx, camel and warthog. The reserve also has a walk-through aviary.

Nature and hiking trails provide an opportunity to form an even closer acquain- tance with an uncrowded, undeveloped sandscape. Easy trails lead past desert flora with name tags and ecosystems with interpretive displays, and over to areas that resemble the open desert of yesteryear.

The Living Desert offers a trio of hikes. Inner Loop is a 0.25-long nature trail that explores palo verde and smoke tree environments. Mile-long Middle Loop leads through a desert wash with views and exhibits of famed San Andreas Fault. Wilderness Loop (5 miles from the parking lot, about 3.5 miles from the top of Middle Loop) travels a rocky canyon, along a ridge about halfway up Eisenhower Peak, and offers great views of the Coachella Valley.

President Eisenhower spent many winters at the El Dorado Country Club at the base of the mountain that now bears his name. Local boosters petitioned the Federal Board of Geographic

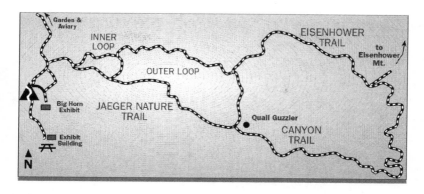

Names to name the 1,952 (coincidentally, 1952 was the year of his election)-foot peak for part-time Palm Springs resident Dwight D. Eisenhower.

DIRECTIONS: From Highway 111 in Palm Desert, turn south on Portola Avenue and drive 1.5 miles south to the park. The Living Desert is open every day October 1 to May 31, 9 A.M. to 5 P.M., with shorter hours and closures in effect during the summer.

Check LivingDesert.org for admission costs and daily program schedules.

THE HIKE: From the exhibit buildings, follow the nature trail. The trail junctions once more and you begin heading up the alluvial plain of Deep Canyon. Walking up the wash observe the many moisture-loving plants that thrive in such environments, including smoke trees, desert willows and palo verde.

Stay right at the next junction and begin the outer loop or Wilderness Loop. Pass plenty of that common desert dweller, the creosote bush, and wind along the base of sand dunes.

The trail climbs out of the wash and into a kind of plain that true desert rats call a "bajada." Junction the south loop of the Eisenhower Trail, climb through a little canyon and wind up the south slope of Eisenhower Mountain.

On the descent of Ike's Peak, get good views of the mountains and the Coachella Valley. Reach a branch of Middle Loop and head west down the brittlebush-dotted floodplain back to the exhibit buildings and main part of the preserve.

PALM CANYON

PALM CANYON, VICTOR TRAILS

3-mile loop with 200-foot elevation gain

The hills and canyons bordering Palm Springs have the greatest concentration of palm trees in the U.S., and in number of trees, Palm Canyon is the uncrowned king of America's desert oases. A meandering stream and lush undergrowth complement over three thousand palms, creating a jungle-like atmosphere in some places.

Palm Canyon is the essence, or at least the original essence, of Palm Springs. Early 20th-century health seekers recognized their discovery for what it was—a true oasis. Here was a palm dotted retreat where ancient springs gushed forth. Here was nature, simple and unadorned.

Some residents championed the creation of Palm Canyon National Monument, in order to preserve the canyons on the outskirt of Palm Springs known collectively as the Indian Canyons—Palm, Murray, and Andreas. The national monument was approved by Congress in 1922 but put under National Park Service protection.

Finally, in 1990, a sizeable portion of the palm canyons came under federal protection with the establishment of the Santa Rosa National Scenic Area, administered by the BLM. More recently, the name was changed to Santa Rosa and San Jacinto Mountains National Monument, a better reflection of the monument's boundaries and mission.

Most visitors stay along the first mile of the main trail amidst the palm trees. After that, it's best to check out the trail map and markers and fashion a route to your liking—along the East Fork, West Fork or making a loop.

Hardy adventurers will relish the challenge of the 15-mile round trip hike up Palm Canyon, gaining 3,000 feet in elevation, before

326

reaching a junction with Highway 74, the Palms-to-Pines Highway.

DIRECTIONS: From Interstate 10, exit on Highway 111 (Palm Canyon Drive) and proceed to downtown Palm Springs. Continue through town on Palm Canyon Drive. At a fork, head straight ahead 2.8 miles on South Palm Canyon Drive to a tollgate where you must pay a fee ($9 per adult) to enter the Indian Canyons, open daily from 8:30 A.M. to 5 P.M. Parking is a short

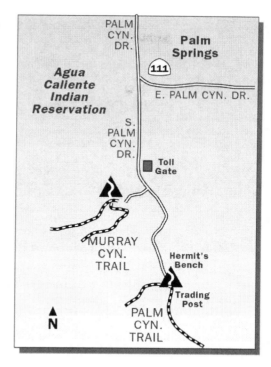

distance beyond the tollgate at the head of Palm Canyon at Hermit's Bench, where there is a trading post and a good view north into Palm Springs. Look for the start of Palm Canyon Trail on the south side of the parking lot.

THE HIKE: From the trading post, the trail heads into the canyon. Some of the California fan palms stand 60 feet tall, with three-foot trunk diameters. Head up-canyon about 0.5 mile, cross over the creek and continue up the left side of the canyon. After another 0.25 mile reach an intersection. Continue farther up Palm Canyon or begin exploring the many paths amidst the palms and loop back on another trail.

As you'll experience, Palm Canyon Trail meanders amidst the palms and along the creek and meets several other paths (including Vandeventer and East Fork Trails) leading along the canyon walls and into the hills.) I like returning via rugged Victor Trail along the cliff overlooking the canyon.

TAHQUITZ CANYON

TAHQUITZ CANYON TRAIL

2 miles round trip with 350-foot elevation gain

Storied Tahquitz Canyon, located just 2 miles as the phainopepla flies from downtown Palm Springs is accessible by tribal ranger-led guided tours and independent hiking.

Highlights of the lovely canyon named after the Cahuilla shaman Tahquitz include ancient rock art, diverse desert flora, an early irrigation system and a 60-foot waterfall featured in Frank Capra's classic 1937 film, "Lost Horizon" starring Ronald Coleman and Jane Wyatt.

As legend has it, Tahquitz, the Cahuilla's first shaman, began practicing his art to good effect, but became increasingly mischievous, then downright dangerous. Such is his power that he can appear to people in downtown Palm Springs or manifest himself as an earthquake or as a fireball in the sky.

The Cahuilla closed the canyon to the public in 1969 when a rowdy crowd left a rock concert and descended into Tahquitz Canyon for several days of partying. In later years, "No Trespassing" signs, locked gates and fences slowed, but did not stop visitors. Most of the hikers and skinny-dippers enjoyed the picturesque falls and were respectful to the serene scene, but a number of vandals dumped garbage on the canyon floor and spray-painted graffiti on the rocks and boulders. Hippies, hermits, hobos and homeless folks took up residence in the canyon's caves.

With proceeds from the tribe's Spa Resort & Casino, the Agua Caliente band of the Cahuilla embarked on a three-year cleanup effort, built a visitor center with educational and cultural exhibits, and reopened the canyon in 2001.

The canyon is chock-full of native plants including brittle bush, creosote, cholla, hedgehog cactus, Mormon tea and desert lavender. Tour leaders detail the many ways the Cahuilla used the canyon's plants for food and medicine.

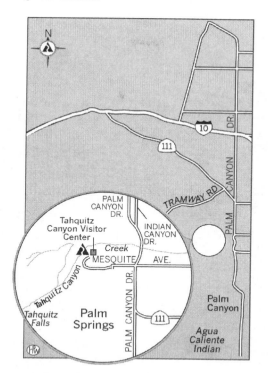

The hiker's view down-canyon over the sometimes smog-obscured Coachella Valley sprawl can be a bit discouraging; up-canyon vistas, however, are glorious. From Tahquitz Peak, a subsidiary summit of Mt. San Jacinto, a lively creek tumbles through an impressive gash in the towering rock walls.

I recommend getting an early start (Tahquitz Canyon Visitor Center opens at 7:30 A.M.) and arriving in time to watch the rising sun probe the dark recesses of the high walls of Tahquitz Canyon. If you decide on a guided hike, take the first (8 A.M.) tour of the day; you'll beat the crowds, beat the heat, and have the best chance of spotting wildlife.

Canyon hiking tours depart from the Tahquitz Canyon Visitor Center at 8 A.M., 10 A.M., 12 noon and 2 P.M.

DIRECTIONS: From Highway 111 in Palm Springs, head south on Palm Spring Drive through downtown to Mesquite Avenue. Turn right (west) and proceed 0.5 mile to the parking area below the Tahquitz Canyon Visitor Center. The canyon is open daily from October through June, 7:30-5 P.M., and in the summer on weekends only. There is an admission fee for adults and kids. For more information: TaquitzCanyon.com

There is a cost for both adults and children, and reservations are strongly recommended.

SANTA ROSA WILDERNESS

CACTUS SPRING TRAIL

From Pinyon Flat to Horsethief Creek is 5 miles round trip with a 900-foot loss; to Cactus Spring is 9 miles round trip with a 300-foot gain

The Santa Rosas are primarily desert mountains and a unique blend of high and low desert environments. Desert-facing slopes of these mountains are treeless, scorched and sparse as the desert itself. Throughout the foothills and canyons, lower Sonoran vegetation – chamise, barrel cactus, ocotillo and waxy creosote—predominate.

In some of the canyons with water on or near the surface, oases of native California fan palms form verdant islands on the sand. With an increase in elevation, the wrinkled canyons and dry arroyos give way to mountain crests bristling with pine and juniper.

The Santa Rosa Wilderness, set aside in 1984, and Cactus Spring Trail, lies within the boundaries of the Santa Rosa and San Jacinto Mountains National Monument.

An ancient Cahuilla path overhauled long ago by the Forest Service, gives the hiker a wonderful introduction to the delights of this range.

The trail first leads to Horsethief Creek, a perennial waterway that traverses high desert country. A hundred years ago, horse thieves pastured their stolen animals in this region before driving them to San Bernardino to sell. The cottonwood-shaded creek invites a picnic.

Continuing on Cactus Spring Trail, arrive at Cactus Spring. Along the trail is some wild country, as undisturbed as it was in 1774 when early Spanish trailblazer Juan Bautista de Anza first saw it.

DIRECTIONS: From Highway 111 in Palm Desert, drive 16 miles up Highway 74 to the Pinyon Flat Campground. Turn south

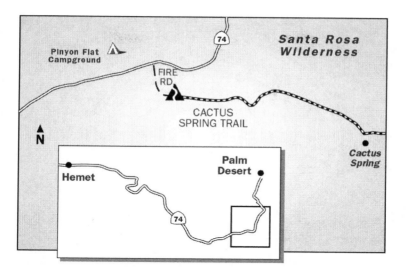

on the road opposite the campground and drive about 0.7 mile to a parking area (also the trailhead for Sawmill Trail), located just before the Pinyon Area Riverside County Transfer Station.

THE HIKE: Walk along the access trail on the east end of the parking area and look for the signed trailhead. Register at the sign-in box located near the trailhead sign; this is your wilderness permit for passage into the Santa Rosa Wilderness.

The trail bears east and dips in and out of several (usually) dry gullies. A half-mile past the sign-in register, a sign welcomes you to the Santa Rosa Wilderness. Cactus Spring Trail does not contour over the hills, but zigzags, almost in random fashion. Bewitching, but easy-to-follow, the path trail finally drops down to Horsethief Creek. At the creek crossing, Horsethief Camp welcomes the weary with flowing water and shade.

Return the same way or explore up and down the handsome canyon cut by Horsethief Creek. To continue to Cactus Spring, cross the creek and climb east out of the canyon on rough and steep trail past sentinel yuccas guarding the dry slopes.

The trail stays with a wash for a time, then gently ascends over pinyon pine-covered slopes. It's rolling wild country, a good place to hide out. Alas, Cactus Spring, located a few hundred yards north of the trail, and difficult to find, is almost always dry.

JOHN MCKINNEY,
HIKING EXPERT

John McKinney is the author of 30 books about hiking, parklands and nature, including *The Hiker's Way* and *Hiking on the Edge: Dreams, Schemes, and 1600 Miles on the California Coastal Trail.*

HIKE for Health & Fitness and *HIKE Griffith Park & the Hollywood Hills* are among the titles in The Trailmaster's Pocket Guide Series, designed to give hikers the information they need in an engaging and easily accessible way.

For 18 years, he wrote a weekly hiking column for the *Los Angeles Times*, and has hiked and enthusiastically described more than ten thousand miles of trail across America and around the world. John, aka The Trailmaster, has written more than a thousand articles about hiking plus numerous trail guidebooks.

A passionate advocate for hiking and our need to reconnect with nature, John McKinney shares his expertise on radio, TV, online, and as a public speaker.

JOHN MCKINNEY'S
TALES FROM THE TRAIL

Hiking on the Edge: Dreams, Schemes, and 1600 Miles on the California Coastal Trail

Until John McKinney agreed to take his epic hike, no one had ever walked along the edge of the state to determine if a California Coastal Trail was even possible. Were the beaches passable at low tide? Could the bluffs be traveled without arrest for trespass? Could a trail be found through the rugged coastal mountains? The intrepid trailblazer found the answers to these questions—and to more profound ones that never occurred to him until he was on his challenging journey of discovery.

Near and dear to his heart, are the unforgettable people he met along the way, including the founding father of whale-watching, backcountry rangers, nuns praying for mercy for the redwoods, and for us all. A saga, a celebration, a comedy, and a lament, this narrative ranks with the classics of California travel literature.

Hiking the Holy Mountain: Tales of Monks and Miracles on the Trails of Mt. Athos Greece

As the Los Angeles Times hiking columnist, John McKinney had a professional purpose for his trip: to hike around the Holy Mountain and write about Mt. Athos as a hiking destination, a spiritual adventure for outdoor enthusiasts. What he encountered there instead was an epiphany that changed his life and a colorful collection of wise Greek monks, who taught him that on this amazing path we call life, we're often compelled to change direction.

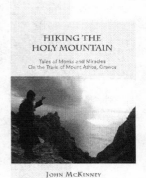

By turns reverent and irreverent, John narrates his progress and setbacks on the trail and within himself, as well a series of miraculous events, including the adoption of his son that took place on—and off—the Holy Mountain. Hiking the Holy Mountain is a powerful one-of-a-kind story of saints and icons, ancient traditions and modern-day faith and family.

THE TRAILMASTER'S "BEST DAY HIKES" SERIES

Perfect for you pocket or pack! The best day hikes in regions all across California. Complete with colorful stories, clear maps, and trusted trail accounts. Great gifts for that hiker in your life!

HIKE ON.

TheTrailmaster.com